CREATIVE CLOTH DOLL COLLECTION

A COMPLETE GUIDE TO
CREATING FIGURES, FACES,
CLOTHING, ACCESSORIES,
AND EMBELLISHMENTS

PATTI MEDARIS CULEA

Brimming with creative inspiration, how-to projects, and useful information to enrich your everyday life, Quarto Knows is a favorite destination for those pursuing their interests and passions. Visit our site and dig deeper with our books into your area of interest: Quarto Creates, Quarto Cooks, Quarto Homes, Quarto Lives, Quarto Drives, Quarto Explores, Quarto Gifts, or Quarto Kids.

First published in the United States of America by
Quarry Books, an imprint of The Quarto Group,
100 Cummings Center, Suite 265-D, Beverly, MA 01915, USA.
T (978) 282-9590 F (978) 283-2742 QuartoKnows.com

Quarry Books titles are also available at discount for retail, wholesale, promotional, and bulk purchase. For details, contact the Special Sales Manager by email at specialsales@quarto.com or by mail at The Quarto Group, Attn: Special Sales Manager, 401 Second Avenue North, Suite 310, Minneapolis, MN 55401, USA.

Library of Congress Cataloging-in-Publication Data available

ISBN-13: 978-1-59253-703-7
ISBN-10: 1-59253-703-0

Digital edition published 2011
eISBN-13: 978-1-61058-016-8

Design: Dutton & Sherman Design, Stephen Gleason Design, and Peter King & Company
Photography: Bobbie Bush, Robert Hirsch, and Allan Penn; Cover Image: Allan Penn
Illustration: Gayle Isabelle Ford and Judy Love; Patterns: Roberta Frauwirth

Printed in USA

TO MY FAMILY, FRIENDS, PUBLISHER, AND
YOU MY READERS, WHO HAVE HELPED MAKE
MY DREAMS COME TRUE.

CONTENTS

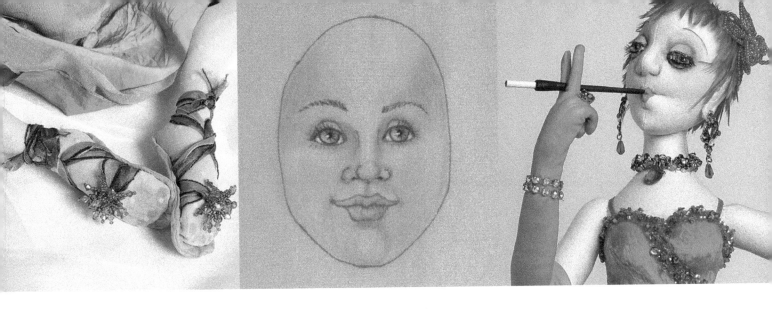

Find instructions for the cover doll, made by Patti Medaris Culea, on our website: www.quarrybooks.com. Search *Creative Cloth Doll Collection*, and print a downloadable pdf.

INTRODUCTION

Creative doll making. These words are at the center of what defines us as doll makers. We are artists who have a passion to create. If others like or appreciate what we do, fine. If not, the love of what we do sustains us. As artists, we think outside the box, whereas others keep within what is familiar. There is no way to predict when our inspirations will come or where they will come from, but when they arrive, we frantically search for the nearest scratch pad.

The book you are holding is actually four-in-one, a compilation of favorite material from my first four books. It is for people who know they have the gift of artistic creativity and want to take their doll-making talents to a higher level. It's also for those who have recently discovered a yearning to be creative—for those who never thought they could be doll makers. My hope is that this book enables you to start with a published pattern and make a doll that's unique. I want to help you learn to create a doll that has your signature, a doll that is truly yours.

Being a creative individual goes beyond scratch pads, needles, thread, sewing machines, and colored pencils. It begins when we rise in the morning. The creative person reflects their calling in the way they dress, cook, go to work, look at the world, interact with others, and think.

This is more than a book about doll making. I hope it will help you integrate creative techniques into many areas of your life—and allow you to take new risks, let go, and have fun! For example, rubber stamps and paints aren't new, but using them on already made cloth figures is a fresh concept. Tyvek has been around for years, mainly for envelopes and environmental suits, but here you'll see how it can be used to create whimsical clothing and beads. And beading! What a wonderful art form. You'll see that when beads are used to embellish a cloth doll, your creation can become magical. Free-motion machine embroidery has been used to create wonderful garments for adults; you'll discover how to use it to change the look of fabric for doll clothing, shoes, wings, and bodices. Fabric collage is commonly found in quilting and garments, but it's also an exciting technique for making doll bodies and clothing.

This book contains patterns for six doll bodies and also for accessories. The doll pattern pieces are designed so that you can mix and match body parts as you wish. At the end of the book is a gallery where family and friends and colleagues have interpreted the patterns in their own style. You'll see the work of beginning doll makers, intermediate doll makers, and some "hall of fame" artists, too. This will give you a lot of inspiration for making a doll that's uniquely yours.

This book is for you, the reader. I hope you enjoy reading each page as an adventure in creativity. Our world is one of heads, threads, beads, and the seeds of new ideas. I'm sure many of you will use the book to come up with new and exciting techniques. I hope you will share your creations with me and with others in the wonderful world of doll making. More than anything, I hope you'll have fun.

God bless,
Patti Medaris Culea

CHAPTER

1

THE BASICS:
Exploring Key Techniques

Gathering the Necessary Supplies

Doll making has changed dramatically over the past several years, with new techniques, supplies, and materials being discovered every day. Many supplies that doll makers use come from places like hardware stores and thrift shops; others come simply from the imaginations of the doll makers themselves.

Just as carpenters and plumbers have toolboxes to house and transport their essential tools, doll makers must have a basic sewing kit. You'll need it at home and, when you travel, to take to classes.

The Basic Kit

Work Space Essentials

Container for water

Containers for mixing dyes and paints

Cover-up or old clothes to wear

Fabric eraser

Hemostats—for turning and stuffing

Large and small finger-turning tools

Latex or plastic gloves

Measuring tape

Mechanical pencil

Paper towels

Plastic work surface

Sewing machine (your closest friend); cleaned and oiled and with a new needle

Sponges—small and large

Stuffing forks

Sweater rack for your clothes dryer or a hair dryer for setting paints and dyes

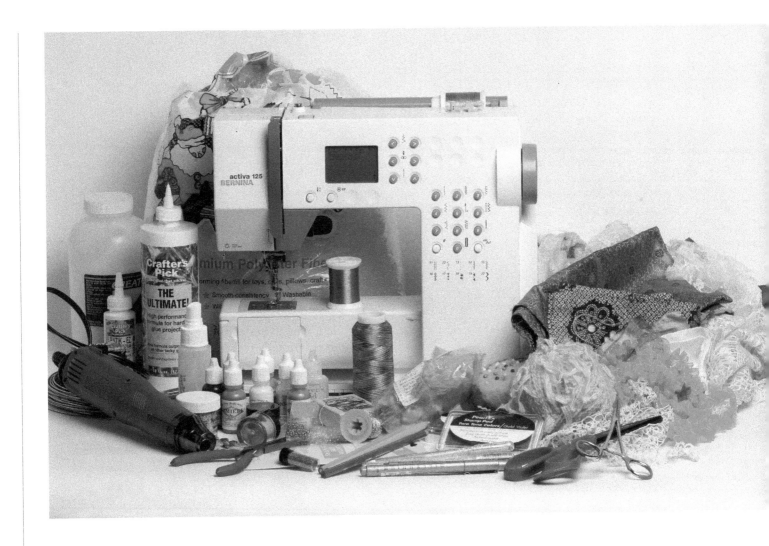

THE BASIC BODY KIT

1/3 yard (30.5 cm) of white or light-colored 100% cotton fabric

colored pencils: light or sienna brown for shading; lighter tan, beige, or flesh for highlights; white for pronounced highlights; carmine red for cheeks; light, medium, and dark colors for eyes; two shades of pink, red, or rose for lips

fabric pens: black, brown, contrasting color for the eyes, red white gel pen

6 pipe cleaners for wiring fingers

stuffing such as Fairfield Poly-fil strong thread for sculpting and attaching arms and legs, color-matched to fabric

textile medium such as Createx Textile Medium or JoSanja Textile Medium

thread to match fabric

soft fabric eraser such as Magic Rub

mechanical pencil

clear plastic quilter's gridded ruler

template plastic (optional)

stuffing tools

sewing machine

turning tools such as the Itsy Bitsy Finger Turning kit or small brass tubes (see Resources, page 302)

needle-nose pliers

wire cutters

THE BASIC SEWING KIT

sewing machine

sewing machine needles: universal points in size 10 and 12; embroidery, metallic, and top stitch in size 12

hand-sewing needles (sharps, milliners, quilter's basting needles, darners, embroidery, chenille)

3" (7.6 cm) -long doll-sculpting needle

size 11/12 beading needle

variety of sewing machine presser feet, such as darning, open-toed, and zigzag

sewing machine tools (for changing needles, oiling, and cleaning)

seam ripper

iron

press cloth

small bottle of Sewer's Aid

extra bobbins

beading threads

straight pins

safety pins

pincushion

thimble

cutting rulers

measuring tape

template plastic (optional)

rotary cutter and self-healing cutting board (optional)

straight-edge fabric scissors

embroidery scissors

paper scissors

pinking shears

hemostats (hand-held surgical clamps) or forceps

large and small tools for turning fingers

stuffing fork

seed beads in various sizes and colors

crystals

accent and drop beads

pencil

small scratch pad

journal

THE BASIC FABRIC-DYEING KIT

Jacquard Dye-Na-Flow paints

Jacquard Pearl-EX pigments

Jacquard Textile Paints

Jacquard Lumiere Paints

Jacquard Silk Dyes

Jacquard Procion MX powder dyes

noniodized salt

Tsukineko Fantastix

Tsukineko Brilliance stamp pads

Tsukineko all-purpose inks

several sizes of soft, flat, and round paint brushes for applying dyes and paints

containers for mixing dyes, such as a plastic ice cube tray

container for water

painter's masks for working with powdered dyes

paper toweling

plastic to cover work surface

TIP

There are many types and brands of colored pencils. They all work fine on cloth, but the best are oil based. These include Sanford Prismacolor (Karisma internationally), Walnut Hollow Oil Pencils, and Van Gogh Colored Pencils.

THE BASIC CLOTHING KIT

cotton batik fabrics

synthetic fabrics such as polyester organza, polyester silkies

silk fabrics such as chiffon, crepe de Chine, dupioni, sand-washed charmeuse

other fabrics such as bridals, brocades, fancies, rayons, tulle or fine netting

paper towels or pattern drafting paper

variegated and metallic sewing machine threads

lace

trims

silk ribbons

wire-edged ribbon

Laying Out Patterns

Before sewing any patterns in this book, look over the pattern pieces. Some have tracing and sewing lines, others have seam allowances. For the pieces that have tracing and sewing lines, trace onto the wrong side of the fabric, double the fabric, and sew. For the other patterns, either trace onto the wrong side of the fabric, double the fabric, and cut out, or make templates, trace, and cut out. Just remember to look at the pattern pieces before jumping in and sewing.

The head patterns have an arrow, which should be lined up with the grain of the fabric. The grain runs along the selvage of the fabric. The selvage is in line with the finished end of the fabric, not the cut end. This is important because it puts the stretch of the fabric where the cheeks are, so when you fill the doll's head with stuffing, it will have a nice plump face, rather than a long, skinny one.

1. Lay out the paper pattern on a table—a light table if you have one. Lay your fabric on top of the paper pattern, with the wrong side of fabric facing you. Using a mechanical pencil, trace all pattern pieces. Trace the darts, too. Double the fabric, and pin it in several places. For pattern pieces that don't have tracing and sewing lines, simply cut the pieces out. For those that have the lines, sew the pieces, and then cut them out.

2. For larger body parts and the legs, use pinking shears to cut them out to avoid the need to go around clipping curves. Avoid using pinking shears for the face and hands because these parts are too small.

AUTHOR'S SUGGESTION

I use a Bernina sewing machine. My normal stitch length is 2.0. When sewing the hands and face on a doll, I lower my stitch length to 1.5. That way I have clean seams and I can sew two stitches between fingers and across the tips of each finger. This also ensures a strong seam that won't burst open. When cutting out the hands, after they are sewn, I leave a scant ⅛" (0.3 cm) seam allowance. For the rest of the body, I leave a full ⅛" (0.3 cm) seam allowance.

3. When sewing the hands and face, use a shorter stitch length on your machine.

4. When sewing the doll's body parts, note the openings. These are important when putting the parts together and turning them right side out. Some pattern pieces have tabs that provide extra fabric for folding down so that it's easier to create a clean hand-sewn seam.

5. After sewing the body parts together, you'll turn the body parts right side out. (Note that the steps for doing this vary depending on the particular project.) Hemostats work well for this step, for everything but fingers. Reach in with the hemostats, grab the end of the foot, leg, or other body part and pull. Use the closed end of the hemostats to go back in and smooth out curves.

Turning Fingers

Although turning fingers does take practice, certain tools are available to make the process easier. You can buy an Itsy Bitsy Finger Turning kit created for doing just that (see Resources, page 302), or you can improvise and buy a couple of tubes from a hobby store that carries model train supplies. The tubes come in various widths; $1/16''$, $3/32''$, $5/32''$, and $1/8''$ (0.2 to 0.3 cm) are good for turning fingers. Just keep in mind that the tubes come in 12" (30.5 cm) lengths, so you'll need to cut them in half first.

If you're using the tubes, begin by inserting the largest tube inside a finger. Then, using the smallest tube, turn over the seam allowance, and push against the finger. Pull the finger up onto the smaller tube. The pressure against the seam allowance will help push the finger inside the hand.

You'll need two hands to do this, so hold the larger tube against your stomach. After you turn each finger, reach in with your hemostats, and turn the hand and then arm right side out.

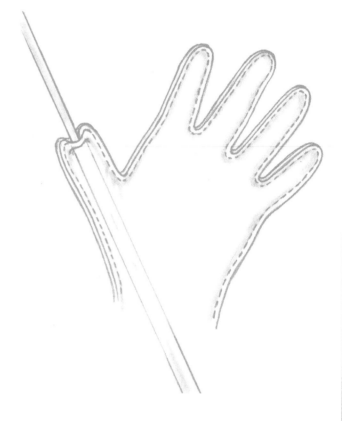

Begin by inserting
the largest tube inside a finger.

Stuffing Body Parts

Use whichever stuffing you prefer, but avoid the type that feels like cotton because this type doesn't sculpt well. When stuffing body parts, except the hands, grab as much stuffing as you can to fit through the opening, and feed the stuffing into the part. Larger bunches of stuffing give a smooth look; smaller bunches, a lumpy look.

To stuff a body part, start by pushing the stuffing into the outside of the part first, and then fill up the inside. This technique helps prevent wrinkling. For small parts like the nose, place a small amount there, and then continue filling in with large amounts of stuffing.

When stuffing the hands, use a stuffing fork to place small amounts of stuffing in the fingers and then hemostats to fill up the hand and arm. (See Resources, page 302, for more information on stuffing forks.)

For a more realistic look, you can insert pipe cleaners into the fingers to give the appearance that the doll has bones in her hands. Pinch back both ends of all pipe cleaners. Bend four pipe cleaners in half, placing one end in one finger and the other end in the finger next to it, until every finger has a pipe cleaner. The pipe cleaners should be in line with each other. The two straight pipe cleaners are for the thumbs. Place these in the thumbs.

To complete the look, push the arm fabric down, and wrap the thumb pipe cleaner around the two bent ends of the pipe cleaners in the doll's fingers, allowing some of the pipe cleaner to stick up in the arm. If the fingers look like they need just a bit more stuffing, you can insert it now. Push back the fabric, and wrap the stuffing around the stuffing fork so it looks like a cotton swab, and then insert it into a finger. Next fill the palm side of each hand with stuffing, and continue filling up the arms around the pipe cleaner.

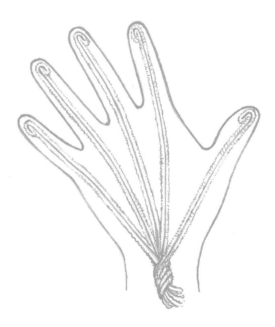

Wrap the thumb pipe cleaner around the two bent ends of the pipe cleaners in the doll's fingers.

To Sculpt a Hand

1 To sculpt the hand, thread a needle with 3.4 yard (0.69 m) strong thread. Place a knot in the single end. Attach this to the inside of the hand, in the seam below the thumb. Push the needle to the outside just in from the thumb, at the wrist. Take the needle and thread across the wrist and into the wrist just short of the seam under the little finger. Come out at the center of the palm.

2 Take the needle across the palm toward the thumb and index finger and push the needle in just short of the seam. Come out just above the thread at the wrist (figure i). Couch the thread by making a small stitch that takes the needle across the wrist thread and into the wrist. Insert the needle through the wrist and then come out at the back of the hand, straight back from the stitch in the wrist. Push the needle back into the hand and come out at the palm. Take a small stitch and push the needle into the palm and down to the wrist.

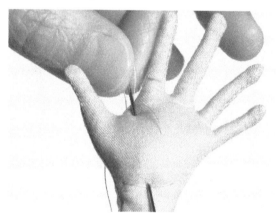

(figure i)
Sculpt the palm of the hand.

3 Take a small stitch where the needle just emerged, then push the needle back into the hand and out at the center of the palm, next to the beginning of the long diagonal stitch made in step 2. Push the needle into the hand, a small stitch this time, and come out at the back of the hand between the index and middle finger.

4 Taking vertical stitches, push the needle into the hand, under the pipe cleaner, and out between the middle and ring fingers (figure j). Push the needle back into the hand, under the pipe cleaner, and out between the ring and little finger.

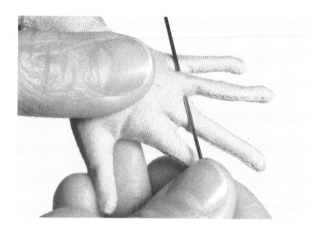

(figure j)
Sculpt the back of the hand.

5 After the hands are sculpted, hand sew each of them to the arms.

6 If your doll will have ears, such as Viviana in chapter 11, cut, sew, and attach them now (see Ears, page 169).

Tip:

Stitching the hand in the recent steps sculpted the lifeline on the palm and lifted the knuckles on the back of the hand.

BASIC SEWING TIPS

- No matter when you last used your sewing machine, it is best to clean and oil it before you start a new project. If you do this often, your sewing machine, no matter how new or old it is, will serve you for years and years.

- Machine needles are another important piece of equipment. Always insert a new needle into the machine for each project. Make sure you have the proper size and type of needle for the fabric and thread. The suitable needle type is listed in each chapter under Materials.

- You may want to dye the fabric for the body. If so, white or light-colored cotton is the best fabric for your doll.

- Make templates of the pattern pieces you will be working with. Transfer all of the markings onto the templates. Place the templates in a zippered plastic bag.

- Some pattern pieces, such as the hands and face, are best traced directly from the patterns, rather than using templates. Use a light table or window to trace these pieces accurately. Other pattern pieces are sewn together before the shapes are cut from the seamed fabric layers. For this process, it is best to first use straight-edge fabric scissors to cut out the general shape from the fabric pieces. Then, after the pieces are sewn, use pinking shears to cut out the detailed shape. By using the pinking shears, you will not need to clip curves. Do not use pinking shears to cut out the face and hands, however. These pieces are too small and need a more accurate cutting technique.

- Seam allowances can be finger pressed open or ironed. This is strictly up to each individual. Some of the seams do not have to be pressed open. Doll makers are not as precise as seamstresses or quilters. We tend to go with the flow.

THE BODY CONSTRUCTION

In this book, there is one body pattern and two variations for the legs. On pages 285–286, you will find three leg patterns. Two pattern pieces are the upper and lower legs for a sitting figure and another pattern piece is for a standing figure. The pattern pieces give you options for the pose you want for the various outfits. Because the focus of this book is on clothing and accessories, the body has a model-type shape. The wardrobe you create will look beautiful on her long, curvy figure. In a sense, you are making your own high-fashion doll with an exciting, fun, and varied wardrobe. Your doll will have something to wear for every occasion.

1. Before starting your doll, note the pattern pieces that need to be traced onto fabric, cut to the rough shape, and then sewn before cutting them out precisely: the Face, Head Back, Ear (Fairy only, see Golendrial, page 144), Arm, Hand, and leg pieces (Upper Leg and Lower Leg for the sitting doll, or Straight Leg for the standing doll). The main body pieces are cut out in detail, and then sewn together. See the Face, Head Back, and optional Ear pattern pieces (page 284).

2. All pattern pieces are templates, meaning you trace them on the wrong side of the fabric with the mechanical pencil. You can use a light table to trace directly from the pattern pieces to the fabric. Or, you can trace the pieces onto template plastic, place the template plastic shapes on the wrong side of the fabric, and trace around them. Trace darts and openings, too. Trace the head pieces onto the wrong side of one half of the fabric, making sure you match the on-grain arrows to the lengthwise grain of the fabric. The grainline is only important for the head.

3. Double the fabric by folding it in half, right sides together. Pin the layers together in several places. Sew seam #1 on the Face. Sew seam #2 on the Head Back, leaving open for turning where marked. With the straight-edge fabric scissors, cut out the two pieces, using full 1/8" (3 mm) seam allowances. Open them up.

> **TIP**
>
> *On my Bernina sewing machine, a normal stitch length is 2.0. I lower the setting for a shorter stitch length of 1.8 or 1.5 when sewing the face and fingers so that I have clean, strong seams.*

4. With right sides together, pin the Head Back to the Face at the top and the chin.

5. Sew all the way around the pieces to complete seam #3 (figure a). Turn the joined pieces through the opening on the Head Back, and fill the shape with enough stuffing to make the head firm. Set the head aside.

(figure a)
Sew the face to the back of the head.

6. With the fabric doubled, trace and then cut out all of the pattern pieces for the body (page 284), using straight-edge fabric scissors. Mark the darts (figure b).

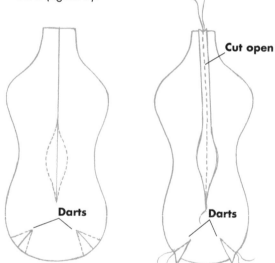

(figure b)
Make darts in Body Back and Lower Body Front.

7. On the Body Back, cut down the center of the back where marked, from the neck down to the hip. Sew in the darts on the Body Back and Lower Body Front.

8. Fold the Body Back in half, right sides together. Starting at the neck on the Body Back, sew down to the opening then continue sewing from the lower part of the opening, curving where marked. This creates a nice curve to the doll's spine. Double stitch the beginning of the neck.

9. Pin the Upper Body Front to the Lower Body Front, starting at the center of the bust and working out to each side. Sew from the center of the bust out to one side (figure c). Repeat on the opposite side of the bust.

(figure c)
Join Body Front pieces at bustline.

10. With right sides together and using a full 1/8" (3 mm) seam allowance, pin the body front to the Body Back, and sew around the sides, from the neck opening down the body and around up to the other side of the neck. Trim the seam allowances with pinking shears. Turn the body right side out by inserting the hemostats into the body, grabbing the end of a body part, and then pulling it through the center back opening. Smooth out the curves with the closed end of the hemostats. Fill the body with stuffing. Plump up the breasts with the stuffing. Set the body aside.

TIP

It is easier to fill up the body until the stuffing starts to pop out of the opening in the back and then close the opening with a ladder stitch (page 200). It helps to insert a pipe cleaner into the neck before filling the neck with stuffing. This keeps the head from getting wobbly.

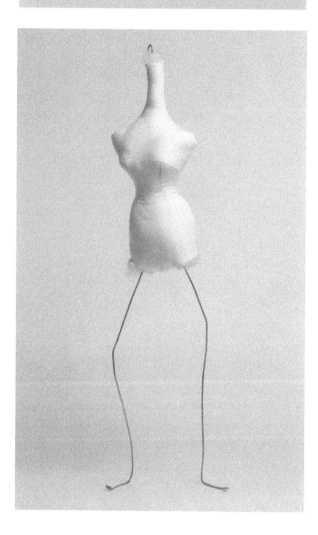

11. Trace two arms onto the wrong side of the fabric. Fold the fabric in half, right sides together. Back stitching at the beginning and end of the seam, sew from the opening at the wrist all the way around. Leave an opening at the wrist. Cut out the arms with pinking shears, leaving a full 1/8" (3 mm) seam allowance. Turn the arms right side out and fill them with stuffing to just below the elbow.

12. Trace two hands onto the wrong side of the fabric. Double the fabric, with right sides together. Carefully sew around the shape, leaving the wrist open (figure d). Be sure you make two stitches between each finger and two stitches across the tip of each finger. (Do not sew down the dashed lines for the attached fingers yet.)

(figure d)
Using a short stitch, sew together the hand fabric layers before cutting out the shape.

13. Cut out the hands with a good pair of sharp scissors. Clip at each side between the fingers and right up to the stitches. This helps prevent wrinkling once the hands are turned. Turn the hands right side out, using brass tubes to help with the fingers (figure e).

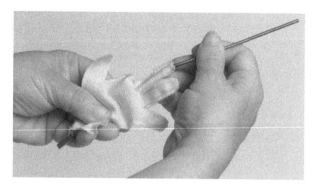

(figure e)
Turn the fingers right side out using small and large brass tubes.

To turn a finger, begin by inserting a larger tube. Using the smallest tube, turn over the seam allowance and push against the finger. Pull the finger onto the smaller tube.

14. After the fingers are turned, topstitch down the center of the two fingers that are attached.

15. Using three pipe cleaners for each hand, wire the hands by folding each pipe cleaner in half and inserting one half up each finger. The straight pipe cleaner is inserted into the thumb. Wrap some of this pipe cleaner around the two used for the fingers to hold everything in place (figure f). Using a stuffing fork, fill just the palm side of each hand. Insert stuffing into the wrists, around the pipe cleaners.

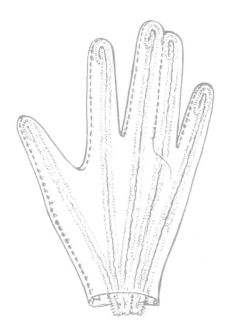

(figure f)
Sew between the joined fingers before inserting pipe cleaners and stuffing the hand.

16. Insert the top of a hand into the wrist of each arm. You will have a bit of the thumb pipe-cleaner sticking out of the wrist. Insert this bit of pipe-cleaner into the arm and finish filling up the arms around the wire. Use a ladder stitch (page 200) to sew the hands to the arms at the wrists. Set the arms aside.

17. Decide if your doll will have jointed or straight legs and follow the instructions opposite or on page 22.

OPTION I: JOINTED LEGS

1. Trace two Upper Legs and two Lower Legs onto the wrong side of the fabric. Double the fabric, right sides together, and pin the layers together in several places. Sew all the way around both of the Upper Legs. Using full 1/8" (3 mm) seam allowances, cut out the shapes with pinking shears and cut a slit at the top, where marked. Turn the Upper Leg right side out through the slit and fill the shape with stuffing. Close up the slit by hand sewing using a needle and thread.

2. Sew the sides of the Lower Legs from the knee all the way down to the opening at the toes. Cut out the shapes, using full 1/8" (3 mm) seam allowances.

3. Fold a Lower Leg at the knees so that the front and back seams match. Sew across the top of the leg, through both fabric layers, stopping short of the matched seams so there is an opening at the center (figure g).

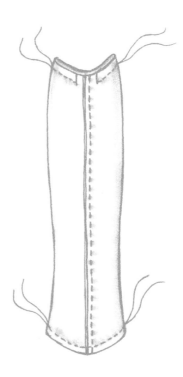

(figure g)
Refold the leg to seam the top and bottom edges.

4. For the feet, draw in a curved pencil line across the top area, as shown, and then sew the edges together following your drawn line (figure g).

5. Turn the Lower Leg right side out through the opening at the top, and fill the shape with stuffing. Close up the opening by hand sewing using a needle and thread.

6. Thread a 3" (7.6 cm) doll sculpting needle with 1/2 yard (46 cm) of strong thread and knot the end. Insert the needle through the top of a Lower Leg. Continue pulling the needle and thread through the Upper Leg at the dot. Go through the top of the remaining Lower Leg. Sew back and forth three times.

7. Continue assembling the doll following the steps for The Body Parts Assembly (page 23).

1. Trace two legs onto the wrong side of one half of the fabric, and then double the fabric, right sides together. Sew from one side of the opening at the toes all the way around the foot and leg to the other side of the toe opening, using full 1/8" (3 mm) seam allowances. Cut out the shapes.

2. Fold the leg so that the front and back seams match and the toe area of the foot is flat and horizontal. For each foot, pin the toes together (figure h).

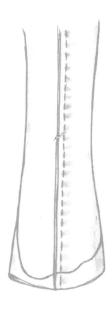

(figure h)
Join the straight leg pieces before seaming the toes.

3. Trace the foot template on page 286 onto the toe area. Sew along the traced lines. Trim the seam allowances with pinking shears. Finish the foot on the remaining leg in the same way.

4. Place the legs so that the feet face forward and cut a slit at the top of each leg on the sides that face each other. Turn through these openings and fill firmly with stuffing. Close up the slit by hand sewing.

The Body Parts Assembly

1. Attach a finished leg to each side of the body using 1 yard (91 cm) of strong thread and a long needle. Attach the thread at the hip, pull the needle and thread through the top of one leg from the inner side to the outer side, then turn the needle and insert it back through the same leg and through. Without breaking the thread, pull the needle and thread through the remaining leg to attach it in the same manner. Sew back and forth three times, and then anchor the thread at the hip, under a leg (figure i).

2. The arms are attached individually. Start by attaching the thread at the shoulder. Insert the needle and thread into—but not through—the arm. Push through just enough to catch some stuffing. Sew back into the shoulder. Go back and forth with the needle and thread three times. Anchor the thread off at the shoulder with a small stitch.

3. Hand sew the head to the neck using a needle and thread and a ladder stitch (page 200) (figure j).

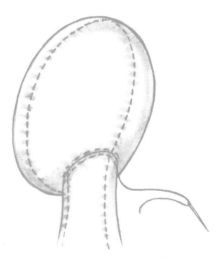

(figure j)
Hand sew the head to the neck.

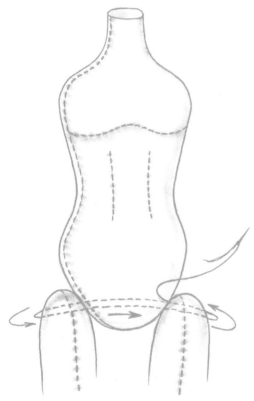

(figure i)
Join the upper legs to the body.

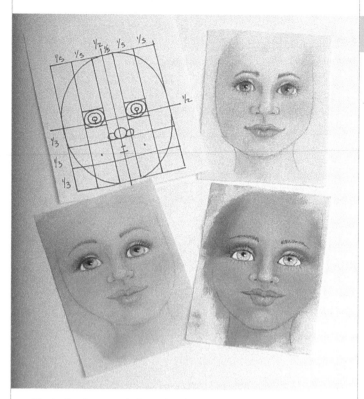

Clockwise from top left: grid, colored pencils, watercolor, paints

Getting Started on the Face

We can thank Albrecht Dürer for giving us a wonderful tool for drawing faces. Dürer was a draftsman, painter, and engraver who lived between 1471 and 1528. He came up with a grid method for drawing. He built a large wooden grid inside a frame, and put his model behind this grid. On a piece of paper, he drew a similar grid, and copied what he saw into his own grid. In this way he was able to create an almost perfect image of the model.

In drawing faces, this same principle can be used, only in our exercise we won't be copying a person. We'll create a new person. Refer to the illustration (below left) as you draw.

1. Using a ruler and a mechanical pencil, draw a rectangle 3½" tall by 2½" wide (8.9 x 6.3 cm).

2. Divide the rectangle in half widthwise and lengthwise.

3. Divide the vertical length into fifths (each unit will be ½" [1.3 cm] wide).

4. Divide the lower half of the rectangle into thirds widthwise .

5. Inside this rectangle, draw a large oval.

6. On the horizontal halfway mark, find each of the one-fifth units where the eyes will fit. Place a small vertical line through the center of each of these.

7. Measure the width of the one-fifth unit for one eye. This measurement will also be the height of the eye. Draw in a square, dropping the lower edge of the square about 1/16" (2 mm) below the halfway mark.

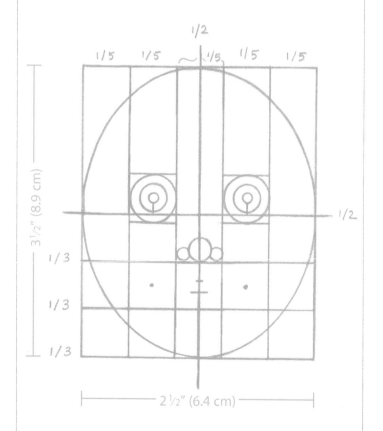

The basic grid for a face
(not drawn precisely to scale)

8. Inside this square, draw a circle. Inside this circle, draw a smaller circle. Inside the medium circle, draw a smaller circle. Before you detail the circles, you'll practice the eyes separately. When you're ready, you'll come back to this grid.

9. The nose is on the first one-third line below the halfway mark. It will fit inside the center fifth square. For now, draw a larger circle, centered above the vertical halfway mark, with a smaller circle on either side.

10. The mouth is on the next one-third line. This line is the base for the lower lip. To find the center of the mouth, measure ¼" (6 mm) up from the one-third line. Draw a small line. Another ⅛" (2 mm) above this line, draw another line. This is for the center of the upper lip.

11. The outside of the center of the mouth is exactly below the smallest circle you drew for the eyes. Draw a dot here, in line with the center of the mouth.

Now we'll practice each of the features.

The Eyes

1. Draw a large circle. Inside this, draw another circle. Inside the second circle, draw a smaller one.

2. The upper part of the eyelid starts slightly outside the larger circle, and curves up and across the top of the second circle. It ends on the outside edge of the larger circle.

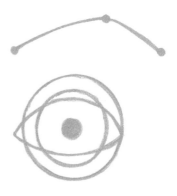

Preliminary eye

3. The lower part of the eyelid starts outside the larger circle, curves down slightly, touches the lower part of the middle circle, and connects with the upper eyelid at the opposite edge of the larger circle.

4. The crease of the eyelid follows the upper arc of the large circle.

5. Shade around the crease of the eyelid, and around the eyeball and iris, as shown. Darken the pupil, and erase a small bit for the highlight that is in the pupil and radiates out to the iris.

Finished eye

6. The eyebrows are slightly above the top of the eyeball. They start straight up from the inside corner of the eye, and stop just past the outside edge of the eyeball. The arch of the eyebrow is above the outer edge of the iris. For each eyebrow, draw a line, and then feather in the separate hairs, following this line.

7. The eyelashes start above the pupils, curve down slightly, and then curve up. Alternate drawing a short lash and a long lash until you reach the end of the eyelid.

8. The lower eyelashes are shorter and not as full. They start just below the lower part of the eyelid, and curve slightly down.

Practice drawing several eyes before drawing eyes into the grid of the face you made earlier.

The Nose

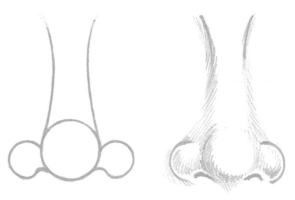

Draft (left) and finished nose (right)

The nose is probably the hardest part of the face to draw. On a doll that has a seam down the center of the face you don't have to draw a nose, but on a flat-faced doll you do. Here's the best way I've found to draw a nice nose.

1. Draw a large circle with one smaller circle on either side.

2. Toward the bottom inside of the smaller circles, draw in the nostrils. They are just two dots for now.

3. Measure the large circle, and double this measurement. Draw a line that length straight up from the large circle . This will be the bridge/base of the nose.

4. From the outside of the large circle, draw a line that curves slightly toward the base you just drew. Repeat on the other side.

5. Outline the flares of the nose. These are the two smaller circles you drew; you will just outline the outside of each circle.

6. Darken the nostrils, and shade in the rounded part of the nose.

When you are comfortable drawing noses, draw one on your doll's face.

The Mouth

Preliminary mouth

1. Draw a straight horizontal line. Draw a vertical line at its center.

2. At this center, draw a small circle. This represents the tubercle (sometimes referred to as the "milk bud").

3. On each side of this circle, draw a larger circle. Keep these larger circles closer to the center than to the end of the horizontal line.

4. Below these two larger circles, and under the horizontal line, draw an oval.

5. Starting at the center of the tubercle, draw a curved line out to the end of the horizontal line. Repeat on the other side.

6. The lower lip starts just in from the end of the horizontal line, curves down under the oval, and then curves up to just before the other end of the horizontal line.

7. Shade the upper lip and part of the lower lip, as shown in the illustration.

Finished mouth

Practice several more mouths, and then draw a mouth onto your doll's face.

Sculpting a Face

Before coloring the doll's face, you'll want to sculpt it, using a needle and thread. As you go from one area to another, pull on your thread. However, look at the doll's face as you pull, because you don't want to pull so tight that you cause wrinkling—you simply want to define the features. Follow the steps below to work your way around the face:

1. Thread a long darning needle with 1 yard (91.5 m) of strong thread. The thread should be in a single strand, not doubled. Anchor this at the back of the doll's head.

2. Push the needle through the head and out the inside corner of an eye (**#1**).

3. Push the needle back inside the head at the corner of the eye and come out at the opposite nostril (**#2**).

4. Push the needle back inside the head at the nostril and come out at the opposite flare of the nose (**#3**).

5. Push the needle back inside at the flare and come out straight across at the opposite flare (**#4**).

6. Push the needle back inside at the flare and come out at the opposite nostril (**#5**).

7. Push the needle back inside at the nostril and come out at the opposite inside corner of the eye (**#6**).

8. Push the needle back inside at the corner of the eye and come out at the outside corner of the mouth (**#7**).

9. Push the needle back inside at the outside corner of the mouth and come out at the outside corner of the eye (**#8**).

10. Push the needle back inside at the outside corner of the eye and come out at the inside corner of the other eye (**#1**).

11. Push the needle back inside at the inside corner of the eye and come out at the outside corner of the mouth (**#9**).

12. Push the needle back inside at the outside corner of the mouth and come out at the outside corner of the eye (**#10**).

13. Push the needle back inside at the corner of the eye and come out at the back of the head, then anchor off.

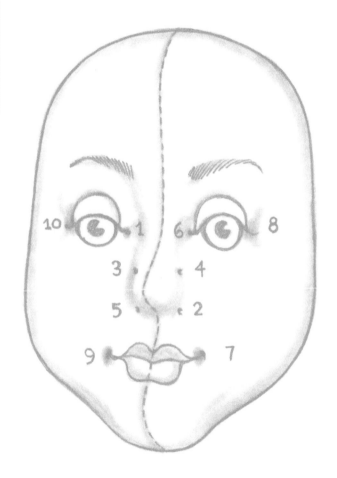

Numbers on the above face correspond to the bold numbers in the text on the left.

Detailing the Face

Once you have a face you are happy with, outline the features with a brown fabric pen.

1. Outline the eyelids, the crease of each eyelid, the eyelashes, the eyebrows, the curves at the base of the nose, the flares and nostrils, and the lips. Erase all the other pencil marks.

2. Using a soft pencil, such as a 2B, add shading down the temples, around the eye crease, down each side of the nose, around the center ball of the nose, and around each smaller ball for the flares. Shade underneath the lower lip and a bit under the nose along the upper lip. This gives the face definition.

[Step 1]
Basic face

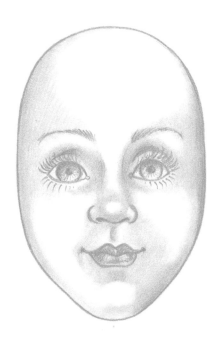

[Step 2]
Shaded face

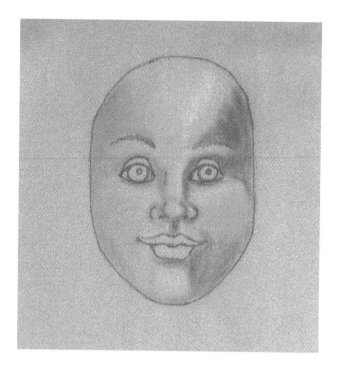

[Steps 1–4]
On the sample, the left side is blended but the right side isn't

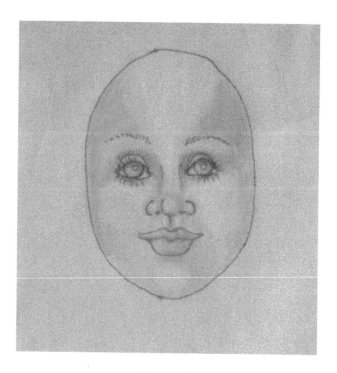

[Steps 5–6]
Eyes and lips are colored

Working on Fabric

It is now time to try drawing a face on a piece of fabric. Assemble a mechanical pencil and some colored pencils. You'll need brown, tan or beige, white, red, and colors for eyes and lips.

1. On a piece of flesh-colored cotton fabric, draw the oval for the face using the mechanical pencil.

2. Lightly draw a grid with a mechanical pencil. Add the features, and outline them with a brown fabric pen.

3. Add the shading, using a brown pencil. Next, use a tan or beige pencil to start bringing in the high lights. Refer to the high-lighting guide. Lastly, use a white pencil at the high points of the face. Apply color to the cheeks. Don't be shy. When you blend the colors together, much of the pigment will rub into the fabric.

4. Once you have the shading, highlights, and cheek color, wrap a scrap piece of fabric around your index finger, and blend the colors by rubbing the fabric. On the sample (above left), the left side is blended but the right side isn't.

5. The eyes are next (see the sample, lower left). This time you'll need three shades of one color, or three different colors in varying shades (a light, a medium, and a dark). Use the lightest color to fill in the iris. With the medium color, follow the edge of the upper eyelid and one side of the iris. The darkest color is last. It actually starts at the inside corner of the upper eyelid and goes across the iris over to the other side of the eyelid. Darken down to the pupil with this color, keeping it along the top of the iris.

6. The lips are filled in with a medium color of red, peach, or rose. With a darker red, color the upper lip and one side of the lip that would be on the shaded side of the face.

7. At this point, seal the face. Iron it to set the colors, and then coat the face with a textile medium. Let it dry before doing the detail work.

8. Use a black gel pen to fill in the pupil.

9. Because you've been coloring a lot on the iris, its outline has been covered. Use a colored pen to outline the iris and draw in the rods that radiate out from the pupil.

10. Use white paint or a white gel pen to add a dot of white on the lighter side of the iris on the pupil and to color in the whites of the eyes.

11. Add a dot of red at the inside corner of the eyes for the tear duct.

12. Draw in the eyelashes. They start just above the pupil on the eyelid and curve down and then up. Alternate short ones and long ones. Stagger them to give a full-eyelash look. See the detailed illustration of the eye (right).

13. Use a red fabric pen to outline the lips and draw in the creases that radiate up on the upper lip and down on the lower lip. Add a bit of white to the lower lip. See the detailed illustration of the lips (lower right).

14. Feather in the eyebrows with a brown pen. Add black if needed.

15. Look at the face you have just colored. If you need to darken any shadows or lighten any highlights, do so now. Add eye shadow if you'd like. Iron the face, again, to set the pens.

These are the basics of drawing a face. The following chapters will cover several ways of coloring and creating faces. It is important to learn the basics, so when you move on from chapter to chapter, you'll know precisely where to place features—or misplace them, if you so desire.

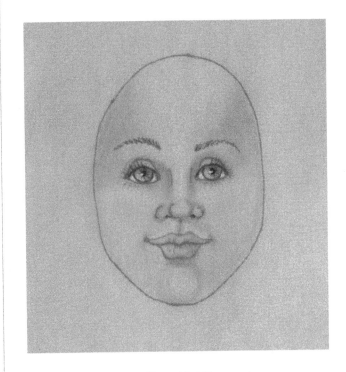

[Steps 12–13]
Detailing the face

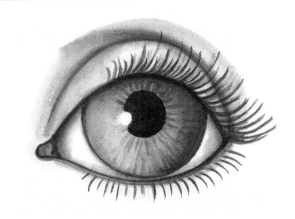

[Step 12]
Close-up of eye

[Step 13]
Close-up of lips

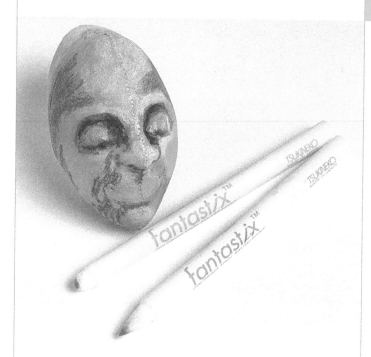

[Steps 1–7]
Color face with oil pastels

[Step 14]
Detail of oil pastel–drawn face

Using Oil Pastels

Oil pastels are probably my favorite painting medium. I use these in my paper journaling, and have found them equally exciting to use on fabric.

1. Start with a finished fabric head, and color the entire head with peach pastel.

2. Next, color in the shadows with a combination of golden brown, medium brown, and violet.

3. Highlight the high points of the face with white.

4. Using pink and red-orange, color in the cheeks.

5. Fill in the eye area with white. Add a bit of the blue for the irises.

6. Color in the lips with red-orange.

7. Add some yellow to the outer part of the eyelids.

8. Using a dampened stencil brush, or Tsukineko's Fantastix, blend these colors.

9. Deepen the crease of the eyelids with more violet and blue-violet. With True Blue, lighten the sides of the irises that would catch the light. Deepen the upper part of the irises with blue-violet.

10. Continue blending as you go along.

11. Add more highlights to the forehead, the center of the nose, and the chin.

12. Darken the center of the lips and the upper lip with red.

13. Spray the face with Krylon's Workable Fixative, or another fixing solution.

14. Add detail work, following techniques described for the other faces.

Finishing

1. Hand sew mohair to the head, starting at the back of the head, and following the seam around.

2. Catch the mohair at its center with the needle and thread.

3. Once you have enough sections of mohair around the seams, fill in at the back of the head. Use your fingers to fluff up the mohair, and then pull it up, toward the top of the head, and secure it with needle and thread. Pull some strands out with a needle.

4. Sew a beaded flower to the hair, near where an ear would be.

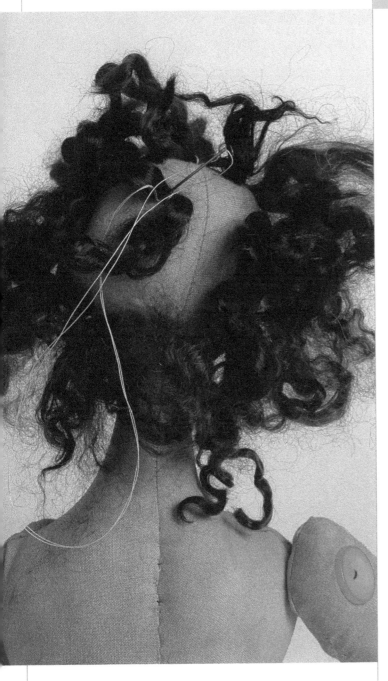

[Steps 1–3]
Hand sew mohair to head.

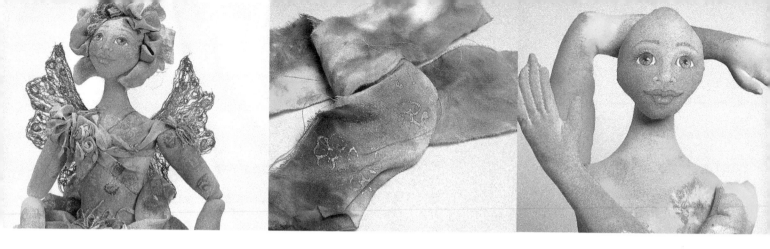

CHAPTER

SURFACES
AND COLORATION:

Working with Dyes, Paints, and Stamps

Beginning Doll

The doll featured in this chapter, Willamae (Doll #1), is a perfect project to start with if you're new to doll making. She's constructed from the pattern found on pages 264 and 265. The pattern is simple. Her head is flat, a perfect canvas for learning the basic principles for drawing a face. Her body is formed with only one pattern piece, and her hands and feet are simple silhouettes for easy sewing.

The first layer of design on this doll is a dyed surface. You'll learn to color the body, mixing several dyes to achieve a pretty flesh color, and then to embellish this layer with stamped designs. Feel free to adapt the palette to your liking as a way to start personalizing your design.

Her clothing is made from silk crepe de chine, which is also dyed and stamped. The simple torn pieces are draped into a lovely outfit and embellished with silk ribbons and ribbon roses. It's easy to transform simple scraps of fabric into fabulous garments by wrapping, gathering, and draping the pieces in interesting ways. If you feel ambitious, you can even add shoes to the ensemble, or go without. It's up to you.

Finally, you'll learn, step-by-step, how to continue to add detail to your doll's face, using pencils, gel pens, and rubber stamps.

Supplies

1/4 yard (23 cm) pima cotton

pins

thread to match

scissors

mechanical pencil and soft eraser

stuffing

stuffing tools

hemostats

hand-sewing needles

strong thread for attaching the head, arms, and legs

3" (7.5 cm) needle to attach legs

fabric marking pens: brown, red, black

plastic bag to cover workspace

paper towel

ice cube tray

Jacquard's Dye-NA-Flow paints: white, ecru, ochre, magenta, sun yellow, turquoise

Jacquard's Lumiere paints: super sparkle, silver, turquoise

paper plate and sponge

rubber stamps

1/4 yard (23 cm) silk crepe de chine

eye droppers

3 yards (2.7 m) 7-mm white silk ribbon

matches and a candle

pie plate with water (optional)

beads

colored pencils: sienna brown, cream, white, carmine red, periwinkle, peacock blue, copenhagen blue, scarlet lake

gel pens: black, purple, white

glitzy yarns

[step 4]
Cut a slit on one side of the head toward the chin.

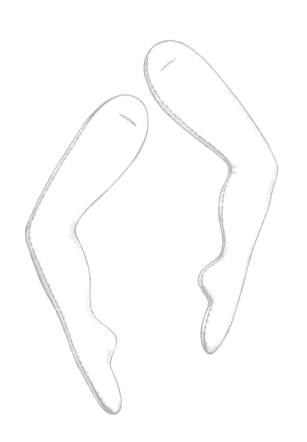

[step 5]
Cut slits toward the top of each leg.

Making the Body

1. Arrange and trace the patterns for Doll #1 onto the wrong side of the body fabric. (See Chapter 1, page 13.) Then double the fabric, right sides together, and pin in several places.

2. Begin sewing the body parts together, leaving a section open, for turning, as indicated on the patterns. *Note:* The head and legs don't have openings; you'll cut a slit later for turning. When sewing the neck, backstitch at the beginning, and then double stitch just the neck sides. This will prevent the seams from busting out.

3. Cut out all body pieces.

4. Cut a slit on one side of the head toward the chin. Make this slit on the side of the head with pencil marks.

5. Cut slits toward the top of each leg. Make sure you have a right leg and a left leg by placing the legs together and positioning the slits on adjacent sides.

6. Turn all pieces, right sides out.

7. This step is optional, but it gives the finished doll a nice look: Follow the markings on the hand template to trace in fingers on the hands and topstitch by machine. Do this before filling up the doll body with stuffing. When topstitching, do a backstitch at the beginning and end of each finger, to keep any threads from coming loose while stuffing.

8. Use the stuffing to fill the main body first. Fill the doll until it feels firm, especially the neck. Fill the head next. Smooth out any wrinkles in the fabric by filling with more stuffing.

9. Place the head on the neck by grabbing the neck with your hemostats and pushing it up into the opening at the back of the head. Pin in place. Thread a regular hand-sewing needle with ¼-yard (46 cm) of strong thread. Place a knot in the end. Ladder stitch the head to the neck. Anchor the thread at the back of the head, and cut.

10. Stuff the legs. After the legs are filled, ladder stitch the openings closed with a needle and thread.

11. Thread a 3" (7.5 cm) needle with 2 yards (1.8 m) of strong thread. Put a knot in the end of the thread, and attach to the side of the hip.

12. Place the leg at the hip, and attach by running a threaded needle through the leg. Go back through the leg, over to the other side, and through the other leg. Go back and forth at least three times, then anchor the thread at the inside of the hip (under a leg).

13. Fill the arms with stuffing, starting with the fingers, using the stuffing fork. Finish filling the arms with stuffing to ¼" (0.6 cm) below the opening. Sew a gathering stitch along the top of each arm. Push the raw edges of the fabric inside as you do this. Tack the arm to the side of the body at the shoulders with a stitch.

14. Repeat for the other arm. The doll is now ready to be dyed, stamped, and clothed.

[step 7]
Follow the markings on the hand template to trace in fingers on the hands and topstitch by machine.

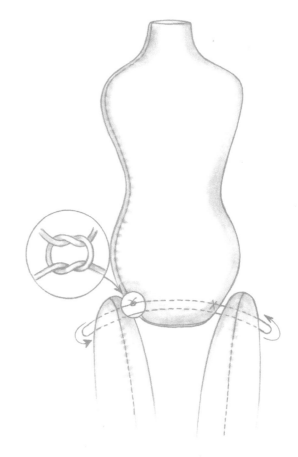

[step 11]
Put a knot in the end of the thread, and attach to the side of the hip.

Drawing the Face

Before dyeing, draw in the facial features. Outline all drawn features with a brown fabric marking pen.

Adding Color with Dye

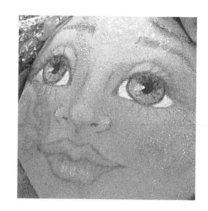

Jacquard's Dye-NA-Flow paints dye just about any fiber but polyester. When used straight from the container, they keep their color; however, when diluted, they do fade a bit. They don't change the 'hand," or feel, of the fabric. They're also nontoxic; therefore, they don't have harmful fumes or much of an odor, so it's unnecessary to wear goggles or a mask when using them.

These paints should be heat set—and, fortunately, that's quite simple to do. If you have a sweater rack for your clothes dryer, set the dryer for cotton, place the dyed doll body on the rack, and dry for 30 minutes. If you don't have a sweater rack, use your hair dryer or a heat gun (found at stamp stores and hardware stores). You can also use an iron to set the colors. When dyeing a doll that isn't going to be laundered, heat setting is unnecessary. Heat setting simply guarantees that the colors won't fade.

To set up a dye space, gather an ice cube tray, some brushes, a container for water, paper towels, and a plastic garbage bag.

1. Lay down the plastic bag to cover the workspace. Next put a layer of paper towels on top of the plastic. The towels will catch any spills and are good for dabbing the brush on when doing some of the dry-brush techniques.

2. Pour a teaspoon (5 ml) of each dye into the different sections of the ice cube tray. Leave a few sections empty for mixing colors together.

3. To create a flesh color, add 1 teaspoon (5 ml) of white, then add a drop at a time of ecru and ochre until you get the shade of flesh you want. Add a drop of magenta to this mixture and a little sun yellow. If the color is too dark, add a bit of water and more white.

4. Brush this mixture onto the flesh parts of the doll body. Working quickly, add other colors, as desired, to cover the entire body. Work quickly because the dyes dry fast, and if you go back and paint next to a dry spot, it will produce a watermark.

5. For cheek color, place a small amount of a skin-toned dye in an empty space of the ice cube tray, and add some magenta. Pick up a small amount of dye on your brush, and dab onto a paper towel to remove excess. Brush her cheeks with this color. The color should bleed.

Any stamp will work on cloth. Intricate stamps are my favorites, such as "Impress Me" stamps by Sherrill Kahn. Because the stamps aren't mounted onto a hard surface, it's easy to bend the stamp around a small arm or other curved parts of the body.

Adding Interest with Stamps

When working with stamps, dab on just a bit of the paint with a sponge. Pick up some paint on the sponge, then dab off any extra paint onto your pallet, thus enabling you to put just the right amount of paint onto the stamp. Have water and an old toothbrush handy; the paints dry quickly and can ruin the stamps if not cleaned as soon as you finish stamping.

Experiment with several colors of paint on a stamp. The colors will bleed together to create other colors. For instance, yellow and blue will make green where the two colors meet, creating some interesting effects.

1. Using the Lumiere paints, place a dollop of each color onto a paper plate. Pick up some paint on a sponge, and dab onto a stamp. Immediately stamp the doll's body. Continue this stamping process until you have the effect you want.

2. Let the paints dry thoroughly. Set an iron to the cotton setting. Set the paints by lightly ironing over the body parts.

Making Clothes

Use silk or cotton for clothing. In the featured doll, silk crepe de chine is used.

1. Wet a piece of the silk crepe de chine thoroughly with plain tap water. Squeeze out excess water.

2. Place small amounts of sun yellow, turquoise, and magenta into the ice cube tray that you used earlier. Scrunch up the silk, and dip into the yellow. With eye droppers, drop magenta and turquoise onto the remaining white areas of the silk. Squeeze out excess dye, and hang the fabric up to dry. Let the colors set for 24 hours, then iron the silk with a warm iron.

3. Using the eye dropper technique only, color the silk ribbons. Ribbons are much narrower than the fabric, so the piece could get too saturated by dipping it into one color first.

Dye-NA-Flow paints will work beautifully on the silk, or you can use any silk dye. Some silk dyes need to be steam set, so be sure to check the manufacturer's labels.

4. Once the fabric is dry, measure the doll's body, and decide how long you want her skirt to be. Tear the fabric to the desired length. (The featured doll's skirt measures 18" x 4" [45.5 x 10 cm]). Light a candle, and carefully run the torn edge along the flame to seal the edge.

5. Using the Lumiere paints and stamps, create designs on the silk. The silk can be stamped before or after it's dyed.

6. For the bodice, tear two strips of fabric 10" x 1½" (25.5 x 4 cm). Wrap these two around each other as shown below.

AUTHOR'S SUGGESTION

Some doll makers place the candle in the center of a pie plate that has about ¼" (0.6 cm) water in it for easily dousing any flames. This is strictly a safety precaution.

[step 6]
Wrap these two strips
around each other.

7. Bring one side up over her shoulders and the other side around to her back. With a needle and thread, tack in place at the back. On one shoulder, tear a long strip of silk, 10" x ½" (25.5 x 1.3 cm), and tie it in various places. Then loop the strip, and tack it to her shoulder. Create some silk ribbon roses or other flowers, and sew these to her bodice. (See the photo on page 37 for ideas.)

8. Her skirt is one long strip of fabric, 18" x 4" (45.5 x 10 cm). With right sides together, sew up the back seam, along the 4" (10 cm) edges. Then gather the waist by hand with a running stitch. Slip the skirt onto her body, and pull the threads to fit the waist. Tack in place.

9. The upper skirt is another strip of fabric, 18" x 4" (45.5 x 10 cm), folded over to create a double ruffle. Hand-gather at the center, and pull the threads to fit at the waist. Leave open at the center.

10. Stamp on her body and her clothing. Add some silk ribbons at her waist and a silk ribbon rose.

Adding Shoes

1. Trace four shoe patterns onto the wrong side of the silk scrap (left over from the skirt and top). Two are for the outside of the shoes, and two are for the lining. Double the fabric, and sew along the solid line, leaving open where marked.

2. Cut out all pieces, and turn two of them right side out. Place the two lining pieces inside the other two, and pin in place with right sides together. Sew along the raw edges from the back of the shoe all the way around. To turn the shoes right side out, cut a slit in the lining at the bottom in the seam, then turn right side out. Finger-press along edges, and slip the shoes onto her feet.

3. Fold a 12" (30.5 cm) length of silk ribbon in half, and tack at the center of the top of the shoe. Bring the ribbon to the back of the shoe, and tack in place. Wrap the ribbons around her ankles as shown in the photo on page 37, then tie in front, just above her ankle, in a bow. Tack in place. Hide the knot under the shoe top. Add some beads at the center top of shoe where the silk ribbon is attached.

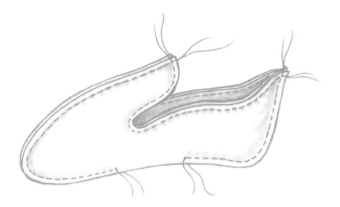

[step 1]
Double the fabric, and sew along the solid line, leaving open where marked.

AUTHOR'S SUGGESTION

The shoes are an optional embellishment. Some of the artists who made dolls from this pattern chose not to make shoes; others did.

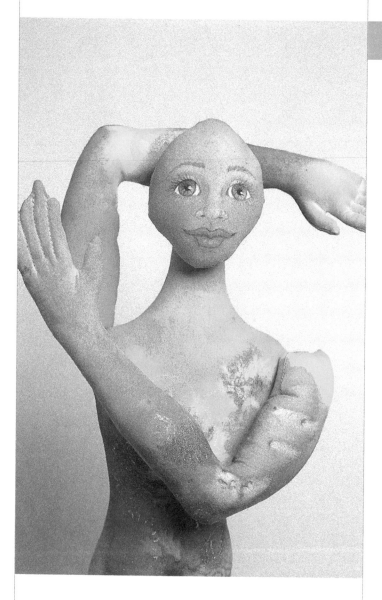

Finishing the Doll

1. Color in the whites of her eyes with the white gel roller. Add a highlight to each pupil on the side that's catching the light. Place a dot of red with a fabric pen or red pencil at the inside corners of each eye to represent the tear duct.

2. Outline her eyelids with the brown fabric pen again. Feather in her eyelashes: Start at the center above the pupil, and draw a short eyelash and then a long one, and alternate between adding a short lash and a long one until you have a pleasing effect. Her lower eyelashes will be shorter and lighter in color. Draw them in with a light touch.

3. The eyebrows are feathered in following the line you drew at the beginning. Always start with the brown pen, and change to black if you feel she needs darker eyebrows and eyelashes.

4. Outline her nostrils and the flare of her nose. Add some more shading and highlights if you feel she needs it. Add eye shadow with other colors.

5. Finish the face with more stamps.

6. For the head piece, loop silk scraps and tack them along her hairline (seam line), and fill in the bald spots with more silk loops. Add a silk ribbon and some glitzy yarns.

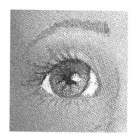

CHAPTER

3

FABRICATIONS:

Working with Tyvek, Liners, and Machine Embroidery

Intermediate Doll

For this project, you'll use the second, intermediate doll pattern. This pattern has a bit more detail. The additional pattern pieces add more shape to the face and body. The doll becomes more like a puzzle, with you piecing the parts together to create a new look. This pattern introduces joints, which you can embellish. You'll create some articulated fingers. Even the foot starts to take on a more realistic shape.

Which fabric should you choose for her body? To give your doll a realistic look, you can make her from a flesh-colored fabric. Or you can dye the fabric after you've made the body, as explained in the previous chapter. To create a more fanciful look, you might consider using a batik fabric. Any type of fabric can be used to make a body—just make sure it has a tight weave and doesn't fray easily.

Arien, the sample doll (Doll #2), was created using a tightly woven pimatex cotton, which was then dyed. In this chapter, you'll discover many ways to embellish your doll's body and clothing. And because the face on this doll has greater dimension, you'll learn how to sculpt it to add even more detail.

Supplies for the Body

$^1/_3$ yard (30.5 cm) pima cotton

good-quality polyester thread

pins

scissors

stuffing

stuffing tools

pipe cleaners

long darning needle and strong thread

hemostats

hand-sewing needles

art supplies

two 25-mm wooden beads for legs

two 20-mm wooden beads for arms

paints and brushes

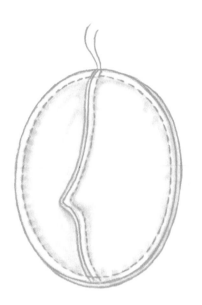

[step 3]
Sew all the way around.

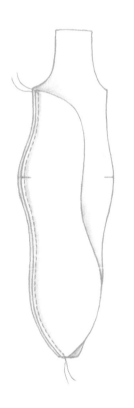

[step 5]
Sew from the center of the bust up
to the shoulder, then from the center of the
bust down to the bottom of the body.

Making the Body

1. Arrange and trace all patterns for Doll #2 onto the wrong side of the body fabric. (See Chapter 1, page 13.) Note those pattern pieces that have a seam allowance and those that don't.

2. Keep in mind that when doing the face and hands, you'll want to use a shorter stitch length on your sewing machine. Sew seam #1 on the Face and seam #2 on the Head Back, leaving open where marked. Cut out the two pieces. Open them up, and with right sides together, pin at the top of the head and at the chin.

3. Sew all the way around. Turn through the opening on the Head Back, and fill with enough stuffing so that the head is firm.

4. Sew seam #3 on the Body Back, leaving open where marked. Cut out all body pieces. (Keep in mind that if you use pinking shears, you won't have to clip curves.)

5. Matching the marks at the center of the bust, pin the Center Body Front to one Side Body Front piece. Sew from the center of the bust up to the shoulder, then from the center of the bust down to the bottom of the body.

    Do the same to the other Side Body Front piece. You now have a full body front.

6. Pin the Body Back to the full body front, and sew from the neck opening down the body and around up to the other side of the neck opening. Be sure to start out with a back stitch at the neck.

7. Turn the body right side out. Fill with enough stuffing so the body is firm. Be sure to plump up her breasts.

8. To stabilize the neck, place a pipe cleaner in it, but allow a bit of it to stick out so the head can rest on it. Close up the opening in the back with a ladder stitch, starting at the bottom of the opening and sewing up toward the top. When doing this, thread a long darning needle with about 1½ yards (1.5 m) of strong thread.

9. Attach the head to the neck by grabbing the neck with hemostats and pushing the neck into the opening at back of head. Ladder stitch the head to the neck.

10. Turning to the legs, sew from the opening at the knee all the way down to the opening at the toes on both sides of the Lower Leg. Cut out.

11. Fold the Lower Legs at the knees so the seams match. Sew along each tab, stopping short of the matched seams to leave an opening at the center.

12. For the feet, draw in a nice curve, as shown, and then sew, following your drawing.

13. Turn the Lower Leg through the opening at the top, and fill with stuffing. Close up the opening using a needle and thread.

14. The Upper Leg is sewn from the opening at the knee around the curve at the top and down to the other side of the opening.

15. Cut out the Upper Leg, fold at the knee, so the seams match. Sew along each tab, stopping short of the matched seam. Turn, and fill with stuffing. Close up the opening using a needle and thread.

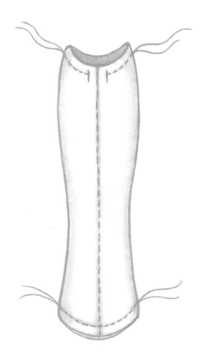

[step 11]
Sew tabs down to the center,
leaving them open at the center.

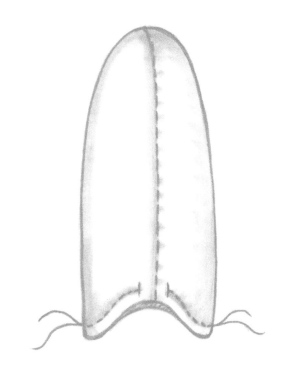

[step 15]
Close up the opening using
a needle and thread.

[step 16]
Join the Upper Leg to the
Lower Leg, using the beads.

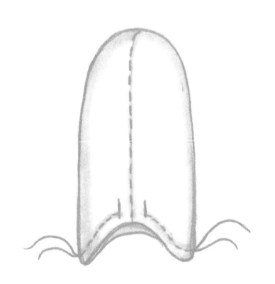

[step 19]
Fold the opening at the elbow
so the seams match. Sew across the tabs,
leaving it open at the center.

16. Paint the two 25-mm beads. After they're dry, join the Upper Leg to the Lower Leg, using the beads:

   a. Thread a needle with about ½ yard (46 cm) of strong thread, and knot the end. Insert the needle at the end of one tab on the Upper Leg.

   b. Go through the bead and into the other side of the tab. Go through the tab and back through the bead to the other side. Do this three times.

   c. If you have enough thread, you can pick up the Lower Leg and do the same thing you did with the Upper Leg. You now have one full leg.

   d. Do the same with the other leg.

17. After your legs are done, attach them to the body, using about 1 yard (91.5 cm) of strong thread and a long needle. Follow the instructions in Chapter 2, page 39, on how to do this.

18. Turning to the arms, sew the Upper Arm from the opening at the elbow around to the other side of the opening. Then cut it out.

19. Fold the opening at the elbow so the seams match. Sew across the tabs, leaving it open at the center. Turn the arm right side out, and fill it with stuffing.

20. Sew the Lower Arm from the opening at the elbow all the way around the fingers and back up to the other side of the opening at the elbow. When sewing around the fingers, be sure to have two stitches across the tips and two stitches in between the fingers. (There are two fingers attached. Don't sew down the dashed lines yet.)

21. Cut out the Lower Arm, clipping in between the fingers and at the curves around the wrist. When clipping between the fingers, clip at each side and right up to the stitches, to help prevent wrinkling once the hands are turned.

22. Fold the arm at the elbow as you did with the Upper Arm, and sew across the tabs, leaving it open at the center.

23. To turn the fingers, use either your favorite turning tool or the tubes described in Chapter 1, page 14.

24. After you turn the fingers, topstitch down the center of the two fingers that are attached. Finish the hands as described in Chapter 2, page 38.

25. Attach the arms to the 20-mm beads as you did with the legs, and attach the arms to the body as you did with the legs.

[step 20]
There are two fingers attached.
Don't sew down the dashed lines yet.

[step 24]
After you turn the fingers, topstitch down
the center of the two fingers that are attached.

Creating the Face

Because this doll has a center seam down her face, you don't have to worry about splitting it in half lengthwise.

The photo below illustrates how the doll's face should be grafted. The left side shows more of the grafting and the right side the finished look. Once you outline your features with a brown fabric pen, you can erase all pencil marks.

Supplies for the Embellishments

¹/₄ yard (23 cm) velvet for skirt

wood block or rubber stamp

iron

diaper liner (Gerber EZ-liner) or disposable diaper

crayons

baking parchment

rayon and metallic sewing threads

³/₈" (0.9 cm) silk ribbon

doilies

needle and thread

¹/₄ yard (23 cm) silk chiffon

dye

double-sided bonding sheet

glitzy yarns and threads

hot air gun

strong water-soluble stabilizer

fabric-weight and medium-weight Tyvek

acrylic or fabric paint or markers

wooden barbecue skewers

¹/₄" (0.6 cm) washers

tapestry needle

size 4 knitting needles

size D crochet hook

aluminum foil

darning or free-motion foot

beading wire

Embellishing the Doll

Clothing and embellishing the doll is the fun part. There are so many new techniques and ideas available. In this section we'll explore several. The dolls in the Gallery section that follows include all of the techniques discussed in this chapter, making them a great source of inspiration.

Transferring Colors and Images

Along with a few basic supplies, a diaper liner can help you transfer color and images onto your doll's skirt in no time at all. If you can't find a box of diaper liners and you don't have a box of disposable diapers handy, ask a friend, relative, or neighbor who does. All it takes is one diaper liner. (Disposable diapers have a lining inside that's the same as the EZ-liners.)

The skirt needs to be done first because it's attached first. Cut a 20" x 8" (51 x 20.5 cm) piece from the 1/4 yard (23 cm) of velvet. Lay it down on an ironing board, velvet side up.

If you have a wood block, that will work best. (If you don't, use a large rubber stamp.) Lay the diaper liner on top of the wood block. Pick out the color of crayon you want, and rub it on the diaper liner. You'll see the design transfer to the liner. Then lay the diaper liner on top of the velvet, crayon side up. Lay a piece of baking parchment on top, and iron over the design area with the iron on the highest setting. Hold the iron in place for about 10 seconds, then move to the next area. Lift up the baking parchment to ensure that the image transfers. Some irons aren't as hot as others, so you may have to go over the image again.

The diaper liner melts into the velvet, leaving the design from your rubbing. Although this technique can be used on other fabrics, it works best on velvet. Also, some people recommend grease markers (Shiva Markers), but crayons seem to work far better. Plus they're easy to find, and they're inexpensive. You'll go through a crayon very quickly, depending on how large a design you want.

Using Free-Motion Machine Embroidery

Sewing-machine embroidery can add your unique mark of creativity to almost anything you make. It is fun, easy, and faster than hand embroidery. Almost any thread will work if the sewing machine is properly adjusted. Experiment to find threads that work best with your machine. Correct thread tension is very important. Usually, the top tension needs to be looser than the bottom. Adjust the machine to allow the bottom tension to pull the top thread down even with the underside of the material. It should not be loose enough to cause loops on the wrong side of your work.

To prepare the machine, remove the presser foot, put on a darning or free motion foot, and lower the feed dog. (On some machines, a lever may raise the throat plate to keep the feed dog from interfering with stitching.) Then, set the machine stitch length and width controls on "O". Always test the stitch tension and setting before beginning your project.

To begin stitching, use the hand-wheel, insert the needle into the fabric, and bring up the bobbin thread. Holding threads taut, take three or four small stitches to lock the threads in place. Clip off the loose thread ends. Continue stitching following any of these basic movements: moving vertically or horizontally, back and forth across the fabric, or moving in small circular or swirl patterns. The movements can form distinct rows of stitches, as shown in the skirt design that follows, or they may be blended by overlapping. To end stitching, move the stitch width regulator to "O". Then, stitch three or four stitches in the same place. Pull the threads to the wrong side, and clip close to the fabric. You can also combine or overlap straight stitches and zigzag stitches.

Adding Ribbons, Silk Strips, and Lace

Once you add a splash of color to your doll's skirt, you can embellish it even more using a few basic techniques. The sample doll skirt here used free-motion machine embroidery, silk ribbons, lace motifs (from an old doily), and torn silk strips to add interest.

Start by placing some variegated rayon thread in your machine and any thread in the bobbin. (The thread in the bobbin won't show.) Starting at the top of the fabric, stitch up and down the length of the skirt. When you're ready to add a silk ribbon or torn silk strip, start at the top and gather the ribbon or strip as illustrated. Continue down the length of the skirt. You can add some strips at the bottom of the skirt and bunch them up tighter.

To add a lace motif, position a doily on the skirt wherever you want that design, and then topstitch it in place.

Finishing the Skirt

Once you have your skirt the way you want it, sew up the back seam and sew in a hem. (If you like, you can use decorative stitching for this.) Then sew a running stitch along the waist. Slip the skirt on the body and pull the threads at the waist to fit. Secure the threads by tying in an overhand knot then tack skirt to waist using a needle and thread.

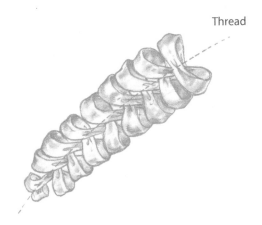

Thread

When you're ready to add a silk ribbon or torn silk strip, start at the top and gather the ribbon or strip.

Adding Glitz to the Bodice

Although the following technique happened by accident, it added glitz to the bodice just beautifully. To begin, tear two 10" x 4" (25.5 x 10 cm) pieces of silk chiffon. Dye them to match the doll's color scheme. As they dry (they'll do so fairly quickly), cut two pieces of double-sided bonding sheet the same size. Peel off the backing on one side of one sheet, and lay the sheet down on an ironing board, sticky side up. Throw bits and pieces of glitzy yarns and threads onto the sheet. Peel off the backing on one side of the second sheet, and lay this on top of your glitzy layer. With your iron on the highest setting, iron the two sheets together, creating a sandwich of glitz.

Set the sandwich aside, and lay down a piece of baking parchment on the ironing board. Place one chiffon piece onto the parchment. Peel off the backing from both sides of the sandwich, and place it down on the chiffon. Put the other piece of chiffon on top of the sandwich. Then put a piece of baking parchment on top of that. With the iron set at the highest setting, press one section at a time until your sandwich is ironed to itself.

Topstitch the silk chiffon sandwich with variegated rayon thread in a random fashion. Then carefully burn it with a hot air gun. You don't want to set it on fire: You simply want to char the silk, to expose the glitzy threads underneath and create a velvety effect.

Finish the bodice by using free-motion machine embroidery edging along the bottom. Place a piece of water-soluble stabilizer under the silk, then stitch. You'll want to start off with some straight stitches and then lock in your design by crossing over each one several times with some short zigzag stitches.

Place the bodice in room temperature water, and dissolve the stabilizer. Let the bodice air dry. Set it aside for now.

Creating Tyvek Beads

Tyvek is part paper and part fiber, so it doesn't tear easily. Express Mail and FedEx envelopes are made from medium-weight Tyvek; clothing and environmental suits, from fabric-weight Tyvek; and housing insulation, from heavy-weight Tyvek. For doll making, medium-weight and fabric-weight Tyvek are best. You'll want to avoid using the heavy-weight Tyvek because it has chemicals in it.

Cut some strips of Tyvek, and color both sides with acrylic or fabric paints, crayons, or markers. Let dry.

Cut these in smaller pieces of varying shapes, about 1" x 3" (2.5 x 7.5 cm). Wrap about three of the shapes and colors onto a wooden skewer, securing them with metallic thread. Using the lower setting on a hot air gun, melt the Tyvek together, to create a beautiful bead.

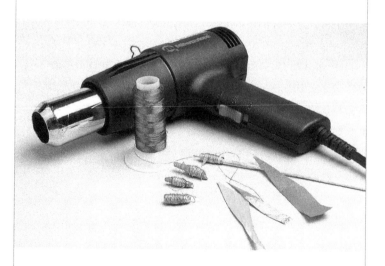

Using the lower setting on a
hot air gun, melt the Tyvek together,
to create a beautiful bead.

Carefully remove the bead from the skewer and make as many as you need to embellish the doll.

Take some Tyvek beads, and string them on some yarn. Tie several overhand knots in the ends to keep the beads from falling off the yarn. Topstitch these to the bottom of the bodice.

Applying Covered Washers

Hardware stores are a great place to find unique doll-making supplies. Washers are a good example.

First you'll need to cover the washers, using some yarn that matches the doll's outfit and a tapestry needle. The stitch used to cover the washers is called "button hole." If you don't know it, it's extremely easy to learn.

Leave the yarn on the spool. Thread the cut end through the tapestry needle, leaving about 1 yard (91.5 cm) to work with. (This means you'll pull 1 yard (91.5 cm) of the yarn off the spool.) Take the needle through the inside of the washer, and come up and under the loose end. Go back through the center of the washer and up under the loose end. Continue doing this until you've gone completely around the washer. Cut the yarn from the spool, and tie at the washer and again at the top. Topstitch this onto the bodice. Make as many covered washers as you want, and attach them to the bodice or leave some for other parts of the clothing.

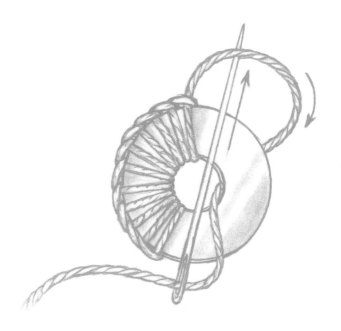

Cover the washers using the "button hole stitch."

Completing the Bodice

Once the bodice is embellished to your liking, pin it to the doll's body. Overlap the raw ends at her back, and ladder stitch or whipstitch it closed. Tuck in here and there using a needle and thread. Because the bodice is so embellished, the threads won't show.

Making Sleeves

The sample doll's sleeves were knitted and then finished with a crocheted edging. An alternative is to create sleeves from fabric. To recreate the knitted look, follow the steps below:

1. Using size 4 knitting needles, cast on 33.

2. Knit 29 rows.

3. Row 30: Knit 3, knit 2 together, repeat 5 times, knit 3.

4. Row 31: Knit.

5. Row 32: Knit 3, knit 2 together, repeat 4 times, knit 2.

6. Row 33: Knit.

7. Bind off, and leave a 7" (18 cm) tail.

8. Thread the yarn through a tapestry needle, and sew the sides together to form the sleeve.

9. To create the edging, anchor glitzy yarn at the bottom of the sleeve with a size D crochet hook. Chain 3. In the starting stitch of the knitted edge, double crochet 2 times. In the next stitch of the sleeve edge, double crochet 3 times. Continue around the edge of the sleeve with 3 double crochets in each stitch, to create a lacy effect.

10. Slip the sleeves onto the doll, and tack them to the shoulders using a needle and thread.

Creating Tyvek Clusters

Paint some light-weight or fabric-weight Tyvek using the colors of your choice. Let dry. Cut out various shapes. Hold these down on tile or aluminum foil with a wooden skewer, and apply heat with a hot air gun. The shapes will curl up on themselves. As you heat them, you can move them around with the skewer. Set them aside to cool.

Apply the clusters to the doll's sleeves to add interest. You might also place some on her head and add some Tyvek beads to the clusters as a further embellishment. The Tyvek remains soft, so you can sew the clusters using a regular needle and thread.

Creating Shoes

Trace the shoe pattern onto a piece of water-soluble stabilizer. Trace two for each foot for a total of four. Then trace two soles.

Place metallic thread in your bobbin and variegated rayon thread in your machine. Lower your feed dog, and use a darning foot or free-motion foot in your machine. (Keep in mind that when doing free-motion machine embroidery, you don't want the foot to touch the plate of the machine.)

Sew the outline of the shoes, then sew in a grid. The grid lays down a base that will prevent your decorative or free motion stitches from falling apart after the stabilizer is removed. To create a grid, stitch horizontally, back and forth across the piece from one side of the outline to the other. Then, stitch vertically, up and down the piece, to create perpendicular lines across the rows, thereby creating a grid. Dissolve the stabilizer.

When the pieces are dry, hand sew the top of the shoes together, and place them on the doll's feet. Hand sew the soles to the bottoms of the shoes while they're on her feet. Catch her feet occasionally to secure them.

Giving the Doll Wings

Trace two wings onto the water-soluble stabilizer. Sew along the outline, then do the grid work. After the grid work is done, set your machine to the zig-zag stitch, and fill in the centers of the design.

When the wings are to your liking, zigzag over some beading wire to stabilize them. Then put them in water to dissolve away the stabilizer. When the wings are dry, tack them to the doll's back.

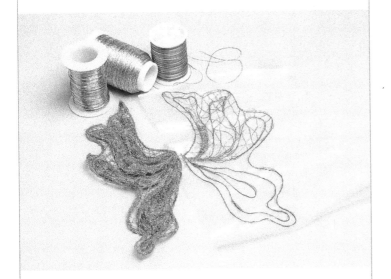

Adding Cuffs to the Wrists

Draw a design on the stabilizer and free-motion machine embroider. When you're done, put the cuffs in water to dissolve away the stabilizer. When they're dry, tack them onto the doll's arms.

Attaching Hair to the Head

On the sample doll, mohair was used. Cluster the mohair, and sew it along the hairline. Fluff it up and arrange it using a felting needle or a needle and thread. Sew some Tyvek clusters toward the front of her hairline. Then add some Tyvek beads.

What a beauty!

CHAPTER

4

BEADING:

Doing Peyote Beadwork and Bead Embroidery

Advanced Doll

So far you've learned how to make a beginning doll and an intermediate doll. In this chapter, you'll learn to make a more advanced doll, Dahlianna (Doll #3). What makes her more advanced? She has a chin gusset, fully articulated fingers, a more complicated bust overlay, and different joints.

After you've made this doll, you can dye her or you can use other fabrics to give the look of flesh. You may even want to make her from patterned fabric for a really unique look. Once the body is fully constructed, you'll learn to create beautiful beadwork to adorn her. The clothing on this doll is made primarily with dyed cheesecloth, to allow her ornamented body to show through.

Supplies

¹/₄ yard (23 cm) pima cotton

matching thread

scissors

hemostats

stuffing

stuffing fork

6 pipe cleaners

hand-sewing needles

3" (7.5 cm) needle and strong thread for attaching the arms and legs

Zig or Micron pens: black, brown, red

16 small buttons or accent beads for joints

cotton or wool batting for joints

Jacquard's Dye-NA-Flow paints in colors of your choice (The sample doll was dyed using magenta, chartreuse, violet, and green. Also, the flesh formula from the last two chapters was used for her face, neck, and part of her chest.)

cheesecloth (the kind found at grocery stores)

5 different decorative yarns for making fabric beads

size 10 or 12 beading needle

Nymo beading thread

beeswax

7 colors size 11 seed beads

accent beads for centers of flowers

small sheet of medium-weight Tyvek

mechanical pencil and eraser

colored pencils

Pentel gel pens: white, black, purple

2 colors size 6 seed beads

floral beads

tapestry needle

heat gun

metallic threads

variegated rayon thread

wooden skewer

silk ribbon dyed to match your color scheme

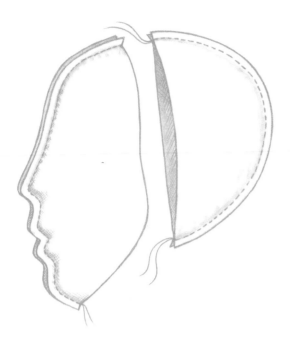

[step 3]
The Face and Head Back have tracing and sewing seams. Sew seam #1 on the Face and seam #2 on the Head Back.

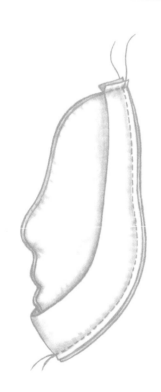

[step 4]
There will be a seam allowance at the top of the Face Gusset. Sew across this now.

Making the Body

1. Arrange and trace all patterns for Doll #3 onto the wrong side of the body fabric. (See Chapter 1, page 13.) Then double the fabric, right sides together, and pin in several places. Trace the Body Front onto a single layer of fabric. (This piece won't be doubled.)

2. When tracing the head pieces, notice that the Face Gusset has a grain line. Fold your fabric here so you have some stretch in the cheek area when you fill it with stuffing.

3. Begin by sewing the headpieces. The Face and Head Back have tracing and sewing seams. Sew seam #1 on the Face and seam #2 on the Head Back.

4. Cut out all three pieces for the head. Pin the Face Gusset, matching from the center of the chin at seam #3 on the Face to seam #3 on the Gusset, right sides together. Sew from the chin up to the top on one side, then from the chin to the top on the other side. There will be a seam allowance at the top of the Face Gusset. Sew across this now.

5. Pin the Head Back to the Face Gusset at seam #4, right sides together. Sew from top down to the X. Do the same on the other side. Keep in mind that you'll want to backstitch when you get to the X so the seam stays together when you fill the head with stuffing.

6. Clip curves, and turn right side out. Fill firmly with stuffing, then set aside.

7. Sew seam #5 on the Body Back, leaving it open where marked. Cut out both body pieces. Sew in darts on both the Body Back and the Body Front.

8. Pin the Body Back to the Body Front, right sides together, and sew from the opening at the neck around to the other side of the opening at the neck. Be sure to backstitch the neck area. Turn the body right side out, and fill with stuffing.

9. Cut out the Bust pieces. Fold each Bust at the dart, right sides together, and sew along the dashed lines. Turn right side out, and place a small amount of stuffing inside the bust "pocket."

10. Pin each Bust piece to the chest of the Body Front. Turning under just 1/8" (0.3 cm), start at the center and hand sew the Bust piece to the chest wall, using a ladder stitch. From the center, go up across the collarbone, down a bit by the "under arm," then leave it open here. Finish hand sewing under the Bust, then fill the rest of it with stuffing, and close up the opening.

11. After you attach each Bust piece, create the collarbone. Using a needle and thread, start at the center, hiding the knot under the breast. Come out about 1/4" (0.6 cm) from center top of the Bust. Take about a 1/4" (0.6 cm) length stitch across, heading toward the shoulder with the needle going into the Bust and up to the top where you attached it to the chest wall. Hide the stitch at the top, and go back down to 1/4" (0.6 cm) below this seam, next to the stitch you made above. Go across toward the shoulder as before and then back inside the Bust piece up to the top. Keep doing this up and down stitch until you come to the end of the Bust at the shoulder. Anchor the thread, and cut. What you've done is sculpt the collarbone. As you do the up and down stitches, pull a bit to define the "bone." Do the same to the other Bust.

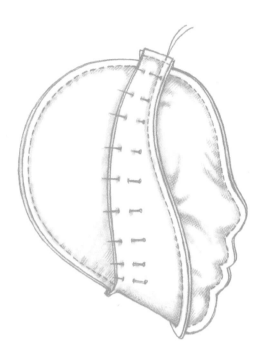

[step 5]
Pin the Head Back to the Face Gusset at seam #4, right sides together.

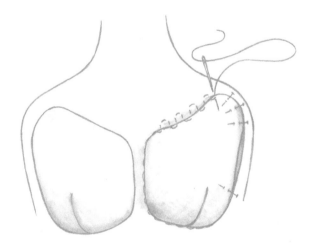

[step 10]
Turning under just 1/8" (0.3 cm), start at the center and hand sew the Bust piece to the chest wall, using a ladder stitch.

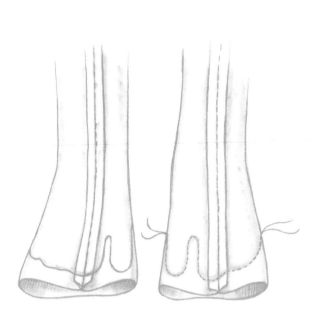

[step 13]
Draw in a big toe and then the other toes together. Make sure you have both a right and a left foot.

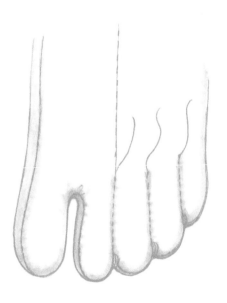

[step 14]
Sculpt the other toes using a needle and thread.

12. The upper legs are extremely easy. Sew all the way around both Upper Legs. Cut them out, and cut a slit on one side of each leg. Turn through this slit, and fill with stuffing. Close up the slit using a needle and strong thread.

13. To make the lower legs, sew from the opening at the toes around and down to the opening at the toes on the other side, leaving open where marked toward the top of the leg. Cut out the Lower Legs, then draw in the toes before turning. Note that this doll has a separate big toe. Fold the feet so the seams match at the toes. Draw in a big toe and then the other toes together. Make sure you have both a right and a left foot.

14. Next, follow your drawing and stitch the toes. Clip around the curves and in between the big toe. Turn the leg right side out through the opening at the top of the leg. Fill with stuffing, making sure to fill out the big toes. Sculpt the other toes using a needle and thread. First, draw with a pencil where you want the toes to be. Attach thread to the bottom of the foot (her sandals will cover it), and come out at the bottom of the toe, in between two toes. Sew a running stitch from top to bottom, back up to top, and down through fabric to bottom. When you come to about $1/8''$ (0.3 cm) from the end of the toe, wrap the thread over the top of the toe, and go into the fabric. Do this with each toe.

Finish by drawing in toenails with the brown Zig pen, and paint her toenails with paint or fingernail polish.

15. Trace four joints onto the wrong side of your fabric. Layer this with batting at the bottom and the fabric on top. The drawing is face up. Sew all the way around. Cut out the joints, and cut a slit in the drawing side on one layer only. Turn through this slit, and close up opening using a needle and thread.

16. Attach the joints to the legs with accent beads or small buttons. These joints show, so use nice beads or buttons.

17. Attach the legs to the body where marked.

18. Sew around the Upper Arm, leaving it open where marked. Cut it out, and turn through this opening. Fill with stuffing, and close the opening.

19. Sew the Lower Arm from the opening at the wrist around to the other side of the wrist opening. Turn, and fill to ¹/₂" (1.3 cm) above opening.

20. With a shorter stitch length on your machine, sew the Hands from the opening at the wrist around the fingers to the opening at the wrist on the other side. Follow the instructions in Chapter 3, page 53, for sewing fingers. Cut out the Hands, and finish as described in Chapter 1, pages 14 and 15, for both turning and wiring them.

21. After the Hands are done, insert them into the arms and ladder stitch at the wrists, leaving a small place open to finish filling up wrists with stuffing. Close up this opening.

22. Trace four joints as you did with the legs, and sew. Turn, close up the openings, and attach to Upper Arm and Lower Arm as you did with the legs.

23. Attach the arms to the shoulders, using the long needle and strong thread. Run the needle back and forth through the body as you did with the legs.

24. Draw the features on her face, then sculpt as described in Chapter 1, page 28.

25. Now dye the face and body and color the face. You can also refer to Chapter 5 for more ideas on faces.

26. While you have the dyes out, dye the cheesecloth. Dry everything thoroughly, then heat set everything either by placing the doll and the cheesecloth on a sweater rack in your clothes dryer or by ironing.

Embellishing with Beads

The techniques featured here include making a wrapped bead, making a simple peyote-beaded flower, and doing free-form peyote beadwork, which helps to create an undulating look by using different sizes of beads.

Beading is a fun way to add texture and interest to your doll. This art form has been around forever, and many terrific books are available on the history of beading.

1. To make a wrapped bead, cut each of the five different yarns into 3-yard (2.7 m) lengths. Tie one of the ends together. Move down about ½" (1.3 cm), and take 1 yarn and wrap it around the others until you get a shape that looks somewhat like a bead.

2. To secure this "bundle," thread your beading needle with 1½ yards (1.5 m) of beading thread. Put a knot in the end, and anchor this thread under the yarn bead. String on enough beads to go over the top of the yarn bead. Run the needle under the bead, and string up more beads to do the same. Keep adding rows of beads to add interest to your yarn bead.

3. Wrap another yarn around the rest of the yarns underneath your bead for about ½" (1.3 cm). Wrap another yarn bead. This time use one of your other yarns, and secure the yarn bead by coming out under the bead and then going over it, down under the bead and up again.

4. Continue wrapping and creating beads, sometimes using seed beads and other times using yarns to secure the yarn beads. You can do some latticework with yarns, too, or you can do needle lacing or crochet.

5. When you've gone the full length of the yarns, tie an overhand knot to secure everything. Set this aside for now. You can use this for her headband, which you'll complete toward the end of the project. (If you did it now it would be in the way.)

6. For the peyote-beaded flowers, you'll need the seed beads, beading needle, and nymo thread. Even if you haven't done peyote beadwork before, these flowers are simple to make, and the leaves are made using the same steps.

7. Start by cutting a 1-yard (91.5 cm) length of the nymo thread. Thread the beading needle with this. (To make threading easier, lick the eye of the needle, then thread it.) Because no stress will be placed on these petals, single thread is sufficient. Also, it helps to wax the thread with beading or beeswax to prevent the thread from knotting up. Pick up 12 of the size 11 seed beads, all in a single color. Run them to the bottom of the thread, leaving a 3" (7.5 cm) tail.

8. Skip beads 12, 11, and 10, and go through bead 9. (You're heading back toward the tail.) Go only through one bead, bead 9. Add a bead, skip bead 8, and go through bead 7. Add another bead, skip bead 6, and go through bead 5. Add a bead, skip bead 4, and go through bead 3. Add a bead, skip bead 2, and go through bead 1. Now you've done peyote beadwork and learned the peyote chant: Add, skip, go through! Fun, right?

9. At the bottom where your tail is, tie the two threads together in an overhand knot, twice. Head back the other way by adding a bead, and go through the "up" bead (the last bead you put on in the previous row). You've still skipped a bead, the "down" bead, or bead 1 where it all began. Continue on by adding another bead, skip the "down" bead, and go through the "up" bead. Add another bead, skip the "down" bead, and go through the "up" bead. Stop. You want to see two more "up" beads. Next, add two beads (you'll do this only once on each side), go back down toward the tail, and go through the "up" bead. Add a bead, skip the "down" bead, and go through the "up" bead and on down through the last two beads. This technique is different, but the beadwork here is the end of one petal, and it needs to be thinner than the midpart of the petal.

[step 8]
Add interest with
peyote beadwork.

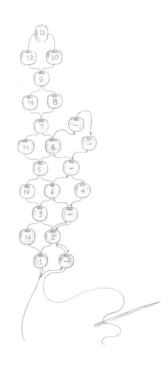

[step 9]
At the bottom where your tail
is, tie the two threads together in
an overhand knot, twice.

10. Your needle is at the bottom of the work. Take the needle over to the next bead at the bottom, and go up through two beads. Add a bead, skip the "down" bead, and go through the "up" bead. Add a bead, skip the "down" bead, and go through the "up" bead. Stop. You're at the same point as you were on the other side. Add two beads, go down toward the bottom and through the "up" bead, add a bead, and go through the next three beads. You're at the bottom again. You now have one complete petal.

11. Next to this petal, create two more petals using the same color beads. The bottom part of your flower—the three petals that are connected—is done. Secure the petals by weaving your thread in and out of the beads at the bottom of each petal.

12. Change colors, and create three more petals. These will remain on the top of the three lower petals. Secure them using a needle and thread.

13. At the center of each flower, add an accent bead. This can be a beautiful Austrian crystal or any another type of bead. Make as many flowers as you want. Change your colors around. The sample doll has 15 flowers.

14. Use the same pattern for the leaves, but do only half of the petal. So instead of having two sides with points, you'll have only one side. This creates the look of a leaf.

15. Start tacking the petals to her arms, then string some green beads along her arm to create the look of vines. Add some leaves to the vines, and continue tacking on the flowers.

16. Before tacking flowers to her bodice, you'll want to add some clothing. Her bodice is done the same way as for Doll #1 in Chapter 2. Loop two strips of cheesecloth around each other, then tie it at the back. Sew it in place using a needle and thread. Cut some smaller strips of cheesecloth, and arrange them at her shoulders.

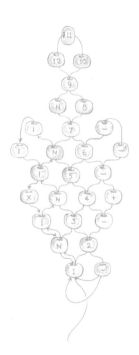

[step 10]
Your needle is at the bottom of the work. Take the needle over to the next bead at the bottom, and go up through two beads.

17. Once her bodice is in place, you can tack on some flowers. Leave room for some free-form peyote beadwork.

18. To begin, thread a beading needle with 2 yards (1.8 m) of beading thread. As with the flowers, you don't need to double it. You'll need two colors of size 11 seed beads and one color of size 6 seed beads. Pick up two of each of these beads on your needle and thread. Six total. Add a bead, skip bead 6 and go through bead 5, add a bead, skip bead 4 and go through bead 3. Add a bead, skip bead 2 and go through bead 1. When adding the beads, change sizes. Keep doing these rows until you have the length you want. Add some accent beads every once-in-awhile to give a more undulating effect.

19. Once you have the look you want, tack it to her bodice. Add more flowers and leaves.

20. Tack a flower on each of the arms where you attached them to the body. These add a nice touch to cover those stitches.

21. To make her skirt, use a strip of the cheese-cloth, and tack it to her body just below her waist. Cover that with a narrow strip of cheesecloth that has been dyed a different color, then cover that with some fancy yarns. Sew on some accent beads here and there along the top edge of the skirt.

22. Make some Tyvek beads. (See Chapter 3, page 58.) Add them to some of the yarns, and tack along her waist. Allow the Tyvek beads to dangle from the waist. Slip some larger beads on the bottom of the cheese-cloth strip that's at her waist.

23. Her headpiece is another strip of cheesecloth that's wrapped around her head and tied at the top. Wrap the yarn beads you created around this, as shown on the sample doll, and secure in place using needle and thread. Add some more strips of cheesecloth at the top and a beaded flower to one side.

24. Her shoes are done using free-motion machine embroidery on water-soluble stabi-lizer. Trace the bottoms of her left foot and her right foot onto the stabilizer. Next lay the stabilizer on top of her feet, and trace the design you want. Sew in your design, and dissolve the stabilizer. (See Chapter 3, pages 60 and 61, for more on this process.)

25. Attach her sandals to her feet using a needle and thread. Secure a few beads here and there, then add some silk ribbons and some beaded flowers to the top.

CHAPTER

5

COLLAGE:

Working with Fabric, Beading, and Photo Transfers

The Collage Doll

This sample doll, named Down Memory Lane, uses several forms of collage. To begin with, she combines all three patterns—her body is from Doll #2, her arms are from Doll #1, and her head, hands, and legs are from Doll #3.

Before the body is made, a decorative fabric is created using collage techniques. Then the main body parts are cut from this fabric. Her face, hands, feet, and upper chest are all done in flesh tones. More detailed face instructions are discussed in this chapter along with using a different type of stamping material. Remember: It's good to experiment with different mediums. Also, don't let a label throw you off—if you like a product, go ahead and try it on fabric.

Incorporating collaged materials into your dolls will open up a whole world of design possibilities. You can also use collage to explore all types of textures and themes, transforming your doll into a true work of art.

Supplies

photos

photo-ready fabric

scissors

rayon and metallic threads for machine embroidery

fabrics for making collage body (batiks, prints, solids, and so on)

fat quarter-pima cotton for face, bust, hands, and feet

threads to match

stuffing

stuffing and turning tools

yarns (including glitzy ones)

fine netting

pins

face supplies

Tsukineko's All Purpose Inks: sand, white, autumn leaf, cherry pink, and other colors of your choice

paint brushes and containers for mixing paints

paper towels

Tsukineko's Fantastix (looks like empty markers)

Brilliance stamp pads

rubber stamps

hand-sewing needles

strong thread for sculpting

beads: beading needles and thread

accent beads

old lace or trims

crochet hook

tulle

Lucet

[step 1]
In the sample doll, squares and stars were
cut from various fabrics, in various sizes.

[step 2]
Peel off the paper backing, and cut
out the photos you want to use.

Making the Body

1. Before cutting out the body parts, create a collage of fabrics and designs to form the main part of the doll's body. In the sample doll, squares and stars were cut from various fabrics, in various sizes. The smaller square had a "window" cut in the center.

2. Using the photo-ready fabric, have some pictures copied onto the fabric. If you have a copy machine at home, you can do this easily yourself. If you don't, you can go to your local copy center. Peel off the paper backing, and cut out the photos you want to use.

3. Place the shapes and photos on the main fabric, and free-motion machine embroider them in place.

4. Using Body for Doll on page 268, make your templates. On the Center Body Front, draw across the bust and add a seam allowance on each side, above and below the drawn line. Make a template from this.

5. On the wrong side of the collaged fabric created, lay out the body pieces, except for the top of the Center Body Front, which you'll do in flesh or white fabric. Following the construction of this pattern in Chapter 3, page 50, put the body together. The only difference will be the Center Body Front, which you'll sew together at the center bust then match to the Side Body Front as in Chapter 3.

6. The legs (but not the feet) are from the Doll on page 271. Simply draw a line at the ankle, adding seam allowance. Then trace the feet from Doll on page 267, adding a seam allowance at the ankle.

7. Then trace the Upper Leg and Lower Leg (minus the feet) onto the wrong side of one fabric. (The sample doll uses striped fabric for one side and the created fabric from step 1 for the other side.) Sew as instructed in Chapter 4, page 68.

8. Sew the feet as instructed in Chapter 3, page 51.

9. Fill everything with stuffing. Insert the feet into the Lower Leg, and ladder stitch at ankle.

10. One side of the arms uses a pretty fabric that's created in a unique way: On the right side of one fabric, lay down all kinds of yarns and metallic threads. On top of this, place some fine netting. Pin in several places.

11. Free-motion machine embroider this together to make a beautiful piece of fabric.

12. The sample doll uses the arms from the Doll on page 265, and the hands from Doll #3, page 270. Trace two arms onto the wrong side of your fabric of choice, then use the above fabric as the other side, and pin the right sides of both fabrics together. Sew, cut out, turn, and fill with stuffing.

13. The hands are done as in Chapter 4, page 69, with the exception that they're separated from the arm. Follow the instructions for turning, wiring, and filling them with stuffing. Insert the hands into the arms at the wrist, and ladder stitch them together.

14. The head is created from Doll #3, page 269, following the instructions in Chapter 4, page 66.

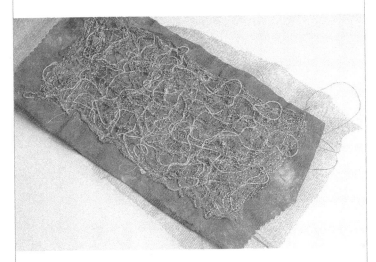

[step 10]
On the right side of the fabric, lay down all kinds of yarns and metallic threads.

Coloring the Face and Chest

1. Draw and sculpt the face, according to the instructions in Chapter 1, page 28. Then add color either using Tsukineko's All Purpose Inks or dying your doll as you did in the other chapters.

2. For the flesh, mix sand, white, and autumn leaf. Add water, then brush on the entire face and chest.

3. While the color is still wet, pour some left-over flesh color into a container, and add a couple drops of cherry pink for her cheeks. Dip a brush in the ink, and dab it on some paper towels. Now dab it on her cheeks. If it's too bright, use another brush and add more flesh color.

4. Pour some flesh color into another container, and add about 4 drops of sand to this. Add the shading to the side of her face that will be in the shade.

5. After the face is dry, use the Fantastix, and load them with the inks of your choice. Color in the iris by starting with a light color then adding dark to the side of the eye in the shadow.

6. Do the same with the lips.

7. When this is all dry, color in the whites of the eyes with the white ink.

8. After the face is dry, use your pens to add detail.

9. Using the Brilliance stamp pads, stamp her chest and face as you wish. On the sample doll, a Fantastix was dabbed on the Brilliance ink pad and then brushed on her eyelids and eye creases, and stamped images were added for more color.

10. Color or dye her hands and feet. (If you are going to sculpt her toes, do so before coloring.)

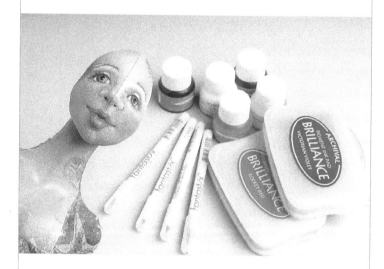

[step 9]
On the sample doll, a Fantastix was dabbed on the Brilliance ink pad and then brushed on her eyelids and eye creases, and stamped images were added for more color.

Embellishing the Joints

Using some leftover fabric, beads, and yarns, you can embellish the joints in a truly unique way. You'll want to make at least four of these joints, to go along with the collage theme and to replace the joints from the pattern for Doll #3, Chapter 4. You can also make a fifth one, and add it to her belt as the sample doll shows.

1. Cut two 12" x 1" (30.5 x 2.5-cm) strips from three of your fabrics, on the bias.

2. With right sides together, sew these strips, lengthwise, into tubes.

3. Turn using the brass tubes you use to turn fingers or whatever other tool you prefer to use.

4. Decide how you want your colors to go, and cut one strip 1½" (4 cm) long, one strip 3½" (9 cm) long, and the last one 2½" (6.5 cm) long.

5. Cut another piece of fabric (a different color from above) so that it measures 1½" x 1" (4 x 2.5 cm). Finger press one long edge under ⅛" (0.3 cm).

6. Sew the strips together at the top. Fold the short one in half, and position it so that it's facing you. The longer one goes on either side of this, looping it down and up; the medium one, on the outside of the longer one, looping down in front and up.

7. Cover the top of the bundle with the piece of fabric you cut in step 5. Fold under the back, and ladder stitch up the back. Sew along the folded edge, catching the loops as you sew. This secures them so they don't fall out. About ⅛" (0.3 cm) down from the top, sew a running stitch around the top. Leave the needle and thread in for the time being. The strap will be done next, then the dangle will be finished.

8. From one of the tubes, cut a ¾" (2 cm) length. Tuck one end in the top of the bundle, and pull the threads to fit tightly around the strap. Poke the raw edges of the top of the bundle under, and hand stitch the bundle to the strap.

9. The top of the strap is covered with a circle of fabric. Cut out a ¾" (2 cm) circle. Sew a running stitch along the edge, and start to pull. Place the top of the strap inside, and pull circle to fit snugly around the strap. Sew in place.

10. Wrap glitzy yarn around the top of the strap, then run it down to the bundle around the dangles. On the center loop at the bottom, sew a drop or accent bead.

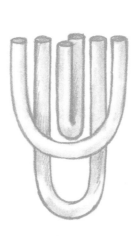

Attaching the Joints and Finishing the Legs

1. Sew one joint at the bottom of her Upper Leg and at the top of her Lower Leg—that is, one on each side of her leg. Do the same on her other leg.

2. Sew her legs to her body, as done in Chapter 4, page 69.

3. Paint some lace to match your color theme. When it's dry, cut two 7" (18 cm) lengths, and hand sew a running stitch along the top edge. Pull to gather, and fit where the feet meet at the ankle. Tack in place.

4. Dye an appliqué motif, and hand sew at ankle of one leg and on the thigh of the other leg.

Finishing the Arms

1. After her hands are dry, color in her fingernails with either the inks or a marker.

2. Using the inks, color a piece of old lace. (Thrift stores are a good place to find old lace if you don't have some handy.)

3. Tack the lace to the arms. Have a bit of it spill over onto the hands.

4. Attach the arms to the body at the shoulders with a needle and strong thread, as done in Chapter 2, page 39.

5. To cover the area where the arm is attached, add a crocheted ruffle:

   a. Using a size G crochet hook, chain 14.

   b. Row 2: Single crochet in each chain.

   c. Row 3: Chain 1 and half double crochet two in each single crochet.

   d. Row 4: Chain 2 and double crochet two in each half double crochet.

   e. Row 5: Chain 1 and half double crochet in each double crochet.

   f. Anchor off, and sew the completed ruffle to the arm at the shoulder.

Adding the Clothing

Because the doll is so colorful, less is more when it comes to clothing her. Besides, you don't want to hide your beautiful collage work underneath layers of clothing. The sample doll is clothed in a simple tutu and a snazzy belt.

1. The tutu is a 20" x 5" (51 x 12.5 cm) piece of tulle. Fold this in half, and hand sew a running stitch along the raw edges. Pull to fit just below her waist, with the opening in the back, then tack in place.

2. The belt is made of two tubes of fabric and a length of yarn that was braided using a Lucet. If you don't have a Lucet, braid some yarn together to the length you want. Measure around her body below her waist to get your measurement.

3. Once you have your tubes and braid made, sew them together at each end, then fit the belt on her body to cover the raw edge of her tutu. Sew in place.

4. At the center, add one joint similar to her leg joints, or add a button or an accent bead.

5. The edging around her bodice is also done on a Lucet. If you don't have a Lucet, make another braid with yarns. Tack this in place. Add an appliqué motif if you wish.

Attaching the Hair

1. Attach mohair to the top of her head, as done in Chapter 3, page 61.

2. Around the mohair, gather a length of the painted lace, and fit it around her head. Then tack it in place.

CHAPTER

6

PAINTING
AND EMBELLISHMENTS:

Coloring a Face and Beading Accessories

Magdalene

Head pattern (pages 280–281) is used on this doll to give a more adult look. Fabric paints are used to add dimension to the face. These give more vibrancy as well. Body pattern (pages 276–277) is used, but with changes to a leg and an arm, and some tucks added in the body. These change the positioning of the doll. Using simple tucks here and there on any cloth doll body can add excitement to its body attitude.

Materials

½ yard (46 cm) white cotton for the body

thread to match

6 pipe cleaners for the fingers

good-quality stuffing

¼ yard (23 cm) batik cotton for the bodice and shoes

¼ yard (23 cm) polyester fabric for the skirt

5 yards (4.6 m) each of 3 different yarns for embellishments

rayon and metallic sewing machine thread

mohair for hair

scraps of organza in 3 colors for embellishments

water-soluble stabilizer (Mokuba's Free Lace is an excellent choice)

5 colors of seed beads, size 11

five 6-mm Miracle beads

one hundred 4-mm crystals

beading thread and needles

1' (30 cm) 24-gauge beading wire

fabric paints (Jacquard's Textile and Lumiere, or Stewart Gill's Byzantia and Alchemy, are good choices)

Jacquard's Dye-Na-Flow in yellow, white, and red

Portfolio Series Water Soluble Oil Pastels

Tsukineko's Fantastix (optional)

Krylon's Workable Fixative, or other aerosol workable fixative

gesso

acrylic paints

paint brushes in various sizes, including small detail brushes

strong thread for sculpting

rubber stamps

Zig Millennium or Micron Pigma pens in black, red, and brown

gel pens in white, red, and a color for the eyes

various colored markers for acrylic face (colors to outline eyes, eyelashes, lips, and any additional detailing)

Tools

stuffing and turning tools

hand sewing needles

free-motion or darning foot for your sewing machine

Body Construction

1. Sew everything but the head. This project uses Head pattern (pages 280–281).

2. You will note that one leg is straight. I simply redrew one leg by tracing the upper leg, and then shifted the pattern to trace the lower leg (left).

3. After the body is filled with stuffing, sew a ladder stitch on one side of the waist to give it the curve needed so she'll rest on the other side (below, left).

4. Repeat the procedure from step 3 at the inside of the elbow to bend one arm.

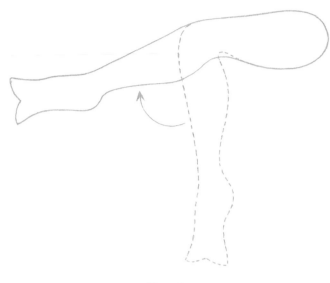

[Step 2]
Drawing a bent leg from the pattern

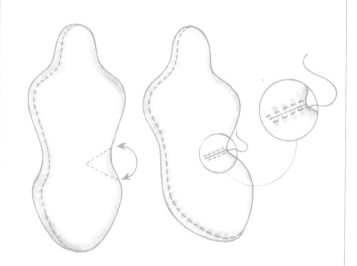

[Step 3]
Adding curves to the body with ladder stitches

The Head

1. Trace the two headpieces onto the wrong side of the fabric, making sure the arrow is on the grain line.

2. Sew Seam #1 on the Face, and Seam #2 on the Head Back. Back stitch at chin and bottom of back of head.

3. Cut out both pieces. Turn the back of the head right side out, and slip it into the Face. Pin them together, right sides together (right).

4. Sew from the top of the head down to the x. Back stitch here.

5. Sew the other side from the top of the head down to the other x.

6. Clip the curves, and turn the Head right side out. Fill it firmly with stuffing. This head can look very narrow if you don't fill out the jaw line and the cheeks.

   Push the stuffing into these areas. You'll be amazed at the amount of stuffing you can pack in.

7. Hand sew the Head to the Neck, using a ladder stitch.

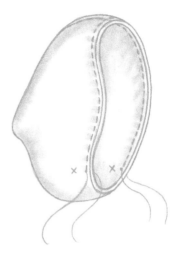

[Steps 3–5]
Sew Head Back to Face, right sides together

[Step 6]
The left head does not have enough stuffing in the cheeks and jaw
The right head is filled correctly

Drawing and Sculpting the Head

1. Follow the instructions in Chapter 1 (page 28), for both the drawing and sculpting of the head. Even though it is slightly different in shape, it is drawn and sculpted in the same manner.

2. After the face is drawn and sculpted, outline the features with a brown fabric pen.

Painting the Head

Fabric paints were used for the sample doll. The following are formulas that I used to mix the flesh and shading colors.

Flesh formula:

Jacquard's Textile, Lumiere, and Dye-Na-Flow Paints

Textile Paints:

1 part Russet

1 part Goldenrod

4 parts White

Mixed with:

2 parts Lumiere Pearl White

1 part Dye-Na-Flow Golden Yellow

Add 2 parts water.

1. Paint all flesh parts with this formula.

2. For shading, use 2 parts flesh formula mixed with $\frac{1}{2}$ part Russet Textile Paint and $\frac{1}{4}$ part Violet Dye-Na-Flow. You could mix with brown, but I find these colors warmer and more realistic.

3. Shade down the sides of the nose, around the upper crease of the eyelid, under the nose and around the flare of the nose, under the lower lip, and along the temples.

4. Using 1 part White Textile Paint mixed with 1 part Pearl White Lumiere, add highlights to the forehead, down the center of the nose, on both flares of the nose, on the center of the chin, on the cheekbones, and on the brow. Refer to the photo for placement of the highlights.

[Step 6]
Fill in eyes with white paint

5. For the cheeks, put a small amount of the flesh formula in a container, and add Magenta. Load up a brush with this color, and dab quite a bit of it onto a piece of paper towel. Blush her cheeks with this brush.

AUTHOR'S SUGGESTION

The technique described in Step 5 is called dry brushing. It gives you more control with the paint.

6. Use the white paint to fill in the entire eye area.

7. Magdalene's irises are next. They are two shades of blue: a light blue and a medium blue. Fill in the irises with the light blue (or the light color you want to use). You'll use a small brush for this. With the medium color, darken the side of each iris that is in the shadow.

8. The eye shadow on the sample doll is a metallic blue with pewter added. With a small brush, color around the upper crease of the eye, and a bit under the eyelid. This gives a vampish look.

9. While the eye shadow is drying, color the lips. Again, use two shades: a medium and dark red, rose, or other color of your choice. Fill in the lips with the medium color. Next, use the darker color on the upper lip and the side of the lips that are in shadow. Let her lips dry.

10. When the eyes are dry, use a small brush and black paint to add the pupil.

11. Add a dot of red to the inside corner of each eye.

Close-up of finished face

12. Color the rest of the body with the paints of your choice. Magdalene has a red upper body and arms, and yellow legs.

13. After the body is dry, use rubber stamps and Lumiere paint to stamp her body.

14. After the body is stamped, let it dry for 24 hours, then heat set. There are several choices for heat setting. Place the doll on a sweater rack, in a clothes dryer set on the cotton setting for 30 minutes, or in an oven set at 225°F (105°C) for

15 minutes. Whatever you do, don't microwave her. There's enough wire in her wrists to cause her to fry. Plus, it wouldn't be good for your microwave.

15. When the doll is dry, it is time to do the detail work. Start by outlining the eyelids with a black Zig or Micron pen. Use this same pen to draw thin eyebrows. With a white gel pen, add a dot of white to each pupil.

16. Dot the nostrils with a brown pen, and draw the flare on each side of her nose.

17. Use a red pen to outline the upper and lower lips, and draw the creases. For the center of the mouth, use a brown pen. A red pen just doesn't show up.

18. Using a contrasting gel pen, outline the irises and draw in the rods that radiate out from the pupil. Use the black Zig or Micron pen to draw in the eyelashes.

AUTHOR'S SUGGESTION

When using Lumiere on rubber stamps, have some water and an old toothbrush nearby. Lumiere, or any metallic or pearlized paints, will dry quickly on the stamps, clogging them up. As soon as you are finished stamping, clean the stamps with water and the toothbrush.

Using Acrylic Paints

Acrylic paints are a bit different from fabric paints. Actually, most fabric paints are simply acrylic paints with a textile medium added. This allows the fabric to be painted without the paint making the fabric stiff. In painting a cloth doll head with acrylic paints, you get an entirely different look.

When painting with acrylics, you have to work quickly. They dry almost immediately. You can add products called extenders to the paint to slow the drying time. Golden has one called Acrylic Glazing Liquid that gives you approximately 45 minutes to work on the face before the paints dry.

1. Start with a head that has been filled with stuffing, and cover it with gesso. Allow it to dry, and then sand it with fine sandpaper.

2. Do this two more times. It takes about three coats of gesso to seal the head.

3. Once the last coat of gesso is dry (this generally takes about one hour), paint the head with the paints of your choice.

I find working with acrylics most appropriate for creating a whimsical or fantasy doll.

Artist Arley Berryhill used acrylic paints
to add texure to Lady in Red's expressive face.

Artist Li Hertzi used acrylic paints over the
entire body of Wide Open to show off her bright, energized posture.

[Step 5]
Zigzag yarns to seams of bustier.

Creating Clothing

1. Cut two each of the Bustier pieces (pages 280–282).

2. Pin the Center Front Seam #1 to the Side Front Seam #2, wrong sides together. Zigzag stitch these by machine, from the top to the bottom. Do the same with the other side.

3. Pin the Back piece together at Seam #4, wrong sides together, and sew from the top to the bottom.

4. Pin the Front Bustier to the Back at Seam #3. Zigzag stitch by machine, wrong sides together.

5. Using one of your yarns, zigzag stitch the yarn to both sides of the seam by machine.

6. With right sides together, sew the shoulder seam, joining Seam #5 to Seam #6.

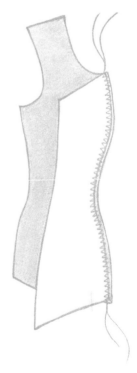

[Step 2]
Sew Center Front to Side Front using a zigzag stitch.

Skirt detail

7. Machine sew the yarn along the upper edge of the bustier all the way around, starting on the left side front. When you reach the right side front, zigzag down the front.

8. Machine sew more yarn to the arm openings, as described above.

9. The bottom of the bustier is left unhemmed. This will be covered up with the embellishments.

10. The skirt is 20" (51 cm) wide by 8½" (22 cm) long. Machine sew the back seam, right sides together.

11. Turn under a hem ⅛" (3 mm) wide. Zigzag stitch in place. Edge the hem with yarn by machine sewing the yarn in place.

12. Machine sew a running stitch along the waist, and pull to gather. Slip the skirt onto the body, and hand sew it in place, just below the waist.

13. Slip the bustier onto the body, and adjust to fit at the center front. Pin it in place.

14. Sew crystals down the front of the bodice to close it, and to give the look of sparkling buttons. Mark the bodice so that the crystals are ⅜" (1 cm) apart.

15. To make the ruffles that create the edge of the bustier, cut 11 circles from each of the 3 pieces of organza. You'll have 33 circles.

16. Place these, one by one, between two sheets of water-soluble stabilizer. Pin in place.

17. With the rayon thread in the upper threader of your machine, and the metallic thread in your bobbin, free-motion machine sew lacy edges around each of the circles. (See photo, page 98.)

[Steps 16–18]
Free-motion machine sew on circles of fabric

18. In free-motion machine work, the key is to create a base of threads for the top machine threadwork to lock onto. It is important to make sure that, as you sew, your threads connect with each other. Start on the circle of fabric, and then run along the edge. The samples were sewn with circular machining around the edges. This circular sewing was done several times, going around and around along the edge of the fabric.

19. Dissolve the stabilizer according to the manufacturer's recommendation. Let the circles dry.

20. When they are dry, place three circles on top of each other, alternating the colors.

21. Sew them together at the center in a circle. Pull the thread to gather them, and then hand sew them along the edge of the bustier. At the center front, sew a beaded flower. The instructions for the flower are at the end of this chapter (page 101).

22. Cut three different yarns into 10" (25 cm) lengths. You'll need enough of these to put one between each of the ruffles. Tie the yarn bundles at the center, and then hand sew them between the ruffles.

23. At the shoulders, tie the bundles into a bow, and hand sew along the edge of the bustier.

24. Cover the wrist area with beads or trim to hide the seams.

[Steps 7–8]
Hand sew a beaded flower at center of Shoe Top.

The Shoes

1. Cut out four Shoe Soles from the same fabric. Set aside.

2. Trace two Shoe Tops on the wrong side of the fabric. Double the fabric, right sides together, and sew along Seam #1. Cut out both Shoe Tops. Turn, right side out.

3. Cut a slit down the center of one of the Shoe Soles. You'll do this for both shoes.

4. Pin the Shoe Tops to the Shoe Soles that aren't slit, right sides together. On top of these, pin the Soles that have been slit.

5. Sew all the way around the outer edge of the shoe along Seam #2.

6. Turn the shoes through the slits, and push out the sides of the shoes.

7. Place the shoes over the feet of your doll. Hand sew three of the yarns, cut in 24" (61 cm) lengths, along each of the Shoe Tops. Start attaching them at the center of the shoe, and at the center of the yarn. Follow the upper edge of the Shoe Tops. As you hand sew the yarns, they will go through the foot, too. This secures the shoes to the feet.

8. When you get to the sides, wrap the rest of the yarns around the legs, and tie them in a bow about mid-shin. With a needle and thread, tack the yarns to the legs.

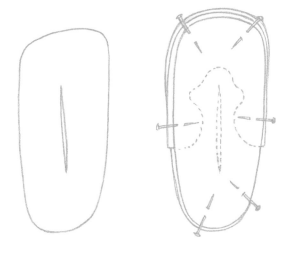

[Steps 3–4]
Cut a slit in one Shoe Sole and pin to remaining shoe parts.

Beaded Flowers

These beautiful flowers can be used on dolls, garments, quilts, jewelry, and any number of creations. If you are familiar with peyote beadwork, you'll find them very simple to make. If you aren't familiar with peyote beadwork, you'll still enjoy the process.

1. Assemble your supplies: Miracle or Wonder Beads, size 11 seed beads, beading thread, and needles.

2. Thread a beading needle with 2 yards (1.8 m) of beading thread. Don't tie a knot at the end of the thread.

3. Needle up enough size 11 seed beads to wrap around the Miracle Bead. You'll measure around the bead for now. Take the beads down towards the tail and tie them in a circle, using an overhand knot.

4. You'll now start doing a circular peyote stitch. Place one seed bead on the needle.

5. Skip the bead that is next to the bead that the thread has passed through, and go through the next bead.

6. Add another bead, skip a bead, and go through another bead. Continue this around the circle.

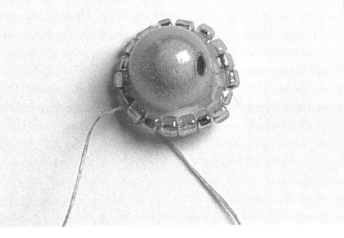

[Step 3]
String beads to wrap around Miracle Bead.

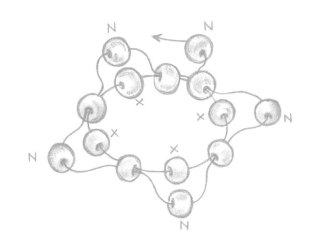

[Steps 4–6]
Circular peyote stitch

AUTHOR'S SUGGESTION

If you have an even number of beads on your circle, you'll need to do what is called a "step up" in peyote beadwork. This means that when you come out of your last bead in the circle, there won't be room to add another bead. You will go through the bead that is sticking up; it's called an "up" bead.

If you have an odd number of beads in your circle, you'll be able to add a bead, and then go through the "up" bead.

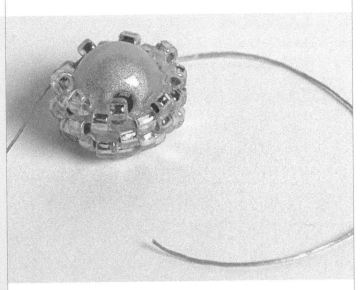

[Steps 6–8]
Creating rows of peyote beading, before stringing Miracle Bead

7. Continue around the circle three more times. After the third row, pull your beads and the beads will pull up into a cup.

8. After you have made four rows (the base row and the first row of peyote are considered Row #1), it is time to thread the Miracle Bead.

9. Weave down to a center bead in a three-bead stack.

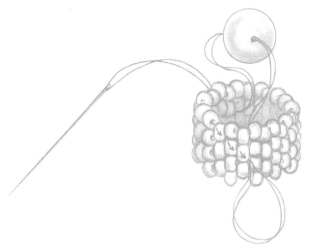

[Steps 9–11]
Add the Miracle Bead at the center of the peyote "cup."

10. Go to the inside of the cup, and pick up the Miracle Bead with the needle. Go straight across to the other side, and through a middle bead.

11. Go back inside and through the Miracle Bead, and over to the original side. Go into a seed bead, and then weave up to an "up" bead along the top edge.

12. Come out the "up" bead, and pick up four seed beads, one crystal, and one seed bead.

13. Skip the last seed bead, and go through the crystal and the #4 seed bead.

14. Pick up three more seed beads, and go over to the next "up" bead.

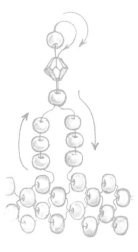

[Steps 12–14]
Create the beaded petals with seed beads and crystals.

15. Continue doing this around the top of the cup.

16. For the next series of "petals," change colors of seed beads and crystals. With your needle, weave down to the next "down" bead. This will be between the petals you just made from one "up" bead to another. You'll now go from "down" bead to "down" bead.

17. Make another row of petals in the same manner. When you are finished, weave the needle down to the bottom, and attach the flower to the shoes, bodice, hair, or wherever.

CHAPTER

7

1940s
HAUTE COUTURE:

Fashioning a Stylish Suit

HELEN

In this chapter, we'll explore efforts in 1944, by some of the New York and Paris designers, to create a more feminine suit design. This suit pairs a traditional square blouse with a shorter pleated skirt. The underwear is soft and feminine. And, with apologies to Uncle Sam, in this book, our gal wears nylon stockings! (In case you were wondering, silk stockings were gone by 1942.)

MATERIALS

basic body

¹/₃ yard (30.5 cm) small-print rayon for the jacket and jacket lining and shirt.

¹/₄ yard (23 cm) small-print rayon for the blouse and jacket cuffs

¹/₄ yard (23 cm) low-loft quilt batting

1 yard (91 cm) pattern drafting paper or tissue paper

¹/₄ yard (23 cm) of silk fabric or a vintage silk scarf or handkerchief for the camiknickers

one half of a pair of nylon knee highs

25" × 18" (63 × 45.7 cm) cotton fabric for the hat, purse, and shoes

scraps of cotton fabric for lining the purse and shoes

9" × 4" (22.9 × 10.2 cm) netting or tulle for the hat

1¹/₂ yards (1.4 m) ¹/₂" (12 mm) wide lace for the trim on the camiknickers and garters

¹/₄ yard (23 cm) stretch lace for the gloves

1 yard (91 cm) of ¹/₄" (6 mm) wide lace for the trim on the gloves

¹/₄ yard (23 cm) double sided bonding sheet such as Wonder-Under or Vliesofix

thread to match

14" (35.6 cm) florist wire for the hat brim

black machine sewing thread

beading thread

size 11/12 seed beads in color to match the doll's theme

8 flower-shaped beads for embellishing the garters

2 doll-sized buttons for the camiknickers

8 small buttons: 1 for skirt, 2 for shoes, 5 for blouse

8 small snaps for the blouse, purse, and skirt

hairnet

doll hat-pin

mohair for hair

TOOLS

basic clothing and sewing kits, pages 10-12.

CAMIKNICKERS

Camiknickers were very popular during the early 1940s. Helen's delicate version of the one-piece undergarment was made from an old silk scarf. Garters for the stockings complete the effect.

TIP

Silk can be very tricky to work with. To gain some control over this light, slippery fabric, spray the silk with a liquid stabilizer product called Perfect Sew. Once dry, it gives the fabric a crisp hand so that it cuts and sews like cotton. When your garment is finished, simply rinse it in water to restore the silk to its original drape.

1. Trace all of the camiknicker pattern pieces onto tissue paper or pattern drafting paper. Pin the traced shape to the wrong side of the silk scarf or handkerchief that has been doubled, right sides together. The camiknickers Bodice Front is pinned on the fold.

2. Cut out all of the pattern pieces from the fabric using straight-edge fabric scissors.

3. Set aside one Bodice Front and two Bodice Backs for the lining. Work on the remaining bodice pieces as follows: Sew the darts on the front. Pin the side seams of the front to the side seams of the back, right sides together, and sew seam #1 as pinned (figure a).

Note: All camiknicker seam allowances are 1/8" (3 mm) unless otherwise noted.

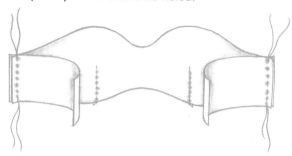

(figure a)
Assemble the bodice.

4. Dart and join the remaining bodice front and backs, following the same instructions in step 2, above, to make the lining. Set the assembled piece aside.

5. With right sides of the Center Front fabric pieces together, sew seam #2.

6. Pin one side of a Center Front to a Side Front, right sides together, at seam #3, and sew (figure b). Attach the remaining Side Front to the other side.

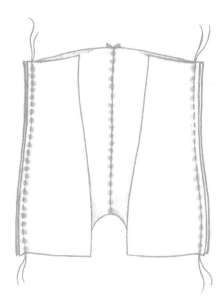

(figure b)
Attach the Side Fronts to the Center Front.

7. Sew the darts in the Center Back fabric pieces, then sew the 2 pieces together at seam #4, right sides together, leaving open where marked. Do not sew the crotch.

8. Pin the joined backs to the fronts, right sides together, and sew down the sides along seams #5 (figure c).

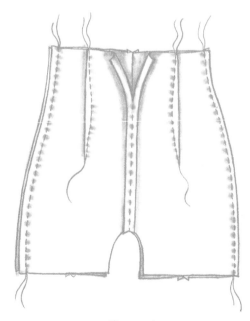

(figure c)
Join the front to the back at the sides.

9. With right sides together, pin the lower part of the camiknickers (the joined back and front) to the bodice at seam #6, and then sew from one opening to the other side around the bodice.

10. Pin the small lace to the bodice at the top starting along the center back edge, with the bottom edge of the trim aligned with the top edge of the bodice, right sides together (figure d). Sew in place.

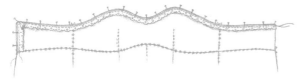

(figure d)
The lace is at the top of the bodice when the lining is sewn and turned.

11. Pin the bodice lining to the bodice, right sides together, and sew across the top and down both sides at the back, catching the edge of the lace between the seam allowances (figure e). Turn the bodice lining to the inside of the garment. With needle and thread, hand sew the lining to the inside of the bodice, turning under a small hem as you sew.

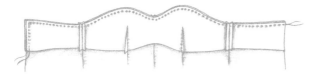

(figure e)
Attach the lace and join the lining.

12. Fold up a ⅛" (3 mm) deep hem along the legs of the camiknickers. Baste in place. Pin the small lace to the right side of the hem, on the outside of the hem. Sew the lace in place.

13. Pin the front and back along the crotch, right sides together. Sew from one hemline of a leg opening to the other side (figure f).

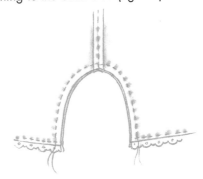

(figure f)
Seam the crotch after the legs are hemmed.

14. Hand sew snaps to the opening at the top of the camiknickers Bodice Back on the outside on one side, and on the inside of the other side. Sew one just below the top edge and another one just above the seam where the bodice meets the lower part of the knickers. On the outside, sew small buttons at the snap locations.

15. Measure more of the small lace for the straps and hand sew them in place, as marked on the Bodice Front pieces. Slip the camiknickers on the doll and mark the placement of the straps on the back of the bodice. Remove the camiknickers from the doll and hand sew the straps where marked.

16. Cut four 1" (2.5 cm) lengths of the small lace for garters. Hand sew these at the front and back of the legs to represent the garters.

17. Take one stocking from a pair of nylon knee highs, and turn it wrong side out.

18. Machine sew, using a stretch stitch and black thread, from the bottom of the stocking up to the top, on one side. Repeat on the other side of the same stocking. This will create two doll stockings.

19. Cut out the stockings close to your stitching, turn them right side out, and slip them on the doll's legs. Hand sew the garters to the top of the stockings. Use a flower-shaped bead at each stitching point to add a nice embellishment.

Using black thread in the sewing machine when sewing the stockings creates the effect of dark back seams that were popular during this era.

THE BLOUSE

1. Trace all of the Blouse pattern pieces onto tissue paper or pattern drafting paper. Pin them to the wrong side of the blouse fabric of choice that has been doubled, right sides together. Cut two Blouse Backs and one Blouse Front. The Blouse Front is cut on the fabric fold.

2. Mark and sew the darts on the Blouse Front. Pin in the pleat on the Blouse Front, and on the right side of the fabric sew down the entire pleat line.

Before sewing up the side seams of the Blouse, it is best to insert the sleeves.

3. Fold over the pleat to the left of the Blouse Front. Pin it in place.

4. With right sides together, sew the Blouse Front to the Blouse Back at seam #7, the shoulders.

5. Cut out one Blouse Front Lining and one Blouse Back Lining, on the fabric fold. Sew the front and back lining pieces at the shoulders, right sides together.

6. Pin the lining to the blouse, right sides together, and sew along the neck, starting at the opening in the back. Clip the curves of the lining, or trim the seam allowances with pinking shears (figure g).

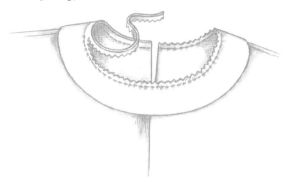

(figure g)
Join the front and back lining at the shoulders, then seam to the blouse neckline.

7. Cut out two Sleeve pattern pieces, and machine sew a running stitch for gathering along the cap of the sleeves as marked.

8. Pull these gathering stitches to fit into the sleeve opening on the blouse. Pin the sleeve in place, and sew it into the arm opening, right sides together.

9. With right sides together, machine sew from the bottom of the sleeves down to the bottom of the blouse along Seam #7 (figure h).

(figure h)
Insert the sleeves before stitching the side seams.

10. To flatten the neck lining, fold it inside the garment and then hand sew it to the inside of the blouse by just tacking it to the shoulder seams and to the pleat on the blouse front.

11. Hand or machine sew a hem in the sleeves and the bottom of the blouse.

12. Turn under a 1/8" (3 mm) hem at the center back openings and machine sew. Hand sew snaps on the blouse opening in the back, and hand sew five small buttons down the front of the blouse.

The Skirt

1. Cut three fabric panels for the skirt, each measuring 9" long by 7 1/2" wide (22.9 × 19 cm).

2. Cut out the waistband using the pattern (page 287). Sew the waistband by folding it in half lengthwise, right sides together, and sewing across each of the ends (figure i).

(figure i)
Fold the waistband lengthwise and stitch across both of the short ends.

3. Sew the three skirt panels together, right sides together, along the short ends.

4. Measure out evenly distributed pleats in the skirt using the waistband as your guide, and pin in the pleats. Iron the pleats flat.

5. With right sides together, pin the skirt to one side of the waistband, right sides together, and machine sew it in place (figure j).

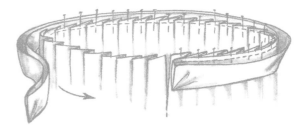

(figure j)
Sew the waistband to the pleated skirt.

6. Fold down the top half of the waistband to the inside of the skirt and hand sew it along the inner edge.

7. Sew the back seam of the skirt, right sides together, leaving a 1 1/2" (3.8 cm) opening below the waistband. Turn under a 1/8" (3 mm) seam allowance and hand sew it flat.

8. Fold the skirt hem in place, iron, and then hand sew the hem. Sew a snap on the waistband at the overlapped opening and add a button on the outside of the waistband (figure k).

(figure k)
Hand sew the long, loose edge of the waistband inside the skirt.

THE JACKET

1. Trace all of the jacket pattern pieces (pages 287–290) on to tissue paper or pattern drafting paper. Cut out all of the fabric pieces from the jacket fabric and lining. Use pinking shears if you are using rayon to help prevent fraying.

2. Machine gather the Jacket Upper Bodice, as marked along the bottom edge.

3. With right sides together, and matching seam #8, sew the Jacket Lower Front to the Jacket Upper Bodice (figure l).

   Note: All jacket seam allowances are 1/8" (3 mm) unless otherwise noted.

(figure l)
Gather the Upper Bodice at the bustline before seaming to the Lower Front.

4. With right sides together, sew the Jacket Back pieces along seam #2.

5. Pin the jacket back to the jacket fronts at the shoulders, right sides together, and sew (figure m).

6. Sew the back to the fronts at the side, seam #10, at this time, right sides together (figure m). Unlike the blouse, the sleeves will be inserted later because the jacket has a lining.

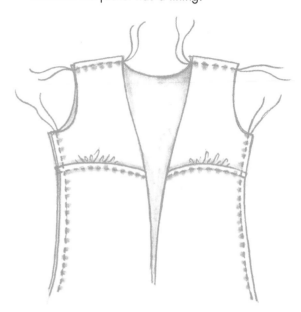

(figure m)
Seam the Fronts to the Back at the shoulders and sides.

7. Following steps 2–6, sew the lining pieces as you did the outside of the jacket.

8. Before sewing the lining to the main jacket, cut the ties. The ties are cut from the same fabric as the jacket. They measure 5 1/2" long by 1 1/4" wide (14 × 3.2 cm). Fold each one in half, right sides together, and sew from one end, down the length of the tie, and leaving open at the other end. Turn them right sides out, using tubes or straws. Iron flat.

9. Pin the tie where marked on the right side of both jacket fronts, with the unstitched edges in the seam allowances and the rest of the ties loose against the right side of the body.

10. With right sides together, pin the lining to the jacket body along the front edges and neckline.

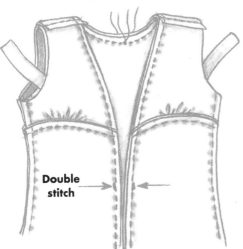

(figure n)
Prepare the lining and attach it to the body.

11. Starting at the back of the neck, sew all the way around the outer seams (figure n). Double stitch where the ties are pinned.

To make sure the ties don't catch in the seam lines, pull them through the sleeve openings.

12. Trim with pinking shears, leaving a scant 1/8" (3 mm) seam allowance. Turn the body and lining right side out. Iron all of the seams flat.

13. With the mechanical pencil, trace two cuffs onto the wrong side of the blouse fabric. Do not cut out the shapes yet. Double the fabric, right sides together, and sew across the top of the cuff. Cut out the shapes, turn each one right side out along the seam line, and iron them flat (figure o).

(figure o)

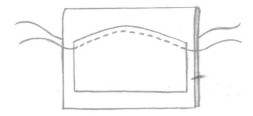

Sew, then cut out the cuffs from the blouse fabric.

14. Machine sew the cuffs at the wrists of the jacket sleeves, right sides together (figure p). Sew just one side of the cuff.

(figure p)
Attach the cuff to the bottom of each sleeve.

15. Sew a gathering stitch at the cap of each sleeve. With right sides together, sew each of the sleeves together along the underarm seam. It helps to open up the cuffs and sew from the top of the sleeve all the way down to the end of the opened-up cuff (figure q).

(figure q)
Sew the underarm seam.

16. Fold back the top half of the cuff, and hand sew it to the inside of the sleeve.

17. Insert the sleeves into the jacket armhole, right sides together. Pin them in place and machine sew the sleeves into the jacket.

> Setting in the sleeves is the trickiest part of making this outfit. It is kind of challenging, but using a ¼" (6 mm) presser foot on your machine really helps. If you do not have this presser foot, use the smallest foot available.

18. Iron the jacket again and it is finished!

Hand-sewn size 11/12 seed beads at the center of the flower design on the jacket add just the right amount of embellishment. This is a delightful technique and is so easy.

THE CUFF-BEADED EDGING

1. Thread up a beading needle with 2 yards (1.8 m) of beading thread, and place a knot in one end.

2. Anchor the thread on the underside of the cuff with a few small stitches and then come out at the top edge.

3. Add three seed beads to the needle and thread. Go back into the cuff next to where the needle and thread first came out. You now have a picot.

4. Taking a tiny stitch, come out the edge of the cuff beside the last bead you added and pull through the hole in that bead (figure r).

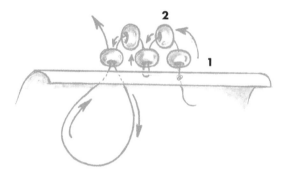

(figure r)
Hand-stitch the picot edging to each cuff.

5. Add two new beads to the needle and thread and pull through the edge of the cuff next to the bead that you just pulled through.

6. Repeat steps 4 and 5 until you have edged the entire cuff with picots. Anchor the thread with a few small stitches and cut it off.

THE GLOVES

In the 1940s and '50s, women did not go anywhere without gloves. In the summer, they generally wore lightweight, lacey, or half-glove versions. Your doll has two fingers that are not separate, so half-gloves are easier to make.

1. Trace two glove patterns (page 290) onto tissue paper or pattern drafting paper.

2. Pin the traced pattern pieces onto the wrong side of doubled stretch lace fabric.

3. Sew along the tracing and sewing lines as shown on the pattern pieces, leaving open at the wrist where marked. Cut out the stitched shapes with straight-edge fabric scissors, using ⅛" (3 mm) seam allowances. Tear away the paper

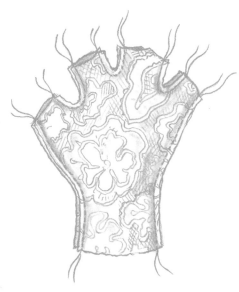

(figure s)
Sew the gloves with the paper tracing in place.

4. With a needle and thread, hand sew the trim along the wrist edge of the gloves. Tuck in the raw edges of the lace around the doll's fingers.

Delicate lace gloves stitch up with ease when a paper tracing of the pattern piece is used as a stabilizer while stitching.

1. Trace two Shoe Top pattern pieces (page 289) onto the wrong side of the fabric.

2. Pin a Shoe Top to the (uncut) lining fabric, right sides together, and sew along both of the tracing and sewing lines, at the top edge and the toes. Cut out the lining with pinking shears and turn the piece right side out (figure t). Make the second lined top in the same manner.

   Note: all seam allowances are ¹/₈" (3 mm) wide unless otherwise noted.

(figure t)
Sew the toe and the top opening to the lining fabric before cutting out the lining.

3. Open up the back so that the lining and fabrics match and, with right sides together, sew this opening closed (figure u).

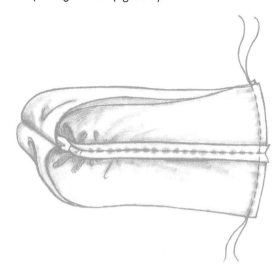

(figure u)
Join the Shoe Top and the lining along the back seams.

4. Fold the lining to the inside and iron.

5. Cut out two Shoe Soles pattern pieces (page 291) from the fabric and two from the lining fabric. If necessary, trim the lower raw edges of the lining to the same length as the outer shoe. First, though, make sure that the seam lines for the toe and foot openings are at the edges.

6. On both of the lining pieces, cut a 1" (2.5 cm) long slit down the center. Set aside one shoe and continue with the following steps.

7. With right sides together, pin the bottom edge of the shoe top to the Shoe Sole. Starting at one side of the toe opening, sew around the outer edge.

8. Pin a lining to the Shoe Top with right side of the sole lining to the wrong side of the Shoe Top (figure v). Sew all the way around the outer edge.

(figure v)
Sandwich the Shoe Top and lining inside the sole pieces.

9. Clip through the seam allowances along the curves and then turn the shoe right side out through the slit in the lining. Make sure that the shoe top is turned right side out.

10. Cut out the Cardboard Sole Insert (page 290) and slip it into the shoe through the opening in the lining. This insert gives the bottom of the shoe stability. Repeat steps 7–9 for the remaining shoe.

11. Cut out all the heel patterns (page 289). You need four Heel Sides, two Heel Fronts, two Heel Backs, and two Heel Bottoms.

12. With right sides together, pin one Heel Side to one Heel Front, and sew down the length of seam #9. Join another Heel Side to the same Heel Front at the remaining seam #9.

13. Pin the Heel Back to the two Heel Sides, right sides together, and sew down each seam #10. You now have a square-looking shape.

14. Pin the Heel Bottom to the lower edges of the heel that you just created, right sides together.

15. Sew the Heel Back to the Heel Bottom along seam #11, as pinned. At the corner of the Heel bottom, make sure that the previously stitched vertical seam (#10) is caught in the stitching. Leave the needle down in the fabric. Lift the presser foot, pivot the heel pieces, and lower the presser foot so that you can sew seam #12, which joins the Heel Bottom to the Heel Side. Continue stitching around the pinned heel pieces, pivoting at the corners and catching the bottoms of each vertical seam (figure w). At the end of the current seam, you will be catching the bottom of vertical seam (#9). Then you will sew seam #13 to join the Heel Bottom to the Heel Front. The last edges to be joined are a Heel Bottom to a Heel Side, with another seam #12.

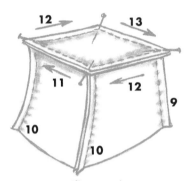

(figure w)
Join the Heel Front, Back, and Sides before adding the Heel Bottom.

16. Turn the heel right side out, and fill it with stuffing. Pin the heel to the bottom of the shoe and hand sew it in place (figure x).

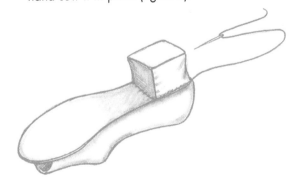

(figure x)
Hand sew the stuffed heel to the bottom of the shoe.

17. Cut a 3″ × ³/4″ (7.6 × 1.9 cm) -wide piece of fabric on the bias for the ankle strap. Fold the strap in half lengthwise, right sides together, and sew down the length of the strap, using a scant ¹/8″ (3 mm) seam allowance. Sew one end closed. Turn, using a turning tool.

18. Measure the length of strap needed to wrap around the ankle and attach to the back of the shoe. Cut the raw end of the strap to fit. Hand sew the raw end to the inside of the shoe back. Slip the shoe on the doll's foot, wrap the strap around her ankle, and pin it toward the back.

19. Hand sew the strap to the shoe and add a button (figure y).

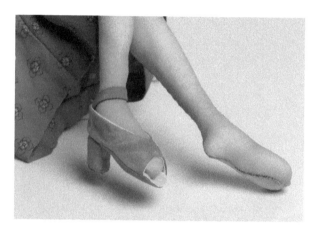

(figure y)
The ankle strap secures the shoe permanently to the doll's foot.

The Hat

1. Trace all of the pattern pieces (pages 288, 290, and 291) onto the paper side of a double-sided bonding sheet such as Pellon Wonder Under or Vlisofix. Iron the bonding sheet onto the wrong side of the hat fabric. Cut out all of the pieces and peel off the paper backing. Be sure to cut out the hole for the center of the Hat Brim.

2. Lay the fabric Hat Brim on the right side of the fabric and cut out another Brim for the lining.

3. Using an iron, fuse the wrong side of the Hat Top, Hat Side, and Hat Brim cut from hat fabric (not lining) onto a piece of quilt batting. Cut out the shapes.

4. With right sides together, sew the back seam of the Hat Side.

5. Pin the Hat Top to the Hat Side, right sides together, and sew along the edge (figure z).

(figure z)
Seam together the Hat Top and Hat Side.

6. Pin the inner edge of the Hat Brim to the bottom of the Hat Side, right sides together, and sew (figure z).

7. Pin the Hat Brim lining to the Hat, right sides together, and sew along the outer edge (figure aa).

(figure aa)
Seam together the Hat Brim pieces.

8. Clip through the seam allowances of all curved seams. Turn the hat, right sides out, and iron it flat. Measure a piece of wire to fit around the outer edge inside the brim of the hat, and secure it in a circle. Insert the wire and machine sew along brim, just inside of the wire, to keep it in place.

9. On the inside of the brim, hand sew the inner edge of the Hat Brim lining to the Hat Side, for a finished look.

10. Arrange the netting or tulle on the top of the hat. Hand sew it in place.

THE HAIR

1. Hand sew the mohair in place in clumps around the head of the doll. Each clump of mohair is spaced 3/4" (1.9 cm) apart. Follow the seam of the head as you hand sew it to the head. Catch each clump in its center with the thread. This secures it to the head. Fluff it up with your fingers. If you need more at the center of the head add a couple more clumps.

2. Cut a small piece of the hair net and tie the raw ends in a knot. Slip this over the doll's hair and secure it to the head using a needle and thread (figure ab).

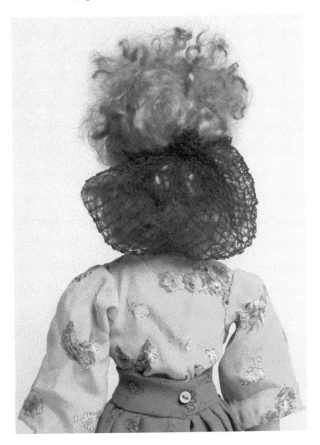

(figure ab)
Sew on clumps of mohair and cover the back with a hair net.

3. Secure the hat to the doll's head with a hat pin. *Note: The pretty fabric flower on her hat is explained on pages 148-149.*

THE PURSE

1. Trace the Clutch Purse template (page 291) onto the wrong side of a piece of lining fabric. Pin this piece to the purse fabric, right sides together. Pin a piece of thin quilt batting against the wrong side of the fabric.

2. Sew around the outer edges, leaving open where marked. Cut out all of the joined layers with pinking shears, and turn the purse right side out through the opening so that the batting is in the middle. Iron flat.

3. Machine sew the opening closed.

4. Fold the clutch at the first fold line, right sides together. Sew both side seams through all layers (figure ac). Be sure to back stitch at the top edge of each seam. Turn the clutch right side out.

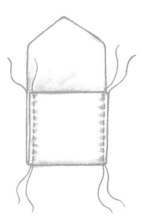

(figure ac)
Sew the sides of the purse.

5. Fold down the clutch flap along the second fold line. Sew a fabric flower (page 148-149) to the outside. Sew a snap inside of the flap. Sew the other side of the snap on the body of the purse. You now have a clutch purse for your doll to carry all her treasures.

Congratulations! You have made it through a chapter with a ton of information. You learned basic sewing techniques and are now ready to get adventurous. Warm up your imagination—in the next chapters you will have fun with nontraditional techniques for clothing design.

CHAPTER

8

1960s COLLAGE:

Layering Appliques, Fiber, and Transfers

ELIZABETHE

In this chapter, existing pattern pieces are used to create a mixture of mod, hippie, and high-fashion clothing; it will be a collage of styles made with collage techniques.

MATERIALS

basic body pattern pieces, with jointed or straight legs, as desired (pages 284–286)

1/4 yard (23 cm) flesh-colored batik cotton for doll body

1/4 yard (23 cm) purple batik cotton for skirt edging

1/4 yard (23 cm) polka-dot cotton fabric for legs

12" (30.5 cm) square red cotton for shoes

1/4 yard (23 cm) silk chiffon or silk chiffon scarf

1/4 yard (23 cm) white or cream-colored silky polyester fabric for skirt

1/4 yard (23 cm) tulle or fine netting in cream or color to match your theme

1 yard (91 cm) of 5" (12.7 cm) -wide lace for skirt

1 yard (91 cm) of 1/3" (1 cm) -wide trim for skirt

32" (81.3 cm) of 1/4" (6 mm) -wide ribbon for boot laces

20" (50.8 cm) yarn for headband, such as Knitting Fever Macao ribbon yarn

scraps of lace, metallic threads, ribbons, and yarns for collage

snippets of brocade, metallic, silk fabrics for collage

2 yards (1.8 m) of two different yarns for purse strap and tassel

Meadowbrook Industries Angelina Heat-Bondable Fiber (Hot Fix) in colors to match your theme. (*Note: Make sure you use the Meadowbrook product, as there is another version. Angelina is sold through Textura Trading [see Resources, page 302] or at local quilt and yarn shops.*)

decorative machine threads

threads to match

1 snap for skirt

1 small button for skirt

2 sheets Jacquard Inkjet Print on Silk

heat-transfer inks or paints

image to print on silk

size 11/12 seed beads in 5 colors

size 6/7 seed beads that coordinate with the size 11/12 seed beads

accent beads to match your color theme

beading thread

costume jewelry

colored pencils

white gel pen

Zig Millennium or Micron Pigma pens: black, brown, red

Mohair or Tibetan goat hair

4 sheets white printer or copy paper

small sea sponges, one for each color

1 sheet cardstock paper

2 sheets of baking parchment paper

double-sided, iron-on, water-soluble stabilizer such as Floriani Wet N Gone Fusible Dissolvable Stabilizer, Freudenberg Solusheet/Vilene 541, Mokuba Free Lace, Brother/Foundation Aqua-Melt Water-Soluble Stabilizer

TOOLS

basic body, clothing, fabric-dyeing, and sewing kits (pages 10–12)

free-motion or darning presser foot

size 12 topstitch or embroidery sewing machine needle

THE BODY AND FABRIC COLLAGE BODICE

The Bodice (or blouse) is made from fabric created using collage techniques. You are creating your own fabric to use for the bodice. This Bodice includes her upper body and arms. Instead of making separate clothing, the decorated cloth is used to make several body parts.

1. Before the body of the doll is made, the collage work needs to be done. Collect the materials for this and clear a space on a table. You will need the flesh-colored batik fabric, silk chiffon or silk scarf, and all your bits and pieces of brocade, lace, fabrics and threads, silk fabric, and yarns, as well as the tulle or fine netting.

2. Place several colors of Angelina between two protective sheets of parchment paper. Set iron at a medium temperature and press for about three seconds. If you overheat the Angelina, it will lose its sheen. Let the sheets cool, then remove the Angelina fiber.

3. Choose the silk chiffon or silk scarf to be encrusted with embellishments. Tear the Angelina into smaller pieces and place them onto half of the silk surface, then throw down snippets of fabrics, threads, and yarns. You will want a scattering of snippets. Allow the Angelina fibers to show. On top of this, lay the other half of the silk. Pin through all layers in several places.

4. With decorative thread in the upper threader of your sewing machine, and any thread in the bobbin, free-motion sew all over the layered items. (See the tip on page 148 for more guidance on free-motion embroidery stitching.) Be sure to sew the lines of stitching closely together, as you will be cutting out pieces of this fabric for parts of the body.

5. Cut the flesh-colored batik fabric in half. On the wrong side of one piece, trace the Face, Hand, Head Back, and Upper Body Front pattern pieces. On the other piece of fabric, trace the Arm, Body Back, and Lower Body Front. Cut the Upper Body Front from the batik fabric. Sew, then cut out and finish assembling, the Hands and head. (See steps 1–5 and 12–15, on pages 18 and 20–21).

6. Iron the double-sided, iron-on stabilizer to the wrong side of your collage fabric. Peel off the paper backing.

7. Lay the collage fabric, bonded side down, on the right side of the batik fabric where the arms and remaining body pieces are traced. Iron it in place. Cut out all but the arms. Fold the fabric in half where the arms are traced and sew, then cut them out (figure a) (step 11, page 20).

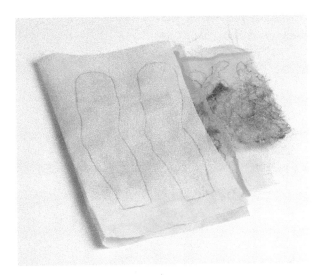

(figure a)
Overlay the collage fabric on the batik fabric.

8. Following the instructions for sewing the body in Chapter 1, page 23, sew the body pieces, including joining the Upper Body Front to the Lower Body Front.

9. The legs are traced and sewn using the polka-dot fabric following the sewing instructions in Chapter 1 for jointed legs (page 21) or straight legs (page 22). Fill all of the body parts with stuffing and sew them together.

10. Following the beaded-edge illustration and instructions (page 114), and using the size 11/12 seed beads, bead the collage-fabric bodice of the Body Front. Bead the seams where the hands were sewn to the arms.

THE SKIRT

1. Gather the inks or paints, sponges, patterns for the leaf and flower designs (page 292), cardstock paper and the printer or copy paper. Trace the leaf and flower onto the cardstock and cut them out using paper scissors.

> **TIP**
>
> *Heat-transfer inks or paints are used mainly for coloring polyester fabrics. They do not transfer well onto natural fibers. They are a wonderful way of coloring fabric and they leave the hand (personality when draped) of the fabric very soft and natural. Because theses paints are heated to transfer the colors, this single step also permanently sets the colors.*

2. Pour the inks or paints onto a piece of cardstock. Using the sponges, pick up the inks and dab them onto the copy paper. Place the templates down, one at a time, and dab onto them. Remove the templates and set them down in another area of the copy paper. This gives you shadow images (figure b). The colors used on the sample doll were yellow, bottle green, ultramarine, and claret.

(figure b)
Paint on paper.

3. Let the papers dry completely and then place them, colored side down, onto the right side of the silky polyester fabric, which is cut into a 7" × 24" piece (17.8 × 61 cm).

> Does polyester have a right or wrong side? It is hard to tell. Look at the selvedge (the edges). You will see little holes where the fabric was attached to the loom. The holes will feel smooth on the right side of the fabric, whereas the wrong side will feel bumpy at those spots.

4. Place a protective sheet on your ironing board. Place the fabric on the protective sheet and, on top of the fabric, the paper. Set the iron at the hottest setting and iron, holding it in place for about 8 seconds. Lift up a corner of the paper to see if the color has transferred to the fabric. If not, hold the iron in place a bit longer.

5. Because the templates of the leaves and flowers were painted, their images can be transferred to the fabric. Place them, colored side down, onto the right side of the fabric and iron them to transfer the images. Cover them with a protective sheet before ironing. This adds a positive image to the fabric.

6. Copy the image desired for the skirt onto the ink-jet-silk. Peel the paper backing from the silk and iron double-sided iron-on stabilizer to the back of the silk.

> The sample doll used a drawing I did. I scanned the drawing and placed it into Adobe Photoshop. I then made a picture package with four images on a page, which reduced the drawing to the proper size for the skirt. I printed two of these images onto the silk. If you want to use my drawing it is included on page 292.

7. Cut out the images and iron them along the bottom of the polyester fabric. Machine sew with decorative thread in the needle around the images. Any thread can be in the bobbin as it will not show. You can free-motion or straight stitch around the images.

8. To take up some of the bulk along the waistline, sew seven darts along the top (24" or 61 cm) edge of the fabric (figure c). Each dart should be ⅛" (3 mm) deep and approximately 3¼" (8.3 cm) apart.

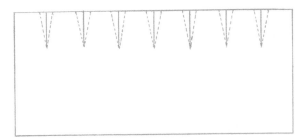

(figure c)
Sew seven darts in the skirt waist.

9. With a straight stitch set for a gathering stitch length, machine sew along the top edge of the skirt.

10. Following steps 2, 4, 5, and 6 of the skirt assembly instructions in Chapter 7 (page 111) cut out and sew the waistband, and attach the skirt to the waistband.

11. Trace the Skirt Edging pattern onto the wrong side of the fabric chosen for this, which has been cut 9" × 24" (22.9 × 61 cm). Use a colored pencil so you can see your traced lines. You will need to move the edging pattern piece as you trace it along the top edge of the fabric. Fold the fabric in half widthwise (fold so that the edging is finished on both sides), right sides together. Machine sew along the traced lines. Cut out the stitched shape with pinking shears and using ⅛" (3 mm) seam allowances. Turn the edging right side out and iron it flat.

12. With right sides together and raw edges even, pin the Skirt Edging to the bottom of the skirt. On top of the edging, place the 5" (12.7 cm) -wide lace. Machine sew the layers in place. Turn down the edging and lace and iron flat.

13. Collect the narrow trim and pin it along the seam where the Skirt Edging meets the skirt bottom. Machine sew the trim in place. With right sides together, sew from about 2" (5 cm) below the waistband down to the bottom of the skirt. Where the skirt has a raw edge below the waist band, sew both sides under (figure d).

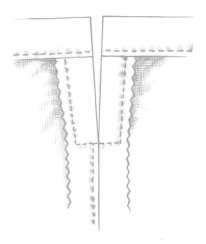

(figure d)
Sew the skirt back seam, leaving the waist opening.

14. Following the Cuff Beaded Edging instructions (page 114), bead the bottom of the skirt edging with size 11/12 seed beads. When you get to the points, add beaded fringe (page 201). Use the accent beads for this (figure e).

(figure e)
Add beaded fringe to the skirt.

15. Hand sew snaps in place on the waistband and sew a button on one side of the waistband. Place skirt on Elizabethe.

THE VEST

1. The vest is made using the Jacket Lower Front, Jacket Back, and Jacket Upper Bodice (on pages 288–290). This is from the jacket used for Helen and is simply redrawn. Follow the illustration (figure f) and draw the pattern for the vest. Use tissue paper or pattern drafting paper to redraw these pieces. Shorten the Jacket Lower Front and Jacket Back so that the vest will fall just below the doll's waist. Draw a narrow pattern for the trim for the front of the vest. In the illustration, you will see a dashed line to represent this trim. Do not make the vest pattern piece narrower at center front. The trim is fused on top of the vest fabric piece.

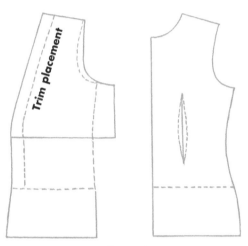

(figure f)
Draw the vest pattern using Helen's jacket pattern pieces.

2. Cut out two sets of the front and back pieces from the fabrics you have chosen. On the trim, before cutting it out, iron some double-sided iron-on stabilizer on the wrong side of the fabric. Cut out two sets of trim, peel off the paper backing, and iron in place on the fronts of the vest fabric shapes.

3. Sew the shoulder and side seams on both sets of the fabric shapes. With right sides together, pin one set to the other. Sew all the way around the outer edges of the vest, leaving the armholes open. Turn the vest right side out through one of the armholes and iron it flat.

4. Hand sew the armholes together by turning under the raw edges as you sew them.

5. Following the Cuff Beaded Edging instructions (page 114), bead along the bottom edge of the vest and up around the outer edge of the trim.

6. To embellish the vest, some of it has to be done after it is on the doll, but the beaded fringe can be made first. Thread up a beading needle with 1 yard (91 cm) of beading thread. Tie a knot in the end and anchor the thread at the back of the vest, opposite the edge where you want the fringe. Take the needle through the vest and come out at the edge. String on several size 11/12 seed beads, then a size 6/7, more size 11/12 beads, another size 6/7, and so on. At the end of the length you want, add an accent bead and then a "stop" bead. Skip the "stop" bead and go up the beads you just added and into the vest edge. Create as many of these fringes as you like until you have the look you want. Do the same on the other side of the vest.

(figure g)
Add beaded fringe to the vest hem.

7. Place the vest onto the doll. Hand sew a piece of costume jewelry on one side of the vest, near the doll's bust. On one bottom edge of the vest, hand sew another piece of costume jewelry. Under this, string on beads to create the loops that you see on the sample doll (figure g). Go from one side to the other.

Costume jewelry is so fun to use on dolls. I love going to thrift stores and buying old earrings and necklaces. I take them apart and use the bits as embellishments for my dolls. Old rings can become crowns for a smaller doll.

8. Trace the General Shape pattern (page 292) eight times onto the sleeve fabric. Fold each shape in half diagonally as shown (figure h), with right sides together, and sew with a $1/8$" (3 mm) seam allowance, leaving one area open for turning. Turn each shape right side out through this opening and hand sew the openings closed.

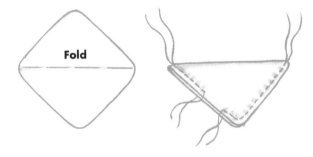

(figure h)
Fold the shapes in half diagonally and stitch.

9. Place two of the shapes together and sew a gathering stitch at the back, catching the shapes together. Pull and you will get a nice looking cluster. Create four of these clusters and hand sew all of them to the vest, at the shoulders, to represent cap sleeves.

Stefania Morgante created a collage bodice using feathers, dried clusters from trees, organza, and crocheted wire.

1. Using the Shoe Top, Shoe Sole, Heel Side, Heel Front, Heel Back, Heel Bottom (page 289), and Boot Top (page 292) trace all of the pieces onto the wrong side of the red cotton fabric. When you get to the toe of the Shoe Top, round it out (figure i).

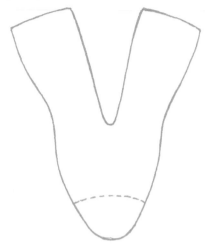

(figure i)
Draw the toe on the Shoe Top.

2. Follow the instructions for sewing the shoes found in Chapter 7 (page 116). The only difference will be that you will not have to sew the toe opening. Slip the shoes onto the doll's feet.

3. Trace four Boot Top pattern pieces (page 292) for the top of the shoes (figure i). This turns the shoes into boots, which were more common during this era. Double the fabric and sew along the entire length of seam #1 on two of the pieces. On the remaining two boot pieces, sew seam #1 but leave an opening in the center of the seam. Cut them out of the fabric using 1/8" (3 mm) seam allowances.

4. Open up each of the boot pieces and, with right sides together, pin two pieces to each other, making sure that each pair has a piece with an opening in the seam. Sew all the way around the outer edges. Turn the boots right side out through the opening you created earlier. Iron flat and pin the boots to the doll's legs, just above the heels of the shoes. Hand sew the boots in place using a ladder stitch (page 200).

5. Cut two 16" (40.6 cm) lengths of ribbon to match the doll's boots. Starting at the top, hand sew the ribbons to the edges of the boot openings, crisscrossing them as you go down the boot front. When you get to the top of the foot, tie the ribbons into bows and tack them in place.

6. Thread up a beading needle with 1 yard (91 cm) of beading thread. Place a knot in the end and tack it into the foot, under the shoe so that it does not show, at the top edge of the boot, by the ribbon. Using the size 6/7 and 11/12 seed beads, add embellishments along the edge of the shoe and the boot. Start by placing a size 6/7 bead, then a size 11/12 bead on the needle and thread. Skip the size 11/12 and go through the size 6/7 bead and then insert the needle and thread into the shoe. Move over 3/8" (1 cm) along the edge of the boot and do another bead stack. Continue this along the edge of the boot top and shoe top.

Anne van der Kley used the jacket pattern to create a patchwork vest. Note the unique way Anne created the doll's hair with threads stitched together on a serger.

THE HAIR AND HEADPIECE

1. Color the face as you wish. I copied the way Zandra Rhodes used to wear eye make-up during the late '60 s and early '70s. Eyes were very important during this time period, with heavy make-up and false eyelashes. Lips were paler, as were eyebrows. Follow the instructions in Chapter 1 (page 24) for coloring a doll face.

2. If you are using the Tibetan goat hair, follow steps 4, 5, and 6 (page 155), for cutting and attaching this type of hair to the head.

3. Cut a 20" (50.8 cm) length of yarn and a 1½" × 24" (3.8 × 61 cm) strip from the silk scarf. Tie the scarf and yarn together near each end, leaving a bit of the ends loose for embellishments. The sample doll used Macao ribbon yarn.

4. Thread up a beading needle with 1 yard (91 cm) of beading thread. Tie a knot in the long end and attach it to the knot at one end of the headband. Place 9 of the size 11/12 seed beads on the needle and thread and wrap around the headband, twisting this as you tack in place (figure j). Add nine more seed beads, changing colors if you wish, and continue around the headband wrap When you get to the end tie knot, leaving at least 3" (7.6 cm) free. Tie the headband around the doll's head and tack in place.

(figure j)
Wrap beading around the silk and yarn.

5. Add beaded fringe from the knot created when the wrap was placed on her head.

THE PURSE

1. Create another piece of collage fabric with a 9" × 4" (22.9 × 10.2 cm) piece of batik, snippets of fabrics, lace, ribbons, threads, and yarns, and the tulle or fine netting on top.

2. Using the General Shape pattern piece (page 292), cut two of these shapes from the collage fabric. Pin the shapes together, right sides together, and sew along three of the edges. Turn right side out and turn down the raw edge. Hand sew a hem and, at the same time, sew beads along the opening.

3. Cut two pieces of yarn, each 6" (15.2 cm) long and add seed beads as you did on her headpiece by wrapping the yarn with sets of nine seed beads. Hand sew each end of the beaded yarn to the sides of the purse, to create a handle. Add some beaded fringe if desired (figure k).

(figure k)
Embellish the handle with beads.

4. Hand sew a tassel to the bottom point of the purse. To make your own tassel wrap yarn, fabric scraps, and beaded threads around a small piece of cardboard. Slip the fibers off the cardboard and secure them at the top by wrapping it with yarn. If you have added beaded threads, do not cut the bottom of the tassel.

Congratulations, you now have a beautiful, hip doll straight from the '60s with a touch of the '70s and a bit from the twenty-first century.

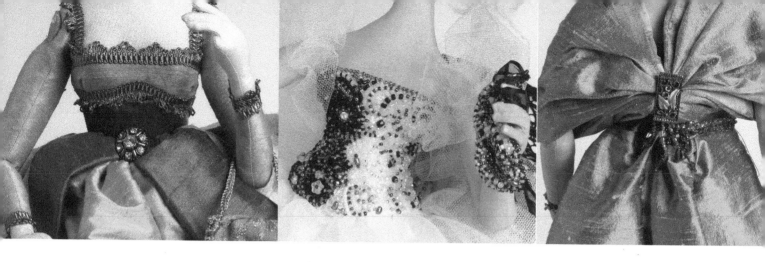

CHAPTER

DRAPING FOR A FORMAL AFFAIR:

Working with Beads, Lace, Satin, and Silk

CHRISTINA LEFEVRE

Elegant, sophisticated, regal. These words seem to describe the doll for this chapter. Working with silks and beads gives a feeling of satisfaction when the project is finished.

MATERIALS

basic body with straight legs (pages 17–22)

stand for 18" (45.7 cm) doll

1/2 yard (46 cm) copper-colored silk dupioni

1/4 yard (23 cm) bridal lace

1/4 yard (23 cm) silk satin or silk charmeuse, natural colored or color to match your theme

sewing machine thread in color to match the silk dupioni

upholstery or strong quilting thread in color to match silk dupioni

size 11/12 seed beads in two colors

size 8/9 seed beads in two colors

size 14/15 seed beads in two colors

accent beads: drops, flower-shaped, 6 mm (1/4") marguerites

4 mm (5/32") bicone crystals in two colors

pieces of costume jewelry or decorative buttons for dress, hat, and shrug

paper toweling

mohair for hair

thread to match mohair

TOOLS

basic clothing and sewing kits (pages 10–12)

THE PATTERN DRAPING

1. Make the doll body using the straight leg pattern. Assemble the body, but wait to attach the arms after the gown is made and placed on the body. Secure the doll body with a stand so it is easy to work with. Decide what type of evening dress you want and collect the fabrics, paper toweling, mechanical pencil, and straight pins. You will be creating your own evening gown using the draping method.

2. Cut a piece of paper toweling the size you want for the costume you have in mind. Arrange the paper toweling around the body. Pin it in place (figure a), cutting it to fit at the back. The sample doll will have a separate bodice, so a shorter length of paper toweling is pinned around her bodice. Pin a longer piece of paper toweling to the body for the skirt, depending on the type of gown you are creating. Cut it to the length you want.

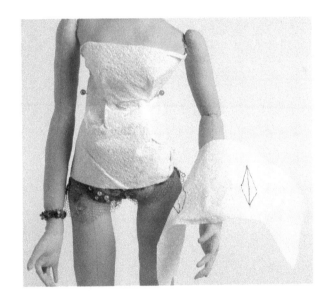

(figure a)
Pin the paper toweling to the doll.

3. Mark the seams and darts on the pinned paper toweling with a mechanical pencil. Pin in the darts (figure b). As you pin the darts, make any corrections needed. Remove the paper toweling from the body and cut out the shapes from the paper toweling. These are your paper patterns.

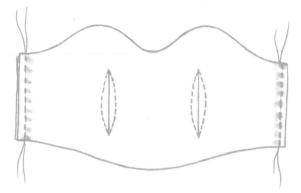

(figure b)
Pin the darts and mark the seams on the front and back.

If you are going to bead the bodice, make the pattern about ¼" (6 mm) larger. The beadwork pulls the fabric in a bit. Without the extra width, the bodice would be too small when placed on the doll.

THE BODICE

1. Pin the paper toweling pattern to the silk dupioni fabric and cut out the pieces.

2. Sew in the darts and sew the seams together. Place the bodice on the body again to make sure it all fits. A beaded bodice needs to be lined to give the bodice more stability to handle the weight of the beads. Cut out and assemble a second bodice. Sew the two bodice pieces together, right sides together. Turned the joined bodice right side out.

3. Thread up a beading needle with 1 yard (91 cm) of beading thread. Place a knot in one end and tack it to the underside of the bodice. Stitching through both layers of the bodice fabric, bead the upper edge of the bodice. Following the bead embroidery instructions (page 114), bead the bodice. The sample doll has three rows of backstitched beading along the top edge, one row of picots above the top row of backstitching, stacked single stitchbeading, and a simple fringe (figure c).

(figure c)
Graph of beading techniques on the bodice.

A close-up of the beaded bodice shows how beading can bring elegance to a simple garment.

The Skirt

1. The skirt is slightly gathered at the waist. With the elaborate bodice, the skirt will not be the focal point. A full skirt would overpower the gown.

2. Cut the paper-toweling skirt pattern from the silk dupioni. Machine gather it at the waist.

3. If desired, dye the bridal lace to match or contrast the skirt fabric. Machine-hem the bottom of the skirt, using a matching color thread. Lace will cover the stitching, so there is no need to hand sew a hem. Along the bottom of the skirt, hand sew the bridal lace in place. With right sides together, machine sew the center back seam from the hem to the waist. Turn, right side out, and place the skirt on the body. Pull the gathering threads to fit at the waist. Hand sew the skirt directly to the body.

Some of the dyed bridal lace was used for Christina's underwear. The lace was hand sewn onto the doll. It is very easy to do and adds a lovely touch. Adding underwear is explained in Chapter 10 (page 146).

4. Place the bodice onto the doll and hand sew it together at the back with the beaded edges overlapping at the back and over the skirt.

The Bracelets

1. It is much easier to sew the bracelets to the wrists before attaching the arms. Anchor the beading thread at the wrist and thread up enough beads on a beading needle to wrap around the wrist.

2. Insert the needle through the first beads added, to make a circle and tack this row to her arm in at least three places. Thread up another row of beads and attach them to the arm. Add a third row. Anchor that row to the arm.

For this doll made by Dorice Larkin, the entire bodice is embroidered with beads.

3. Embellish the bracelet with marguerites. Come out a bead from her wrist and into a marguerite. Add an anchor bead (size 14/15 seed bead). Skip the seed bead and push the needle back through the marguerite and into the bead on her wrist. Insert the needle through five seed beads on the wrist and add another marguerite. Continue around the wrist, adding more marguerites.

A marguerite is a copy of a vintage bead made by Swarovski. The company has started making them again, and they are beautiful accents for any project. They are shaped like flowers and come in several sizes.

The Shrug

Rather than sleeves for this doll, a shrug added a nice finishing touch.

1. Cut 17" (43.2 cm) long by 6" (15.2 cm) wide piece from both the silk dupioni and the silk satin (for the lining). With right sides together, sew along the two long edges, leaving open at each short end (figure d).

(figure d)
Join the shrug to the lining along the long edges.

2. Turn the shrug right side out through one end, and with right sides of the silk dupioni together, sew across the ends. This closes the piece into a tube shape (figure e). Hand sew the lining closed.

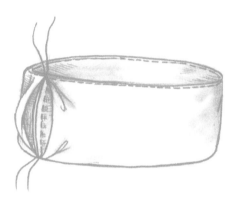

(figure e)
Join the short ends of the silk dupioni.

3. Place the shrug on the doll and pin the two pieces together at the back. Hand sew these two sections together with strong thread. When you slip this off the doll, it will look like a bow.

4. To hide the stitches, hand sew a decorative button or piece of costume jewelry at the center and then create some beaded fringe (step 6, page 128) to hang down from the centerpiece.

If the beads on the bridal lace and the costume jewelry do not match the colors on the dress, color them with markers. As long as the garments are not laundered, the color will last the lifetime of the doll. You do not need special markers. Any colored marker will work. The pearls on the bridal lace and the costume jewelry of Christina's shrug and headpiece were colored with Pantone markers.

The Shoes

1. Follow the instructions for the shoes in Chapter 7 (page 116), but omit the heels. If you are making the shoes from the silk dupioni, you will want to stick with flats, rather than heels. Christina is a dancing girl, so flats are definitely what she wants to wear.

2. After the shoe is made, collect your beading materials and tools. Using the beading needle and thread, anchor the thread with several small stitches at the back of the shoe (where the heel would be). Thread up about thirteen size 11/12 seed beads and backstitch them around the top edge of the shoe top. Do two rows of beading. You can change bead colors with each row, if you wish.

3. Starting at the heel, come out of a bead on the top row and add five size15 seed beads. Skip a bead that is attached to the shoe and go into the next attached bead with the needle and thread. Come out that same bead. Add five more size 14/15 seed beads and make another picot. Continue all the way around the shoe top adding the five-bead picots.

4. At the center front of the shoe top, add some crystals and single-bead stacks (figure f).

(figure f)
Add crystals and single bead stacks to the shoes.

5. At the toe, add beaded edging (page 114).

It is easier to bead the shoes before placing them on the foot. Once beaded, slip the shoes onto the feet, and then tack them in place with a needle and thread.

The Hat and Hair

1. Collect the silk dupioni. Cut a piece 17" (43.2 cm) long by 4" (10.2 cm) wide. Fold it in half with the short ends meeting. Sew from the opening to the folded end. Repeat on the other side (figure g).

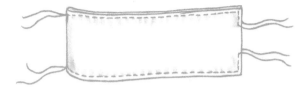

(figure g)
Sew the long edges of the silk dupioni fabric strip.

2. Turn the fabric piece right side out and close up the opening by hand sewing with a needle and thread. Twist the piece into the shape you want and secure the shape's folds by hand sewing with a needle and thread. Before attaching the hat to the doll's head, the hair needs to be sewn onto the head.

3. Following the directions in Chapter 7 (page 119), attach the hair. Arrange in the style you want, then secure with a needle and thread.

4. Once the hair is where you want it, hand sew the hat to the head. As you sew the hat in place, secure the doll's hair into its style. Hand sew a decorative button, or costume jewelry, to the hat.

For Christina's decorative jewelry pieces, the starting point was an inexpensive bracelet strung on stretchy plastic. The plastic was cut away, leaving the beautiful pieces for accents on the purse, hat, shrug, and skirt. These bracelets are great sources of fun accents for dolls.

Michele Naylor has used a piece of crinkled silk to make a unique hat for her doll.

THE PURSE

1. The squarish General Shape pattern piece (page 292) comes into play again. This time it is used as is. Cut out two shapes from the silk dupioni and two from the silk satin. With right sides together, sew the dupioni shapes together, leaving one corner open (figure h). Repeat with the silk satin shapes.

(figure h)
Join the silk dupioni shapes and the silk satin shapes together.

2. Turn the silk satin piece right side out and slip it into the silk dupioni piece, right sides together. Pin it in place. Sew along the raw edges, leaving open at one corner (figure i).

(figure i)
Sew the silk satin into the silk duponi.

3. Turn the purse right side out. Push out the seam with a pair of hemostats and hand sew the opening closed. With a warm iron, press the top of the purse down. The lining will show, which gives a nice contrast.

4. Use the size 11/12 seed beads and drop beads to sew a bead edging along the edges of the turned down part of the purse. Follow the Cuff Beaded Edging instructions (page 114), but change the look by adding a drop bead where the second ("up") bead would be. On the front of the purse, add three marguerite beads or a decorative button.

5. The handle for the purse is very simple. Using a beading needle, attach beading thread at one side of the purse. String on three size 11/12 seed beads, three drop beads, five size 11/12 seed beads, three drop beads, three size 11/12 seed beads, three drop beads, five size 11/12 seed beads, and three drop beads. Then add three size 6/7 seed beads, three accent beads, three size 6/7 seed beads. End with three drop beads and three size 11/12 seed beads. Attach the strand to the other side of the purse. Christina's purse has a double strap. Create the same pattern as before and attach it to the other side of the purse.

Barbara Willis used a beautiful piece of antique costume jewelry as the accent on her doll's purse.

CHAPTER

10

FAIRY GATHERING:

Styling a Whimsical Ensemble

GOLENDRIAL

Some grownups wag their fingers (don't you hate that?) and say "fairies do not exist." Others will give you the Look and say that fairies are imaginary friends. Do not believe them. Would you be able to see Golendrial if they were telling the truth? My mother and grandmother never denied that fairies exist. In fact, my Grandmother Lefever regaled me with wonderful stories about fairies that lived nearby.

MATERIALS

doll body with straight or jointed legs (pages 17–22)

4" × 6" (10.2 × 15.2 cm) extra doll body fabric for ears

1/4 yard (23 cm) of white 100% cotton for corset and shoe tops

1/4 yard (23 cm) of white or natural colored silk crepe de Chine for skirt

1/3 yard (30.5 cm) cream-colored organza for overskirt and wings

12" (30.5 cm) square of lace fabric for bodice and sleeves

6" (15.2 cm) piece of 3" (7.6 cm) -wide lace for underwear

4" (10.2 cm) square of stretch velvet for purse

scraps of colored silk fabrics for berries, flowers

cloth for wiping ash off skirt fabric

stuffing such as Fairfield Polyfil

machine-sewing threads to match fabrics

upholstery thread to match hair

variegated sewing machine threads for flowers, such as Superior Threads Rainbows #816

metallic sewing machine thread for flowers, such as Superior Threads Metallic #11

Kreinik medium #16 braid in Heather

YLI Candlelight Metallic Yarns in gold, green, and pink

size 14/15 seed beads in five colors for flowers (size 11/12 if you are more comfortable with larger beads)

size 14/15 green seed beads for leaves (size 11/12 if you are more comfortable with larger beads)

size 11/12 crystal-colored size seed beads

size 11/12 gold charlottes

4 mm crystals in various colors for flower centers

small drop beads for baubles

1 accent bead and 1 larger drop bead for purse

beading thread

24-gauge floral wire in color to match your theme, for wings (Note: Beading wire comes on a spool and is used mainly for beads.)

double-sided, water-soluble stabilizer such as Floriani Wet N Gone Fusible Dissolvable Stabilizer, Freudenberg Solusheet/Vilene 541, Mokuba Free Lace, or Brother Foundation Aqua-Melt Water-Soluble Stabilizer

1 pipe cleaner for ears

4" (10.2 cm) square of Tibetan goat hair

paper toweling

several small bells

Jacquard Lumiere paint: halo pink gold, halo violet gold, metallic gold, pearlescent magenta, pearlescent violet, sunset gold, super copper

Jacquard Dye-Na-Flow paint: cranberry red, golden yellow, violet

Jacquard Pearl-EX: antique bronze, brilliant gold, super bronze, super russet

TOOLS

basic clothing, fabric-dyeing, and sewing kits (pages 10–12)

free-motion or darning presser foot

embroidery foot (optional)

lucet (optional)

candle and tin pie plate

You have the option of wiring the fairy body or using the jointed legs so that your doll can sit.

The Ears

1. After the doll is made, trace two Ear patterns (page 284) onto the wrong side of the flesh-colored fabric that you used for the body. Double the fabric, right sides together, and machine sew around the ears, leaving open where marked. Cut out, using a scant 1/8" (3 mm) seam allowance, and turn the ear right side out through the opening.

2. Using a mechanical pencil, draw the outline of the ear lobe (stitching lines on the pattern piece) on the inner side of each ear. With the sewing machine, topstitch along this line. As you do this, leave room between the stitching line and the edge of the ear along the inner edge, for the pipe cleaner to be inserted. Measure the ear with the pipe cleaner and cut to fit the ear (figure a), allowing a bit of extra length at each end (1/4" or 6 mm, total), to be turned back.

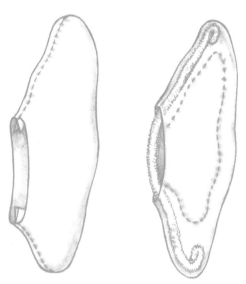

(figure a)
Measure the pipe cleaner.

3. Pinch under the tip at each end of a pipe cleaner and insert it into the ear. The pipe cleaner fits just along the inside edge of the ear. With a needle and thread, close up the opening of the ear using a ladder stitch (page 200).

4. Attach the ears to the side of the head and bend them as shown (figure b). Although the photo shows the hair attached, leave that step for the end of the doll-making process.

(figure b)
Attach and shape the ears as desired.

The Underwear

1. Pin the 6" (15.2 cm) piece of lace to the doll. Hand sew (tack) it in place with a needle and thread (figure c).

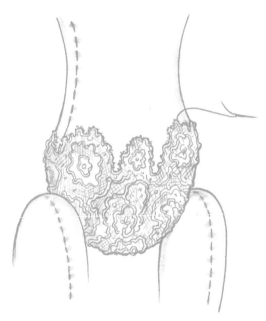

(figure c)
Sew the lace underwear to the body.

2. Wrap the 12" (30.5 cm) square of lace around the entire body at the bust, overlapping at the back, and cut it to fit. The lace ends at the waist. Wrap the leftover pieces around the arms and cut them to fit (figure d). Pin the pieces in place and hand sew the back closed on the bodice. Hand sew the sleeves to the arms. Tuck under the raw edges as you hand sew them in place.

(figure d)
Cover the bodice with lace.

THE SKIRT AND BODICE FABRIC PREPARATION

1. If you want to dye the skirt fabric, use the golden yellow Dye-Na-Flow paint as follows: Wet the silk crepe de Chine with plain tap water. Pour the dye into a plastic container and place the silk in the dye. Squeeze out the excess dye and hang the silk to dry. To heat set the dye, simply iron it at the silk setting.

2. Tear the silk into a piece 24" × 9" (61 × 22.9 cm). Light a candle and place it in a pie tin that is filled with just a bit of water in the bottom.

3. Seal the raw edges of the silk with a candle by running each edge close to the flame. Do not let the fabric touch the flame. If the silk catches fire, immediately dip it in the water. Clean up the ash along the edge of the silk with a damp cloth.

4. Using a paintbrush and Lumiere super copper and sunset gold, paint the edge of the skirt fabric that was sealed with the candle flame. Paint a small section with the copper then the next section with the gold. Change colors as you paint along the edge of the skirt. This paint prevents further fraying and adds a nice finish to the skirt.

5. While the edge of the skirt is drying (and since you have the paints on hand) collect the white cotton fabric and lay it on a piece of plastic. Paint the cotton with sunset gold, super copper, and metallic gold.

> **TIP**
> *I like using my fingers to move the paint around to give a blended look.*

6. While the paint is still damp, rub in some of the Pearl-EX colors (figure e). This gives the cotton a leather look. Again, use your fingers to rub in the Pearl-EX. A darker shade of Pearl-EX will add shadows and a lighter color will add highlights. Set the cotton aside to dry.

(figure e)
Transform white cotton into a leatherlike garment fabric with paints and brushes.

7. Cut a piece of the cream-colored organza 24" × 7" (61 × 17.8 cm). Cut slits along one of the long edges. These slits are random and in varying lengths.

8. Using the candle, run the edge of the organza close to the flame. The edge will melt. Be careful, organza is polyester and will be very hot until it cools. When the raw fabric edges have been sealed, hold the fabric above the flame so that the organza crinkles (figure f). If you hold it too close to the flame, it will burn a hole in it, so watch carefully as you do this.

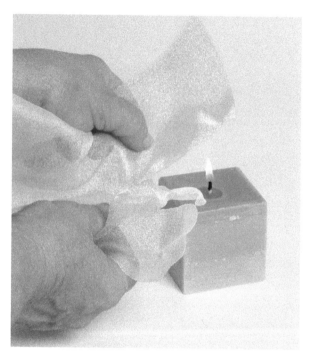

(figure f)
Singe the fabric to seal the raw edges.

THE FLOWERS AND LEAVES

1. Before the corset is made, it is best to prepare the flowers that are made using bits of fabric and free-motion embroidery work. Using a ball-point pen, trace seven flower patterns (page 292) directly onto the stabilizer. Also trace nine leaf patterns (page 292).

2. Cut out seven flowers from scraps of cotton, silk, and other fabric scraps. Place these onto another piece of water-soluble stabilizer. Place another piece of stabilizer over these flowers and pin the layers together.

3. Place variegated thread in the upper threader and metallic thread in the bobbin of your sewing machine. Lower the feed dogs and place a free-motion or darning presser foot on your machine. Set the stitch length to 0 (extremely short) and loosen the upper tension slightly.

4. To start free-motion embroidery, hang onto the ends of the bobbin and needle threads and machine sew a couple of stitches. Cut the loose thread ends, then start sewing. Outline the flower and leaf shapes first, then sew in a grid inside each shape (figure g). The other stitches can lock on to this grid. Make sure this grid touches the outline that was sewn first. If this does not happen, when the stabilizer is washed away the stitches will fall apart. Cut the threads between each shape, doing so either during the stitching or after the stabilizer is dissolved.

TIP

In free-motion machine embroidery, you control the length of the stitches when you move around the fabric. The feed dogs, which usually do this job, are lowered. If your sewing machine does not allow the feed dogs to lower, you can still do free-motion work. The important part is that the presser foot does not touch the plate of your machine. This is what allows you to control the stitches and the movement of the fabric. Move your hands slowly. If you move the fabric too quickly, the sewing machine needle will break.

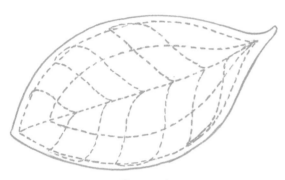

(figure g)
**Stitch a flower and leaf shape, then sew a grid
inside each.**

5. Fill in the flowers and leaves with stitches, making sure that the lines of fill stitching overlap each other inside a shape, and also stitch through the outline of that shape.

6. When you have sewn seven free-motion flowers and nine leaves, it is time to work on the fabric flowers. Sew around the seven fabric flowers that were previously cut from the scraps of fabric and are now sandwiched inside sheets of stabilizer. Sew a few lines from the outer edge to the center of each flower. This stitching simply stabilizes the fabric and prevents fraying, plus it adds a nice touch.

7. Dissolve the stabilizer in lukewarm water. Take the flowers and leaves out of the water and rinse them under running water. Lay them on paper toweling to dry.

THE BAUBLES

1. Trace the Bauble pattern piece (page 294) onto a piece of tissue paper or pattern paper. Cut out at least eleven bauble shapes from cotton, rayon, silk, and velvet fabric scraps.

> **TIP**
>
> *If you stack three to four pieces of fabric and cut out the circles at the same time, this step will go quickly. It helps to cut out the silk and velvet pieces with pinking shears. This prevents the edges of the pieces from fraying as you sew.*

2. Thread up a beading needle with 1 yard (91 cm) of beading thread. Sew a gathering stitch around the edge of a bauble shape. Pull the threads just tight enough to allow you to place a small amount of stuffing inside. Place the stuffing in the circle and pull the threads to close the bauble opening.

3. Tuck the raw fabric edge of the bauble inside.

4. Cut a piece of YLI or Kreinik thread 12" (30.5 cm) long. Tuck one end inside the bauble. Sew the end of the length to the bauble with a needle and thread. Take a few stitches along the top of the bauble to keep the circle closed (figure h).

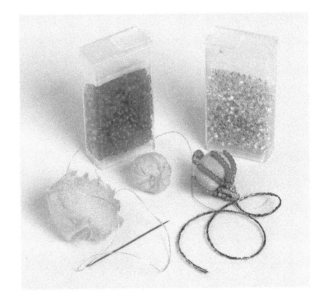

(figure h)
**Fill the fabric circle, add the thread length, and
stitch it closed.**

5. Place nine seed beads of one color on the needle and thread. Move down the bauble and push the needle inside the bauble, pulling it out back at the top of the bauble. Do this several more times, randomly spaced, around the bauble.

6. Push the needle and thread inside the bauble and come out at the center of the bottom. Place a seed bead, a drop bead, and then another seed bead onto the needle and thread. Insert the needle back inside the bauble, close to where you came out, and pull the needle and thread back out at the top of the bauble.

7. Place five green seed beads on the needle and thread. Skipping the last bead, insert the needle in and out of the fourth (second to last) bead. Add three green seed beads to the needle and thread. Insert the needle and thread back into the bauble and out at the top. This creates a leaf (figure i). Make three more leaves along the top of the bauble.

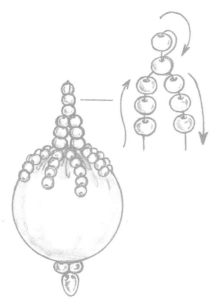

(figure i)
Define the leaves with bead strands.

8. Make another bauble and place it at the other end of the 12" (30.5 cm) piece of ribbon, thread, or yarn. Cut five more pieces of thread and add the baubles to each end of all of them. These will be placed on the corset later.

THE CORSET

1. Trace the Corset pattern pieces (pages 293–294) onto a piece of tissue paper, pattern paper, or template plastic. Cut them out. You will use these as templates.

> Cut out the darts on the template. This makes it easier to trace the darts onto the fabric.

2. Lay the Corset Front template on the wrong side of the painted cotton and trace one using a mechanical pencil. Trace one Corset Back, then flip it over and trace another Corset Back with the template wrong side up. This gives you a left and right side to the back of the corset. Be sure to trace the darts. Leave enough room to cut out the shoe pattern pieces from this fabric.

3. The embellishing is done before cutting the bodice shapes from the fabric. Place variegated thread in the upper threader of your sewing machine. Use a basic sewing thread in the bobbin. The back side of the fabric will not show.

4. Start to randomly sew up and down the fabric, on the right side. Every once in a while, add scraps of fabric and stitch over these. Along the top edge, where you think the top of the corset would be, start attaching the flowers you already made (photo of Golendrial, page 144). Save five flowers to add after the corset is sewn together.

5. Following the traced pattern on the back of the fabric, cut out the corset pieces from the embellished fabric. Machine sew all of the darts. Pin the two back pieces to the front, right sides together, and machine sew seam #3 using a $1/8$" (3 mm) -wide seam allowance. Finger-press the seams flat.

6. Cut a piece of water-soluble stabilizer 4" (10.2 cm) wide by the length of the corset. Pin it in place underneath the top edge of the corset.

7. Free-motion embroider along the raw edge of the top of the corset, along both the front and backs. When you get to the front of the corset, add some of the flowers and sew them in place with free-motion stitching (figure j).

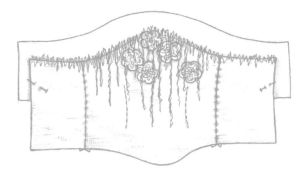

(figure j)
Free-motion embroider to finish the upper raw edge and secure the last five flowers.

8. Cut another piece of water-soluble stabilizer 4" (10.2 cm) wide by the length of the corset and pin it to the bottom of the corset. Free-motion embroider an edging along the lower edge of the corset as you did along the top. This time, add the baubles (page 149) every 3/4"–1" (1.9–2.5 cm).

9. As you did with the baubles, machine sew leaves at each end of a 12" (30.5 cm) length of YLI or Kreinik thread or ribbon. Attach the embellished lengths to the corset, between the baubles.

10. When you get to the back opening, free-motion embroider up one side (raw edge) only. The embellished side will cover the raw edge side when it is placed on the doll.

11. Hand sew a couple of the beaded flowers (at right) on the front of the corset. Set aside the corset.

THE BEADED FLOWERS

Beaded flowers are very easy and add a nice touch to Golendrial's bracelet, corset, and neckline. Embellishments like beaded flowers can be used to hide mistakes and seams.

1. Collect the beading needle, crystals, seed beads, and thread. Cut an 18" (45.7 cm) length of beading thread and place it on the needle.

TIP

It helps to use a piece of beeswax when working with beads. The wax prevents the thread from splitting and knotting. Once the thread is on the needle, hold the start of the thread on the piece of wax with your thumb. Using your other hand, pull the thread so that it moves across the wax. Run your fingers along the thread to clean off any excess wax.

2. Place ten seed beads onto the needle and take them down, toward the tail of the thread. Tie the thread ends together with an overhand knot. This creates a circle of beads.

3. Place seven seed beads onto the needle and, skipping one bead, draw the needle through the next (second) bead. You have now made the first seven-bead picot.

4. Repeat step 3 until you have completed five picots.

5. Place the needle and thread inside the circle and add a crystal. Pull the needle and thread through a bead on the opposite side of the circle. Again, insert the needle and thread through the crystal and then return it to the bead that you first came out. Go inside that one bead and return the needle and thread to the outside of the circle (figure k).

(figure k)
Add picots to a bead circle.

6. Bring the needle over to a bead in the circle that is between a picot. Come out of that bead and make a leaf (page 151). Make another leaf starting at the bead that was skipped before making the next picot.

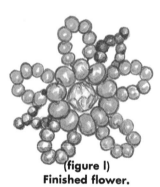

(figure l)
Finished flower.

7. Leave a long enough tail of thread to use it to attach the flower to the bracelet, corset, and neckline. Make as many flowers as desired. The sample doll has thirty-one of these flowers on various places.

THE SHOES

It is easier to put the shoes on Golendrial before dressing her, because the skirt will not get in the way.

1. Trace two Shoe Top pattern pieces (page 293) onto the wrong side of the painted piece of cotton that you also used for the corset. Cut out the shapes.

2. Place the Shoe Top pieces onto a piece of water-soluble stabilizer with the right side of the shoe up, and pin them in place.

3. With the variegated or decorative thread in the upper threader of your machine and metal-lic thread in the bobbin, free-motion embroider along the inner edge of the shoe tops and down onto the shoe. As you get to the sides of the shoes, free-motion embroider the tendrils as shown. The tendrils are stitched only on the stabilizer, without fabric (figure m). Later, these will be hand sewn to the doll's legs.

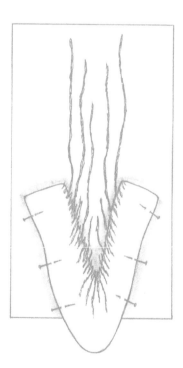

(figure m)
Sew tendrils along the shoe tops.

In free-motion sewing, it is important to lock your threads. What this means is when you leave the surface of the fabric and move onto the stabilizer, you must make sure you catch the threads as you sew up and down. If you do not, when the stabilizer is dissolved, the stitches will fall apart. I find it helpful to zigzag at least one way when I am sewing tendrils on the shoes or other items when working with free-motion machining. This locks the stitches together and prevents them from unraveling once the stabilizer is dissolved.

4. After you are finished with the free-motion sewing, place the shoe tops in lukewarm water to dissolve the stabilizer. Set the top of the shoes aside to dry.

5. While the shoe tops are drying, cut out two Shoe Sole pattern pieces (page 293) from the painted cotton. Using your fingers, fold the Soles in half lengthwise and crease each end of the folded edge. This gives you a guide for pinning the soles to the Shoe Tops.

6. When the Shoe Tops are dry, pin the back seam #1, right sides together, and sew them by machine.

7. Open up the seam allowances and finger-press the seam allowances open.

8. Pin the Sole of the shoe to the Shoe Top, right sides together, matching the crease in the soles, which you made earlier, to the back seam (#1) and the toe's center front (figure n). Starting at the back seam, sew all the way around. Do this carefully so you do not catch the tendrils you created along the top edge of the shoe. Turn right side out.

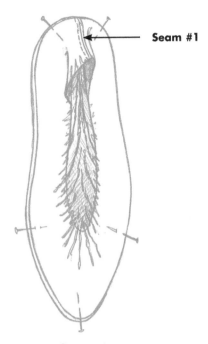

Seam #1

(figure n)
Sew the Shoe Sole to the Shoe Top, taking care not to catch the tendrils.

9. Place the shoes onto the feet of the doll. Because the shoes are larger than her feet, place some stuffing into the toes of the shoes. Fairies always wear pointy-toed shoes. This is so they can push the moss around on the ground when searching for crystals.

10. Hand sew the tendrils to the legs and add seed beads here and there along the tendrils. Add a few seed beads along the edge of the shoe tops.

The Finishing Touches

1. To hide the seams at the doll's wrists, add beads. Thread up a beading needle with 1 yard (91 cm) of beading thread. Place a knot in the end.

2. Attach this thread to the inside of the wrist, over the seam. Thread up enough beads to wrap around her wrist. Close the circle by going into the first bead added. Tack along the strand of beads to her wrist.

3. Sew two more rows of seed beads around each wrist and weave them together to create the look of a three-row bracelet.

4. Hand sew some of the beaded flowers to the circle of beads around her wrist (figure o). Do the same with the other wrist.

5. For the skirt, sew the back seam of the silk crepe de Chine, right sides together.

6. Pin the top edges of the organza skirt to the silk skirt, with the wrong side of the organza against the right side of the silk. By machine, sew a gathering stitch along the pinned top edge. Slip the skirts onto the doll's body and pull the threads to fit snugly. Hand sew the top of the skirt directly to the body.

7. Place the corset over the skirt and bodice. Pin the back opening by overlapping the back's finished edge on top of the unfinished edge. Hand sew the back closed.

8. To give a nice neckline to the bodice, sew some crystal-colored seed beads around her neck and down onto the bodice. Add the beaded flowers along the top edge of the bodice and another one at the center of the neck (figure p).

(figure o)
Weave strands of beads for the bracelets.

(figure p)
For the beaded neckpiece, sew the beads directly to the doll.

The Headpiece and Hair

1. Using three strands of the decorative YLI or Kreinik threads, braid a headpiece. A lucet was used to create Golendrial's braid. A simple braid can be done by hand.

2. Measure the head as you make the braid so that it will wrap around the top of the doll's head. When you have the proper length, secure the end of the braid with a knot. With an overhand knot, tie the two ends of the braid together to form a circle. Leave the ends long and attach beads and free-motion leaves to the ends.

3. Hand sew more of the flowered beads along the front of the headpiece, and a few at each side. The back will not show that much due to the doll's hair.

4. The hair used on the sample doll is an oblong piece of Tibetan goat hair. Cut a piece from the hide side of the hair. You will need a piece 3″ wide by 5″ long (7.6 × 12.7 cm).

> To cut the goat hair, make a snip in the hide, then tear the rest of the way. This keeps the hairs from falling out.

5. To give a nice hairline, pin the hide to the head with the hair side down on the doll's forehead. The length of the hide will be towards the front of her face (figure q).

(figure q)
Sew the Tibetan goat hair to the head.

6. Hand sew this front edge in place with a strong needle and thread. Flip the skin back and pin the skin behind the doll's ears and at each side of the back of her head. Hand sew it in place. If any of the hide shows, tuck it under and hand sew it in place.

7. Place the headpiece on the doll's head (figure r) and hand sew (tack) it in at least three places to keep it from falling off.

(figure r)
Attach the hair before positioning the headpiece.

THE WINGS

1. Trace the Wing pattern (page 294) onto a piece of water-soluble stabilizer, leaving room on the sheet to trace another wing. Fold over the other (untraced) side of the stabilizer on top of the traced wing. Trace on this side. This gives you a right and left wing.

2. Pin the stabilizer with tracings onto a piece of cream-colored organza.

3. Place a decorative thread in the upper threader of the sewing machine and metallic thread in the bobbin. Machine sew, using a straight stitch, around the outline of the wings and along the veins.

4. If you have an embroidery presser foot that has a hole in the front (sometimes called a cording foot), put it on the sewing machine. (For a Bernina sewing machine, this foot is #6.) Feed the beading wire into the hole of the foot. Set the machine for a zigzag stitch, lower the width to 2 (slightly narrow) and the length to 1 (very short).

6. Zigzag the wire to the right side of the wings where marked on the pattern piece(s). When you finish with each line, cut the wire, leaving about 1" (2.5 cm) free at each end.

7. Carefully cut out the wings, making sure you do not cut into the stitches, especially where the wire is attached. Place the wings into lukewarm water to dissolve the stabilizer. Let the wings air dry.

(figure s)
Stabilize the organza to stitch the wings.

8. Once the wings are dry, paint them with Lumiere paints. The sample doll wings were colored with halo violet gold, pearlescent violet, and sunset gold. Start with the darker colors close to the center edges of the wings (pearlescent violet), then apply the halo violet gold and, on the outer edges, the sunset gold.

9. Collect the gold charlottes (or other size 11/12 seed beads) and crystals. Slip three charlottes or seed beads onto a wire at the end of a wing, then a crystal, and finally two seed beads. Cut the wire and pinch under the end to keep the beads in place. Do this to all of the wires on the wings.

10. Pin the wings to the back of Golendrial and hand sew them in place using matching thread. A few couching stitches will secure the wings to her back. To cover your stitches on her back, you can add beaded flowers. The wires in the wings will keep them steady.

Michelle Meinhold is known for her wonderful beadwork. For this sample, she attached seed beads with a peyote bead stitch. It is also easy to follow a cross-stitch pattern to create this type of design.

Kathryn Thompson used a soldering iron and layers of nylon organza to create her whimsical wings. The organza was layered, machine stitched in a free-motion design, and then she used the soldering iron to burn away areas to expose light and the design.

THE PURSE

All fairies need a wee special purse to carry their crystals, threads for bird nests, and a few berries to snack on. It must have a few beads dangling from it and some small bells. The bells are special ones that only other fairies can hear. When you are in the woods, you must let your friends know that you are approaching. Otherwise, you may miss them. Fairies are shy and do not want to be seen by humans.

1. Using tissue paper or pattern paper, trace the Purse pattern (page 293) to make a template. Cut a piece of velvet from this template. Thread a hand sewing needle with an 18" (45.7 cm) length of thread. Place a knot in the end of the thread.

(figure t)
Draw up the edges of a circle for the purse.

2. Attach the thread to the inside top of the circle of velvet and hand sew a gathering stitch completely around the edge (figure t). Pull the thread to close the top of the purse. Do not close the top too tightly. Goldendrial needs enough of an opening to drop her goodies inside. Anchor the thread with several small stitches and then cut off the ends of the threads.

3. Create another braid for the handle of the purse using the same threads you used for the headpiece. Leave about 2" (5 cm) of thread free on both ends of the braid. Place beads and some small bells on the ends. Hand sew the handle to the purse.

4. Thread a beading needle with 12" (30.5 cm) of beading thread. Place a knot in the end. Attach this to the bottom of the doll's purse, on the outside. Pick up a decorative bead, a larger drop-shaped bead, and a small drop-shaped bead. Skipping the small drop-shaped bead, go back through the larger bead and the decorative bead and into the bottom of the purse. Anchor the thread with several small stitches and cut off the thread end.

If you want, hand sew some beads on Golendrial's ear lobes for earrings. Place some crystals and threads in her purse and she's ready. I wouldn't put any berries in right now. They may spoil.

CHAPTER

11

FLOWERS ALL AROUND:

Beading Flowers and Embellishments

Viviana

Visions of Viviana. The inspiration for this doll was flowers, all kinds of delightful flowers: flowers in her hair, in her basket, tattooed on her calves, and sparkling on her clothing. Each flower is a bit different. That's part of our bead-filled adventure. Some flowers are made from seed beads, others are created from fabric and then covered with beads, and others are built around washers found at the hardware store.

Viviana's bodice and skirt are embellished with seed beads. Her shoes and bouquet feature seed beads and washers. The featured flowers are in different forms, but the techniques are easy and can add a wide range of embellishment opportunities for your lovely doll.

Without a doll, a bead is relegated to a communal life in a bead tray. But before we address bead techniques, let's review the basics for making a doll. This chapter includes instructions for making the Basic Doll Body. Keep the doll at 18″ (45.7 cm) tall. This size is just right to "draw a bead on."

Before starting a project, assemble all of your materials. The materials kits listed here include all of the essential items for creating the doll's body, the clothing, and the bead accessories.

Later in the chapter you will find explanations of beading terminology, tools, and materials. We will also cover several basic beading techniques that will be referred to in later chapters.

The Basic Body Kit

* Basic Body pattern pieces (page 295–296)
* ⅓ yard (0.31 m) of tan, light-colored, or batik 100% cotton fabric for the body and head
* mohair, Tibetan goatskin, yarn, fabric, or beads for the hair
* colored pencils: light or sienna brown for shading; lighter tan, beige, or flesh for highlights; white for pronounced highlights; carmine red for cheeks; light, medium, and dark for eyes; two shades of pink, red, or rose for lips
* fabric pens: black for the pupils and eyelashes (optional), brown for outlining all of the features, contrasting color for the eyes, red for outlining the lips and dotting the tear ducts
* white gel pen
* 6 pipe cleaners for wiring fingers
* stuffing such as Fairfield Poly-fil
* textile medium such as Createx Textile Medium or Jo Sonja's Textile Medium
* thread matched to fabric
* strong thread matched to fabric for sculpting and attaching arms, legs, and hair
* soft fabric eraser such as Magic Rub
* mechanical pencil
* clear plastic quilter's gridded ruler
* stuffing tools
* sewing machine
* turning tools such as the Itsy Bitsy Finger Turning kit or small brass tubes (see Resources, page 302)
* needle-nose pliers
* wire cutters
* light table (optional)

The Basic Clothing Kit

❋ cotton batik fabrics

❋ cotton print fabrics

❋ synthetic fabrics such as polyester organza

❋ silk fabrics such as chiffon, crepe de Chine, dupioni, or sand-washed charmeuse

❋ variegated and metallic sewing machine threads

❋ lace

❋ trims

❋ silk ribbons

The Basic Beading Kit

❋ seed beads in various colors: sizes 6, 8, 11, and 15

❋ size 15 charlottes in various colors

❋ size 11 Miyuki Delica seed beads

❋ accent beads: drop, lentil, flower, bugle, triangle, square, and leaf

❋ beading threads: Nymo, FireLine, wax

The Basic Sewing Kit

❋ sewing machine

❋ sewing machine needles: universal points in sizes 10 and 12; embroidery, metallic, and top stitch in size 12

❋ hand-sewing needles (sharps, milliners, quilter's basting, darners, embroidery, chenille)

❋ size 24 (small) tapestry needle

❋ variety of sewing machine presser feet, such as darning, open-toed, and zigzag

❋ sewing machine tools (for changing needles, oiling, and cleaning)

❋ seam ripper

❋ iron

❋ press cloth

❋ small bottle of Sewer's Aid

❋ extra bobbins

❋ straight pins

❋ safety pins

❋ pincushion

❋ thimble

❋ cutting rulers

❋ clear plastic quilter's gridded ruler

❋ measuring tape

❋ template plastic, card stock, or heavy paper (optional)

❋ rotary cutter and self-healing cutting board (optional)

❋ straight-edge fabric scissors

❋ embroidery scissors

❋ paper scissors

❋ pinking shears

❋ hemostats (handheld surgical clamps) or forceps

❋ stuffing fork

❋ pencil

Body made from star fabric, not clothed

THE BODY CONSTRUCTION

The pattern pieces for the Basic Body start on page 295. Do not cut out the pattern pieces before reviewing the construction steps that start below. Some pattern pieces are traced on to the fabric with a mechanical pencil, and then sewn before they are cut out: Face, Head Back, Arm, and Leg. The main body pieces are cut out in detail and then sewn together.

As you sew, backstitch at all openings. This is especially important for the neck.

Have a new needle in your sewing machine and shorten the stitch length slightly. You want a closer stitch, which will prevent the seams from splitting, plus fewer stitches are visible. On a Bernina, for example, rather than the normal 2.0, move the setting down to 1.8 (about 15 stitches per inch [2.5 cm]).

1 Trace the Face and Head onto the wrong side of the body fabric, matching the grain lines. With the fabric folded so there are two layers, machine sew seam #1 on the Face and seam #2 on the Head Back (figure a). Leave open where marked on the Head Back.

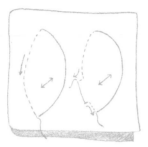

(figure a)
Sew head before cutting the fabric.

2 Cut out the head pieces using full ⅛" (3 mm) seam allowances along seam #1 and seam #2, and open each one up. Pin the pattern pieces, right sides together, at the chin and top of head, matching the seams. Machine sew all the way around along seam #3 (figure b). Clip the curves and turn the head right side out.

(figure b)
Sew front of head to back of head.

3 Fill the head with stuffing and set it aside for now.

4 Trace the Body Front onto the wrong side of the body fabric. Double the fabric and cut it out. Trace all of the darts. Flip the pattern template over when tracing on the reverse side of the body. The Body Back is a single piece. Trace this onto the wrong side of a single piece of fabric and cut it out. Trace all of the darts.

5 After you cut out the body pieces, machine sew all of the darts (figure c). Pin the two Body Front pieces right sides together and sew seam #4.

(figure c)
Sew darts on body front.

6 On the Body Back, cut along the solid line from the neck to the end of the dart (figure d). Fold the Body Back so that the right sides match. Machine sew down dart #1, leaving open where marked. (Note: For fray-free assembly, use pinking shears to trim seam allowances.)

(figure d)
Cut down the center back.

7 Pin the Body Front to the Body Back, right sides together, and machine sew all the way from the neck opening, around the body, to the other side of the neck opening. Leave the neck open at the top. As the neck is sewn, backstitch at either side of the opening.

8 Turn the body right side out and fill it firmly with stuffing. Be sure to plump up the breasts. Ladder stitch opening closed on back. Set the body aside for now.

9 Trace two arms on the wrong side of the same fabric as the body. Double the fabric, right sides together, and pin the layers together in several places. Machine sew from the opening at the wrist all the way around. Cut out, using a full ⅛" (3 mm) seam allowance, and turn. Fill the arms with stuffing from the top to the elbows and set aside.

10 Make a complete pattern piece for a leg by tracing the upper and lower leg shapes onto template plastic and then overlap and tape together the edges as marked. Trace two legs onto the wrong side of the Body fabric. Transfer the slit mark to the right side of each piece. Double the fabric, right sides together, and pin around the shapes. Sew all the way around from the opening at the feet. Cut out the legs using full ⅛" (3 mm) seam allowances, but don't turn the shape right side out yet.

11 Trace the Foot template (page 298) on to template plastic, card stock, or heavy paper. Cut this out using paper scissors. Refold the bottom of the leg and pin the center seams together on the foot, with the fabric right sides together. Lay the template you made of the foot on to the fabric foot and trace around the foot and big toe with a mechanical pencil (figure e). Sew along the traced line. Trim and then clip the curves of the seam allowances.

(figure e)
Trace and sew the foot.

12 Place the legs together with the feet facing each other and cut a slit—only on the side facing you—where marked on each leg. Turn each leg through the opening and fill both legs from the toes to the knee. To allow the legs to bend so the doll can sit, a bit of sculpting will be done with strong thread.

Tip:

To allow the thread to be hidden, make a hidden knot. To do this, when threading the needle, push both raw ends of the thread through the eye of the needle. Go in at the back of the knee and take the needle through the loop that will be at the other end of the thread. Pull this loop closed so no knot shows.

Thread needle to make a hidden knot.

13 Secure the end of the thread on the seam line at the back of the knee (figure f, left). Push the needle inside the leg and come out about ¼" (6 mm) from the seam at the center front of the knee, on the front of the leg (#1) (figure f, right). To sew the knee dimple, take the needle up about ½" (1.3 cm) and push the needle into the leg (#2). Take the needle straight across and out the knee to the other side of the front of the leg about ¼" (6 mm) from the center seam (#3) and in line with the stitch just made. Take the needle down about ½" (1.3 cm) and then push the needle into the knee (#4). Come out on the other side, in line with this stitch, or into the first stitch created. Come out at this point, then take the thread around the back of the leg and back into #3. Pull the thread tightly.

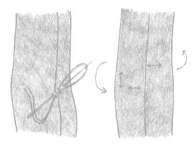

(figure f)
Left: Secure thread without a knot.
Right: Sculpt the leg.

14 The thread will sink into the back of the leg, allowing the leg to bend so that the doll can sit. Anchor the thread at the back of the knee and cut it off. Fill the upper part of the leg lightly with stuffing and sew the opening closed. Still using strong thread, sew the legs to the body starting at the side of the hip. Make sure that the slit at the top of each leg is closest to the body, so it isn't visible when the leg is attached to the body.

15 Trace two hands onto the wrong side of the body fabric. Double the fabric and pin to secure. Backstitch as you start to machine sew at the wrist. Carefully sew around the fingers. You'll need to have at least two stitches across the tips of each finger and two in between the fingers.

Tip:

It is very important to stitch exactly on the tracing lines for the hand and get those two stitches across the tips and between each finger. I always stitch my doll hands by machine with an open-toe presser foot so the pencil line is always clearly visible. The fingers need to be wide enough for a tube to fit inside when turning a finger right side out.

16 Make sure the gap between the fingers is a straight stitch, not a pivot point (V shape). Otherwise, you'll have a difficult time turning the fingers and preventing wrinkles. After sewing the entire hand with tiny stitches, cut out the hand, with a scant ⅛" (3 mm) seam allowance.

17 Using sharp scissors, cut into the inside curves between each finger. Cut to within a fabric thread of the stitching between the fingers.

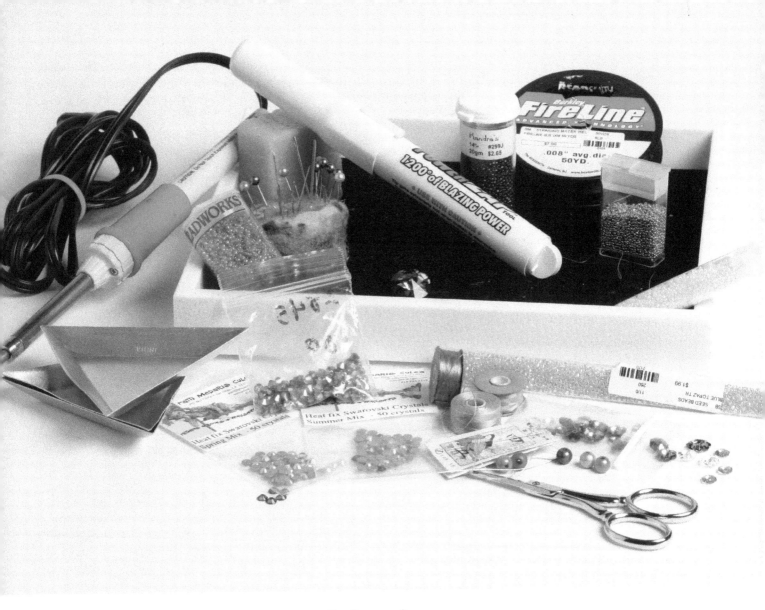

Beading supplies

BEADING BASICS

Because this book is about beading, there are a few essential things that you should know: the different types of beads and tools to make your life easier, and especially, how to get a bead needle threaded.

Many of you will notice that all size 11 seed beads aren't always the same size. This has a lot to do with the manufacturing companies. You'll find that seed beads made in Japan are more uniform. But, again, this varies from one manufacturer to the next. Toho Co. Ltd. and Miyuki Company are my preferred Japanese seed bead companies because both of these companies create even-sized seed beads. You will find that a Toho Treasure size 12 seed bead will be a little different in size compared to Miyuki. That means it's best to stick with one company, if you can.

Delica beads are also made in Japan, by Miyuki. Delicas are perfectly cut so that they fit flat next to each other. Whenever you see a definite design or pattern, such as a beaded pouch, it was made using Delicas. Toho makes a similar bead called an Aiko. Some find that the Aikos are nearly perfect in their uniformity.

Companies in the Czech Republic also make seed beads. Products from this country have smaller holes and aren't cut as precisely as the Japanese seed beads.

Another bead that is called for in the following chapters is a charlotte. This type of bead is cut on one side to give a sparkle effect. Some people consider these the most brilliant seed beads.

Crystals come in all sizes and shapes. Swarovski is the main manufacturer of crystals. There are other companies that make crystals, but they aren't as beautiful as the Swarovski crystals, which are made in the Czech Republic.

Miracle beads are so called because each one appears to have another bead inside it. Actually, the illusion is created by spraying the bead several times with a reflective material and then finishing it with a clear coating. Miracle beads are plastic and made in Japan.

Other types of beads are lampwork (glass), flower and leaf shapes, heat-set crystals (called Hot-Fix by Swarovski), wood, bone, ethnic, and semiprecious. If there is a bead not mentioned here, its use will be explained in the following chapters.

The size beading thread should coincide with the size bead you are working with. For instance, for bead sizes 10 and 11, a size B thread is generally used. For smaller beads, such as size 15, use 00 or 0 size thread. If you're using Japanese seed beads, you can use a B thread for the smaller seed beads. But with Czech beads, you'll need the thinner thread.

The same rule applies to beading needles. The smaller the bead, the smaller the eye of the needle. I find that a size 12 beading needle works with nearly all seed beads, except some Czech beads. Those beads with really small holes I throw away.

Thread conditioners come in several types. Beeswax is preferred by some and others like Thread Heaven, a nontoxic, acid-free conditioner that doesn't deteriorate over time. Beeswax and Thread Heaven prevent the thread from tangling and knotting.

To help keep your beads in place as you work, a piece of Ultrasuede or real suede is very helpful. You can pour the beads onto this surface so that the needle will pick up the beads easily. Or, you can place your working trays onto this surface and they'll stay in place, rather than scooting around.

Ever since the first iron needle with an eye was invented in the fifteenth century, we have had our ups and downs (or ins and outs) trying to thread the evasive small needle. Here's how I've managed to do it—no sure-fire guarantee, but close.

Use very sharp scissors and cut the thread straight across the end. Pinch the cut end between your index finger and thumb. You'll want just a small amount showing. With the needle in your other hand, lay the eye of the needle down on the thread. The thread should go into the eye easily. If it doesn't, lick the eye of the needle and try again. Licking the end of the needle seems to help the thread jump through the eye. I remember my grandmothers doing this and am happy to pass along what I learned from these wonderful ladies to you.

Now that you've threaded your needle...and have your doll in hand, the following chapters will help you put it all together with details on beading techniques and how to use the needles and threads.

EARS

1 Trace two ears from the pattern (page 297) on the wrong side of the fabric used for the body. Double the fabric, right sides together, so that you can see both of the traced ears. Machine sew from the opening all the way around to the other side of the opening of both tracings. Cut out both ears, using scant ⅛" (3 mm) seam allowances, and clip the curves.

2 Using hemostats, turn the ears right side out. Trace the ear stitching lines on the pattern piece onto each ear, making sure you have a right and left ear. Machine sew the stitching line on each ear with matching thread, allowing room between the stitching line and the edge of the ear along the inner edge for the pipe cleaner to be inserted. Cut the threads.

3 Bend back the tip of one end of the pipe cleaner. Insert the pipe cleaner into the ear, in the "casing" along the outer edge of the ear until the tip is in the top of the ear (figure a). Cut the other end of the pipe cleaner about ¼" (6 mm) from the opening of the outer edge of the ear. Bend back this tip and push the rest of that end into the earlobe. Insert a small amount of stuffing in the inner edge of the ear. Close up the opening and hand stitch the ear to the side of the head, where marked on the pattern piece, using the ladder stitch (page 200).

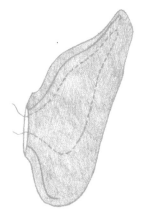

(figure a)
Topstitch ears and insert pipe cleaners.

ARM AND LEG BEAD TATTOOS

1 With the arms and legs still separate from the doll body, select a rubber stamp that is unmounted and has a design that you like. Ink this with the stamp pad and then apply it to the arm (figure b, below). Carefully wrap the rubber stamp around the arm and press with your fingers. Remove the rubber stamp by lifting straight up. It is not necessary to heat-set this stamp, as the design will be covered with beads. The sample doll (page 160) was stamped with Jacquard Pearl Ex Stamp Pad in Gold Violet.

(figure b)
Roll an unmounted stamp over the fabric.

2 Collect three or four colors of size 15 seed beads, two washer flowers (page 175), straight pins, beading needle, and beading thread. At the center of the design, using the beading needle and thread, hand sew the washer flower to the arm or leg. Depending on the amount of thread you have left, start bead embroidering over the stamped design. Use the backstitch (page 199) to anchor the beads to the design.

3 If the design you have chosen has points, as the sample doll has, fuse some heat-set crystals at the ends of the points. The sample doll's design has some curves. In order to follow the curves, place some straight pins along the design. Thread enough beads to follow the pins, then sight along them to help align and anchor the beads using the backstitch (figure c).

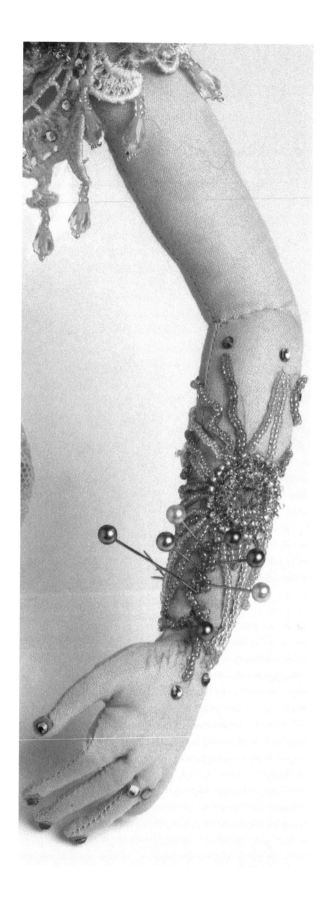

(figure c)
Sight along straight pins to align beads.

4 At the end of some of the shorter points of the design, add a 3 mm bicone crystal by pushing the needle into the arm or leg and coming out at the end of the stamped design. Place a bicone crystal and a size 15 seed bead on the needle. Take the beads to the arm or leg and hold them in place. Skipping the size 15 seed bead, push the needle into the crystal and into the arm. Continue adding the size 15 seed beads to the design.

BEADING CLOTHING AND SHOES

1 Decide on your color theme and pour the Dye Na Flow into containers.

2 Dip the lace for the underskirt into the dye. Remove it from the dye and squeeze out the excess dye. Hang it to dry.

Tip:

I like using an ice cube tray to hold the paint colors. This gives me several mixing containers, plus one for plain water. I color-dip larger pieces of lace because it is faster and easier than hand painting.

3 The rest of the lace is dyed using paintbrushes. Brush on the colors you want, allowing colors to bleed into each other. This creates a third color (figure d). The sample doll was made with Magenta and Periwinkle, with White added along with 30 percent water, creating the pastel colors. When all of the lace is dry, iron to set the colors.

(figure d)
Close-up of the dress

4 Machine sew the short ends of the upper skirt lace, right sides together, to make the back seam on the upper skirt. Before placing the skirt on the doll's body, add some of the heat-set crystals along the lower part of the lace. Next, hand sew some drop beads at various points on the lace. To do this, thread a beading needle with 1 yard (0.91 m) of beading thread. Place a knot in the single end. Attach this to the back side of the lace, behind the spot where you will add a drop bead. Come through to the front of the lace. At each position, add three size 11 seed beads, a drop bead, and three size 15 gold or silver charlottes. Skip the three charlottes, insert the needle and thread back through the drop bead, three size 11 seed beads, and the lace (figure e). Anchor the thread at the back of the lace and cut the thread. Continue doing this along various points of the lace.

(figure e)
Add the drop beads to the lace.

5 For the underwear, pin the lace motif to the body. Hand sew it in place, trimming as necessary.

6 Machine sew the short ends of the underskirt lace, right sides together, to make the back seam on the underskirt. Separately machine sew a gathering running stitch along the waist (upper edge) of both the upper skirt and the underskirt. Pull the threads to loosely gather the edge, then slip it onto the doll and pull tightly. Slip the upper skirt on first, then the underskirt. Adjust the gathers, then hand sew the skirts to the body.

7 Pin the lace motif to the bust, back, and arms of the doll's body. Hand sew it in place. Add a scattering of size 11 seed beads as you hand sew the lace to the body. As with the skirt, add some drop beads to various points along the sleeves (figure f).

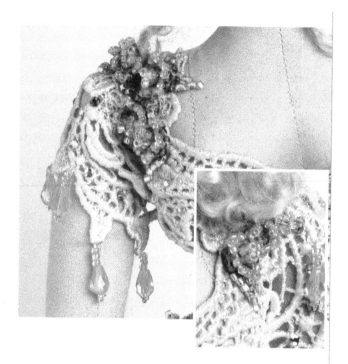

(figure f)
Close-up of sleeves

8 Trace two of the Shoe Sole pattern piece (page 297) onto the wrong side of a cotton fabric of choice. Cut a slit down the center of the drawn soles. Double the fabric, right sides together, and pin it in several places. Machine sew all the way around the traced lines, through both fabric layers. Cut out the shapes using a scant ⅛" (3 mm) seam allowance (figure g). Turn the sole right side out through this opening.

(figure g)
Cut slits through one layer of each seamed set.

9 Cut out two Shoe Sole Inserts (page 297) from cardboard. Slip these inside the soles, through the slits. Hand sew to close up the slits.

10 Collect the size 11 seed beads you want for the shoes. The shoes are made with one color for the shoe top and back, then different color beads for the ruffles and other embellishments. Using backstitch beadwork (page 199), anchor the thread at the back of the heel of the sole and lay down the beads by backstitching along the outer edge of the entire sole.

Tip:

I find it helpful to make a template of the sole. As I draw on to the fabric, I flip over the template for one of the soles. This way, I have a right and a left sole for the shoes. I then cut a slit down the center of the drawn side of each sole. This ensures that I do not cut through both layers when cutting the slit after the shoe is sewn.

11 With the same seed beads, do one row of peyote beadwork (page 199) on each sole, placing the new beads on top of the row applied in step 10. Do not cut the beading thread. Place the sole on to the doll's foot and decide where you want to do the beading to make the shoe back. Using a pencil, mark the placement of the shoe back. Needle over (page 198) to this spot and start adding rows of peyote beading—attached to, and built up from the shoe sole—back and forth, to create the heel. To angle the edges of the shoe back as shown on the sample doll (page 160), as you come to the end of a row, instead of adding a bead, turn the needle and go into the last bead of the current row. Add a bead (this will be the first bead of the next row), skip the next bead, and go through the third bead from the end of the row just worked (figure h). Continue across in peyote as usual. To create an angle at the end of the row, instead of adding a bead, turn the needle and go into the last bead of the previous row, then through the last bead of the current row. Add a bead (this will be the first bead of the next row), and go through the next (second) bead of the row just worked. (Note: Each row of the illustration is shown in a different color. Row colors do not represent a change in actual bead color.)

(figure h)
Angle row ends for shoe heel.
Rows colored for identification only

12 After the shoe back is finished, add two rows of ruffled edging to the shoe as follows: Thread the beading needle with 1½ yards (1.37 m) of beading thread. Place a knot in the single end and anchor it in the fabric in the sole of the shoe, at one side of the shoe back. Push the needle into an up bead at the beginning edge of the shoe back. Come out this bead and add three size 11 seed beads that are a different color from the shoe beads. Take the needle over to the next up bead and go into this bead. You have made a picot (ruffle). Come

out that bead and add another three beads of the same color as the previous picot. Continue doing this along the edge to the opposite side of the shoe back. Change to another bead color and do another row of picots next to the row you just finished. This gives a ruffled effect. Do not cut the thread yet.

13 Slip the shoe on the doll's foot and pin it in place. At this point, anchor the thread you have been working with into the foot of the doll. Anchor the shoe back to the foot in several places, then cut the thread close to the beadwork. Place another 2 yards (1.83 m) of beading thread on the needle and knot the end. Anchor this in the sole, near the place where the instep of the shoe would be. Thread up enough seed beads to go from one side of the shoe to the other side, over the top of the foot. Do not anchor this row to the foot. That is done later.

14 Using peyote beadwork, fill in the shoe top. Do not decrease at the edges (as done on the heel). When you get close to the toe, anchor the shoe top to the foot. To do this, push the needle from a bead into the foot. Move the needle over and come up in between two beads. Go through a couple of beads, then push the needle into the foot. Doing this three or four times anchors the shoe top firmly to the foot (figure i).

(figure i)
Close-up of the shoes

15 As with the shoe back, create picots, with two different colors of size 11 seed beads, along the toe edge and the top edge of the shoe top. Hand sew one of the beaded washer flowers (page 175) to the center of the shoe top.

FLOWERS

Small Five-Point Flower

Viviana has five of these flowers attached at each shoulder. One flower is at the center of her bodice and fourteen are attached around the upper edge of her skirt, at the waist.

1 Thread a beading needle with 1 yard (0.91 m) of beading thread. Wax the thread.

2 Needle up five size 11 seed beads in one color. Tie these in a circle. Add one bead and then go into the next bead in the circle (figure j). (Note: Each round of the illustration is shown in a different color. Round colors do not represent a change in actual bead color.) Add another bead and go into the next bead in the circle. Continue this all the way around. Five new beads have been added. Carefully cut away the tail thread at the knot in the circle. Do not cut the working thread.

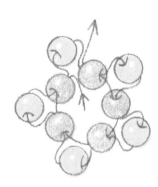

(figure j)
Tie beads in a circle and add five new beads.
Rounds colored for identification only

3 At the end of the most recent row, go through the first bead you added. This is an up bead. You will see four more up beads, which you just added in step 2. In this new row, add a bead and then go through an up bead. Repeat this four more times (figure k). (Note: Each round of the illustration is shown in a different color. Round colors do not represent a change in actual bead color.) Five new beads have been added. Go through the first bead you added in this round. Continue going around the circle, adding three more rounds in the same way. As you add these next rounds, start pulling on the threads so that your beads turn in to a cup.

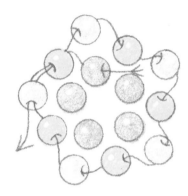

(figure k)
Add another (third) row of beads.
Rounds colored for identification only

4 Change the bead color and thread three size 11 seed beads of this second color. Take the needle into the next up bead of the previous round. Add three of the new color and go into the next up bead. Continue this process all the way around. When you come to the end, you will see that you have created a five-petal flower.

5 Weave the needle down through beads in the previous rows to the bottom, into one of the original five beads. Take the needle inside and up out the center of this bead. Add four of a third color of seed bead. This represents the stamen. Add one bead of another color. Skip this last bead and go back into the four seed beads, and then into the bottom center. Go through one of the original five beads, and then add another stamen. Create two more stamens.

6 After the stamens are made, leaves can be added along the outer edge, on the outside of the flower cup. Change to green seed beads. Going through the flower center from the inside to the outside, come out a bead of the original five. Add five green seed beads. Skip the last bead and go through just the fourth (second to last loaded) seed bead. Add three green seed beads and go over to another bead in the circle of original five beads (figure l). Create another leaf the same way. Leave enough thread to sew the flower to the doll or to the haku lei.

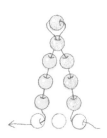

(figure l)
Add beaded leaves to the outside of the flower.

Rounds colored for identification only

7 After two leaves are made, attach the flower to the doll's waist or bodice.

Washer Flower

These flowers are at the center of the shoe tops and on her haku lei (head band).

1 Color a washer with ink from Tsukineko StazOn stamp pads.

2 Collect a painted washer, braids, ribbons, threads of choice, two colors of size 15 seed beads (colors A and B), a 4 mm bicone crystal for each flower, a beading needle, and FireLine beading thread. Cover the washer

with the threads by using the blanket stitch (page 203). Weave the thread and braid tails throughout the blanket stitch at the top. Fasten off the ends and cut off any extra threads.

3 Cut 2 yards (1.83 m) of FireLine and thread a beading needle. Place a knot in a single long end. Anchor this at the top of a blanket stitch on the washer. Place two color A, one color B, and two color A beads on the needle. Push the needle into the blanket stitch next to the one where you came out.

4 From the edge of the blanket stitch, go back into the last bead added and come out this bead. Add one color A, one color B, and two color A beads. Push the needle into the next blanket stitch (figure m). Continue making picots until you have gone all the way around the washer's top edge. When you get to the beads you started with, add one color A, one color B, and one color A. Go into the first bead of the first picot, and then into the first blanket stitch.

(figure m)
Edge washer with beaded ruffle.

5 If you have enough thread left, weave down through the blanket stitches to the center of the washer. Pick up a 4 mm crystal and go over to the other side and into the inner edge of the washer. Go back into the crystal and over to where you started. Do this two more times.

6 After the crystal is seated in the center of the washer, add another round of five-bead picots around the edge of the center (the inner edge of the washer) by working into the blanket stitches as you did on the outer edge. When this row is complete, go back into the threads covering the washer and tack down each of the center seed beads (color B). The goal is to get the top bead of each picot to lay flat against the blanket stitches. This keeps the beads from moving around and covering the crystal.

Marguerite Flower

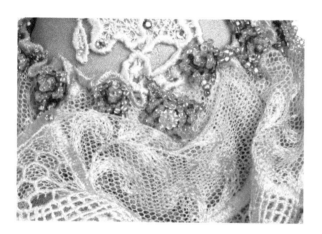

Close-up of marguerite flowers

1 Collect a 6 mm crystal marguerite, size 15 gold or silver charlottes, size 11 seed beads in two colors for the flower (colors A and B) and one color for the leaves, a beading needle, and beading thread. Cut 2 yards (1.83 m) of beading thread and thread the needle with no knot in the end. Wax the thread.

2 Thread sixteen size 11 seed beads of color A. Tie a knot in the thread to form a circle. Work one round of peyote beading on the inside of the circle as follows: Add one bead of color A. Skip the first bead in the circle and then go through the next (second) bead. Add another color A bead. Skip the next bead in the circle and then go through the next bead in the circle. Continue doing this until you have eight beads in the

second round and you are back at the starting point (figure n, left). (Note: Each round of the illustration is shown in a different color. Round colors do not represent a change in actual bead color.)

3 The third round is also worked inside the circle, with color A seed beads. Go through the first bead in round two. Thread one seed bead and then go through the next two beads in round two. Add three more seed beads in the same way, so that the last round-two bead you go through is actually the first bead in round two—the same one you went through at the start of round three.

4 When you get to the first bead you added in the third round, go through that bead. With the same needle and thread, pick up the marguerite bead and a size 15 charlotte, either the gold or silver color. Skip the charlotte and pass through the marguerite, then over to the opposite side of round three, and into a round-three bead. Pass through this bead, then back into the marguerite, through the charlotte, back into the marguerite, and over to another round-three bead that you have not gone through before (figure n, right). This process anchors the marguerite in the center of the flower.

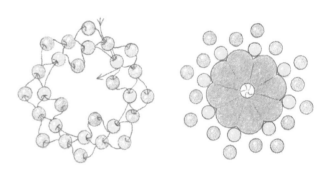

(figure n)
Work a base with peyote beading.
Rounds colored for identification only

5 As round two was worked, the round-one beads that were not used popped to the outside of the circle. These are up beads. Weave through the beads in the previous rounds, coming out an up bead along the outer edge. Thread three size 11 seed beads of color B and push the needle into the next up bead. Continue this all the way around the outer edge (figure o). (Note: Each round of the illustration is shown in a different color. Round colors do not represent a change in actual bead color.)

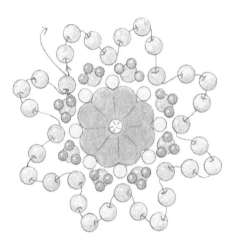

(figure o)
Add the center round.
Rounds colored for identification only

6 Now weave down to a center (round-two) bead in between the up beads and come out one of these. You are now working inside round two. Add three of the color B size 11 seed beads and go over to the next center, or down, bead and continue adding groups of three seed beads all the way around. After the picots are added, weave the needle to the back of the flower and add a beaded leaf or two (step 6 of the Small Five-Point Flower, page 175).

7 Attach the finished beaded flower to the doll skirt or haku lei (page 180). The sample doll has one marguerite flower at the center of the waist. Another marguerite flower was added to the haku lei.

Beaded Mum

1 Cut out three circles of fabric (or use the template on page 298). Thread a beading needle with beading thread and place a knot in the single end. Anchor this to the edge of one of the circles. Hand sew a gathering stitch along the edge. Roll a small amount of stuffing in your hands into a ball. Place this in the center of the fabric circle and pull the thread to close the fabric around the stuffing.

2 Collect size 15 seed beads in the colors you want for the mums. You will also need size 15 charlottes in colors of your choice. The sample doll has gold and silver charlottes at the end of each mum petal (see photo, page 160).

3 Push the needle into the edge of the round fabric ball and come out on the outside, at a spot close to the gathered edge. Thread five size 15 seed beads and then three size 15 charlottes. Skip the three charlottes and go into the last of the seed beads, just through the one bead. Come out this bead and add four seed beads. Push the needle into the ball next to where you added the beads. As you go into the fabric, adjust the three charlottes so that they form a picot at the top of the petal. Take the needle out of the ball, close to where you went in, and add another petal. Add three rounds of these petals, circling the perimeter of the ball.

4 For the rest of the mum, reduce the number of seed beads on each additional petal that you make: thread four size 15 seed beads and then three charlottes. Go into the last (fourth) seed bead and add three seed beads. Go into the fabric, then back out close to where you went in. Continue around the rest of the top of the ball until it is filled in.

Fabric circles, partially made beaded mum,
and finished flower

Six-Point Flower

1 Collect two colors of size 11 seed beads and one accent bead for the center. This accent can be a miracle bead or a 4 mm bicone crystal. Thread a needle with 1 yard (0.91 m) of beading thread. Wax the thread. Thread twelve seed beads of one color. Tie the beads in a circle, leaving a 3" (7.6 cm) tail. Push the needle in to the first bead added and come out that one bead. Add five seed beads of the same color. Skip the next bead in the circle and go into the third bead (figure p, top). (Note: Each round of the illustration is shown in a different color. Round colors do not represent a change in actual bead color.) Come out that third bead and add five more seed beads. Continue around the circle in the same way. At the end of the round, you weave through the same bead that you did at the beginning. You will have six five-bead petals (picots).

2 Push the needle into the first two beads of the petal closest to where your needle just came out (these are round-two beads). Come out the second bead. Thread up five seed beads of the same color. Skip the third bead of the same five-bead petal made in round two and go into the fourth bead. Come out this bead and add one bead. Push the needle into the second bead of the next petal and come out that bead. Add five seed beads, skip the third bead of the same petal,

and go into the fourth bead. Come out that bead and add one bead. Continue in the same way all the way around the circle of petals (figure p, bottom). At the end, add one seed bead as usual and then push the needle into the second bead of the next petal, but now take the needle down to the center circle of beads (round one).

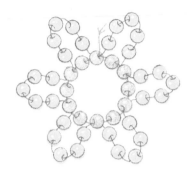

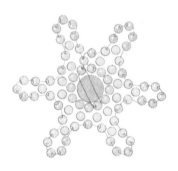

(figure p)
Add central accent bead last.
Rounds colored for identification only

3 Weave down to the bead between the first five-bead petal made in round two. Come out that bead. Following steps 1 and 2, add another row of petals, going from one center bead (between the original petal beads) to the next center bead.

4 Weave down into the center of the circle and pick up the accent bead. Take the needle and push it into a center bead across from the bead you came out. Come out this bead then back into the accent bead and into a bead near where you started. Attach this flower to the haku lei, or wherever you want.

BEADED CUFF

Close-up of beaded cuff

1 Collect the size 11 seed beads, marguerites, and charlottes you want for the cuff on Viviana's right arm. Cut 2 yards (1.83 m) of beading thread and thread the beading needle. Thread enough beads to wrap around Viviana's wrist. If necessary, place a stop bead (page 198) at the end of the thread, then add the seed beads.

2 Following the peyote beadwork instructions (page 199), create seven rows. Place this on the doll's wrist and weave the cuff closed. Push the needle through the top bead and then into the second bead on the opposite side. Come out that bead and go into the third bead on

the side you started on. Come out that bead and go over to the fourth bead on the opposite side. Continue weaving down to the bottom, then back up to the top, in the same way (figure q). This closes the cuff around the doll's wrist.

(figure q)
Weave the ends together to make a circle.

3 Weave through the beads and come out along the top edge. Change colors of seed beads and add a three-bead picot along the edge. To do this, bring the needle out a bead, add three beads, then push the needle down into the next edge bead. Bring the needle out that bead. Add three beads and push the needle into the next edge bead. Continue all the way around the top edge this way.

4 Weave the needle down to the center of the cuff and bring the needle out a bead. Add one marguerite and three silver size 15 charlottes. Skipping the three charlottes, push the needle back into the marguerite then into the seed bead of the cuff. Weave the needle down to the bottom edge of the cuff and add a row of picots along this edge, as done on the top edge. Anchor the thread either in the arm or between the beads and then cut the thread.

HAKU LEI

While living in Hawaii, this was my favorite type of lei. Haku means "head" in Hawaiian, thus, head lei. It is beautiful and will add just the right finishing touch to the doll.

Close-up of haku lei

1 Make a variety of flowers following the instructions earlier in this chapter. Collect size 11 green seed beads, beading needle, and beading thread. Cut 2 yards (1.83 m) of beading thread and place it in the needle. Wax the thread. Thread enough beads to wrap around the doll's head, and then add another five beads. The lei should be a bit loose as adding the flowers, leaves, and buds will make it shrink a bit.

2 Tie these beads in a circle. Work peyote beading for two rounds around the circle, using the green seed beads. Pick up a flower and anchor it to the circle of beads as follows: Push the needle inside two beads at the lower center of the flower then into two beads on the circle. Anchor the flower in this way at least three more times. After the flower is anchored, add two or three beaded leaves as done in step 6 of the Small Five-Point Flower (page 175). Continue adding flowers and leaves until the lei is covered.

3 To create buds, push the needle into a green seed bead at the base of the haku lei. Come out that bead and thread a miracle bead and a size 11 seed bead. Skip the size 11 seed bead and push the needle into the miracle bead and the bead you came out of on the haku lei. Add as many of these buds as you want.

WINGS

1 Collect three different colors of polyester organza, water-soluble stabilizer, decorative machine threads that are thin enough to go through a sewing machine needle, wing template (page 297), and beading wire. Trace the wing design on to the water-soluble stabilizer using a ballpoint pen. Layer the three colors of organza and pin them together with the stabilizer on top. Pin in several places to hold all of the layers in place.

2 Place decorative threads in both the needle and bobbin of your sewing machine. Place a darning or free-motion foot on the machine. Lower or cover the feed dogs, if you can. Lower the stitch length on the machine to 0 (smallest possible satin stitch length). This slows down the feed dogs, which helps with the free-motion sewing if you cannot lower them.

3 Following the drawn lines, machine sew the design. Once the wings are filled in, remove the darning or free-motion foot and place a cording foot on your machine, if you have one. If not, use an embroidery or zigzag presser foot.

Tip:

A cording foot has a small hole in the center of the toe, which allows you to place threads or wires through it. As you zigzag along the item, the material feeding through the hole is controlled to prevent the needle from hitting the threads or wires. On a Bernina, this foot is #6.

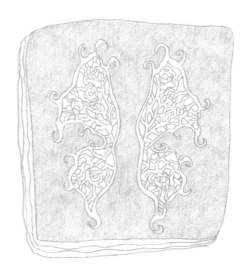

(figure r)
Layer organza and stabilizer with traced wing template.

4 If you have a cording foot, push the wire through the small hole. Set the machine to zigzag and lower the stitch length to ½ (very short). Zigzag along the lines designated for the wire placement (figure r). It helps to not cut the wire from the spool until you have finished placing the section of the wire. Then cut the wire and insert it in the foot and zigzag the wire in place along the next area. Cut the wire, leaving 1" (2.5 cm) tail.

5 Cut closely and carefully around the design, making sure you do not cut through any of the stitches (figure s). Place the wings in a sink of lukewarm water to dissolve the stabilizer. After five minutes, remove the wings from the water and rinse them under running water. Pat them dry with a towel and hang them to dry.

6 When dry, plug in a soldering iron that has a fine tapered point. Once hot, carefully burn away parts of the design. The grayed areas of the template are the parts to be burned away. You may choose to burn away less or more. While the soldering iron is still hot, carefully seal the outer edges of the wings.

7 Once the wings are to your liking, turn on the heat-setting tool and add some heat-set crystals, if you want. You may also hand sew crystals or other beads to the

(figure s)
Stitch wings, add wire, then cut away excess stabilizer.

wings. There are a few scattered along Viviana's wings, arms, legs, and chest. A few were added to her face too.

8 Hand sew the wings to the back of Viviana's body near where her shoulder blades would be.

Tip:

When working with polyester and heating elements, always work in a well-ventilated area. A dust mask is recommended too. Because this product melts, watch your fingers. The burned-away fibers remain hot for about a minute. You might want to keep a small bowl of water handy to soothe hurt fingertips and a fire extinguisher nearby in case something catches fire.

ATTACHING THE HAIR

1 Hair is created last. Otherwise, it simply gets in the way. Collect the hair you have chosen for Viviana. You will also need a hand-sewing needle and strong thread, such as quilting thread. Cut 1 yard (0.91 m) of the thread and thread the needle with this. Place a knot in the single end.

2 Starting at the back of the head near the neck, hand sew a clump of the hair you have chosen. To make sure you have the clump secured, come out one side, at its center, and push the needle into the head next to where you came out, with the clump on the inside of the threads. Follow the seam line around the head, leaving ½" (1.3 cm) gaps between each clump. Add two or three clumps at the center of the head back. Fluff up the hair with your fingers and secure the style you want with a hand-sewing needle and strong hand-sewing thread.

3 Place the haku lei on Viviana's head and arrange. Pin it in place and then, with needle and thread, sew the lei to the head, catching the green base beads as you sew.

Use any brand of craft foam for the finished basket.

BASKET FOR FLOWERS

1 Collect the fabrics you want for the outside and lining of the basket and a tea strainer or other shape for the craft foam. Cut a circle shape from the craft foam (or use the template on page 298). Lay this on the fabrics you have chosen and cut them ⅓" (8 mm) larger. Sandwich the craft foam between the two fabrics with the right sides of both fabric pieces facing out.

2 Using decorative threads in your sewing machine needle and bobbin, randomly stitch all three pieces together. Do not position the stitches too close together, as you want room for the foam to shrink and form in to the shape you want.

3 Preheat your oven to 300°F (150°C). Place the shape in the oven and bake for only 60 seconds. Remove and immediately form over the shape you want. Viviana's basket was formed over a tea strainer. Hold in place for about 30 seconds. The craft foam will not be too hot to handle.

4 Using size 11 seed beads, add a picot edging (page 200) around the edge of the basket. Add accent beads here and there along the outer part of the basket. Make some beaded flowers by following the instructions earlier in this chapter. Hand sew some of them inside the basket, then fill with other beaded flowers, if you want.

Viviana is now ready to finish gathering her flowers and maybe make a neck lei for herself.

CHAPTER

12

WINGS AND THINGS:

Beading an Elaborate Fairy Mermaid

Franalizia of the North Sea

BY PATTI MEDARIS CULEA

In this chapter, in addition to traditional beads, you will learn to make and use many types of synthetic fabrics to create your own unique beads. Essentially, all you need to do is gather the material and apply heat to slightly melt it into a bead form.

The mermaid in this chapter is designed from a combination of shimmering and glimmering elements. Her tail is created using batik fabric and beads. Synthetic organza creates the very light and shimmery beads used along the top edge of her tail. Her flukes, wings (yes, she's a fairy mermaid), and scales use a combination of peyote beadwork and fabrics. None of the techniques used on the mermaid are difficult, but they allow for individual touches and are enjoyable to make, so jump in and have fun!

Materials

* Basic Doll Body (page 163), upper body only (no legs) Note: Do not attach arms.

* ⅓ yard (0.31 m) of batik cotton for the tail, flukes, and scales

* ⅓ yard (0.31 m) of batik cotton in a contrasting color for the flukes and scales

* ¼ yard (0.23 m) of synthetic organza in each of three colors and one in white for the shoulders, base of the tail, beads, and waist

* plastic pellets to fill the tail

* variegated rayon or polyester sewing thread to match your color theme

* metallic sewing thread to match the variegated thread

* strong thread to match the tail color

* acrylic paint in a variety of colors for the organza beads

* embossing powders to match the organza beads

* tacky craft glue such as Crafter's Pick The Ultimate or Jones Tones Plexi Glue

Tools

* basic clothing, sewing, and beading kits (pages 161-162)

* wooden skewer (satay stick) for the organza beads

* size 12/80 metallic or top-stitch sewing machine needle

* hand-sewing needle: sharp or milliners

* dust mask for the organza beads

* heat or embossing gun for the organza beads

* candle and matches for the organza embellishments on tail and shoulders

Bead Supplies

* 10 grams each of size 11 Miyuki Delica seed beads in white and four more colors for the shells, bust, and crown

* 20 grams each of size 15 seed beads in three colors for the scales and flukes and one color for the bracelets

* 20 grams each of size 11 seed beads in the same three colors as the size 15 seed beads for the scales and flukes and one other color (to match the size 8 seed beads) for the bracelets

* 20 grams of size 8 seed beads for the bracelets

* 20 grams of size 11 pink seed beads for the coral

* size 11 x 5.5 mm crystal drops in four colors for the scales and flukes

* 3 mm bicone crystals: fifty in pink for the coral and two in pink for the pair of starfish

* 4 mm bicone crystals: twenty in each of four colors for the flukes and wings

* 10" (25.4 cm) strand of 4 mm freshwater pearls for the waist, coral on the bust, bracelets, and crown

* 1 gram of size 15 silver charlottes for the flukes and coral

* accent beads, such as small shells with holes in them, and other beads for the crown

* circular sequins in five to seven colors for the scales

* three colors of Micro Beads or no-sew beads

* 3 mm Hot-Fix (heat-set, iron-on) crystals in two or three colors for the flukes, belly button, and finishing the doll's body

* Nymo size B beading thread in color to match work

* one spool of 24-gauge beading wire

MERMAID TAIL

To get started on a mermaid, create an upper body, but do not attach the arms.

1 Trace one of each of the pattern pieces for the Mermaid Tail Front and Back (page 301) onto the wrong side of the batik cotton. Double the cotton, right sides together (figure a, left).

(figure a)
Trace, sew, and join the tail pieces.

2 Do not cut out the fabric shapes. Sew seam #1 on the Tail Back and seam #2 on the Tail Front. Cut out both tail pieces using pinking shears. The top edge of the tail should be cut with straight-edge scissors. Pin the front and back tail sections, right sides together. Sew along seam #3 from the top of the hip (widest part) down around the bottom of the tail (point) and back up to the top of the hip on the other side (figure a, right). Turn the piece right side out. (Note: All seam allowances for items in this chapter are ⅛" (3 mm) wide.)

3 Fill the tail to the dashed line found on the pattern pieces with fine plastic pellets. Place a small amount of stuffing on top of the pellets. Slip the tail onto the doll's upper body and pin it in place. Do not turn under the upper, raw edge of the tail. It will be covered later. With a small hand-sewing needle and strong thread, back-stitch the tail to the body. You don't need to be neat, as beads and scales will cover the stitches. Set the body aside for now.

Close-up of the tail

SCALES FOR THE TAIL

1 Trace the Scales pattern (page 300) onto the wrong side of two colors of batik fabric. You will need to trace a total of seven scale strips. Trace three on one batik fabric, and four on the contrasting batik fabric. Each finished strip will become a row on the mermaid's tail. Double the fabric, or place another color on the other side. Pin these right sides together. For each of the seven traced scales, sew along the scalloped edge (seam #4) and, at both ends, seams #5 and #6 (figure b). Cut out the shapes with pinking shears. Turn right side out and press the scales flat with an iron. Do not press open the seam allowances.

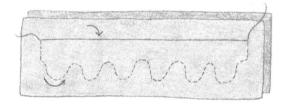

(figure b)
Sew together pairs of scales.

2 Now it is time to cross-stitch bead along the finished seam line of seam #4. Collect the size 15 and 11 seed beads, the crystal drops, sequins, FireLine thread, and a beading needle. Cut 1½ yards (1.37 m) of the FireLine and thread this in a size 10 or 12 beading needle. Place a knot in the single end.

3 Starting at the X marked on the pattern piece, push the needle from inside the scales to the outside where marked on the pattern to start the beading. Take a small stitch in the seam, and then come out close to the edge (figure c, left).

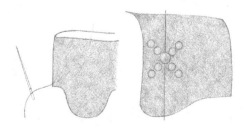

(figure c)
Straddle seam #4 with beaded
cross-stitch edging.

4 Needle up two size 15 seed beads, one size 11 seed bead, and two size 15 seed beads (all of the beads are in one color). Diagonally cross the line of beads over finished seam #4, and push the needle through only the layer of fabric on the underside of the scale, close to the seam line. As you push the needle in, be careful to avoid catching the top fabric. Angle the needle up, on the underside of the scale and come out. You're making an X that straddles the seam line, so the needle must come out in a spot on the underside that's directly in line with the place you started the previous strand on the upper fabric layer. Needle up two size 15 seed beads and go in to the size 11 seed bead on the previous strand. Push the needle into the seam under the size 11 seed bead and come out the other side of the seam. Push the needle back into the size 11 seed bead and add two more size 15 seed beads. Angle down on the top side of the scale and push the needle into the fabric (figure c, right).

5 Continue creating the beaded cross-stitch until you come to the place marked at the bottom center of the scale on the pattern. Push the needle from the last bead added out of the fabric at this mark and add two size 15 seed beads, one size 11 seed bead, three size 15 seed beads, one crystal drop, and three size 15 seed beads. Skip the last three size 15 seed beads, the crystal drop, and the other three size 15 seed beads. Push the needle into the size 11 seed bead and the last two size 15 seed beads.

6 Anchor this cluster by pushing the needle into the seam, under the size 11 seed bead and coming out at the back (bottom fabric layer) of the scale. Needle up two size 15 seed beads and push the needle into the fabric then out about ¾" (1.9 cm) in from the fabric edge, directly in line with the drop cluster. Needle up a sequin and one size 11 seed bead. Skip the seed bead and push the needle into the sequin and into the fabric (figure d). Come out next to the size 15 seed bead above the crystal drop cluster.

(figure d)
Create a crystal drop cluster at the center of each scallop.

7 Continue steps 4, 5, and 6 until you come to the end of the strip (row). Anchor the thread in the seam line and cut the thread. Set the row of scales aside. With each set of scales, change the colors of the beads. The doll shown on page 96 starts with crystal at the bottom, then purple, blue, and pink. The other rows repeat in reverse: blue, purple, and then crystal. Set the scales aside for now.

WINGS, FLUKES, AND FINS

1 On the wrong side of a batik fabric trace two Wings, three Large Flukes, and four Small Fluke patterns (pages 299–300). Either double the fabric or pin a different batik fabric to the fabric with the tracings. Place the fabrics, right sides together.

2 With matching thread in your sewing machine, a lower stitch length (1.5 on a Bernina), and the fabric layers held together, sew from the opening at the top all the way around each fluke. On the wings, sew from the openings all the way around. Backstitch at the openings to keep the seams from splitting when turning each piece right side out. Cut out all pieces, clipping through the seam allowances at the curves. Turn right side out using a small pair of hemostats. Push out the curves of the wings and flukes by inserting the hemostats inside the turned fabric.

3 Place decorative machine threads in both the upper needle and bobbin of the sewing machine. Either free motion or topstitch along the inside of the flukes. Follow the guidelines on the wings. Be sure to leave small openings for the beading wire.

4 Without removing the wire from the spool, bend back the cut end and pinch it closed with either the needle-nose pliers or hemostats. Insert this end into a fluke where marked with a wire placement line. Measure the other end along the outside of the fluke, along the next closest wire placement line. Cut the wire to fit and bend back the cut end. Insert it into the fluke at the second line (figure e). Do this one more time, to wire the remaining lines on the fluke. Do the same with the wings and remaining flukes, following the markings on the pattern pieces.

(figure e)
Topstitch a decorative pattern on flukes
and insert wire.

5 Collect the size 11 and 15 seed beads, crystal drops, 4 mm bicone crystals, charlottes (optional), FireLine thread, micro or no-sew beads, tacky craft glue, and size 12 beading needle. Cut the FireLine in 1½ yard (1.37 m) lengths. Thread the needle with the FireLine.

6 Place a knot in the single end of the FireLine. Insert the needle inside the top of a fluke and come out in a seam. Take a small stitch in the seam to anchor the thread.

7 Set the wings aside. Following the picot edging (page 200), edge the flukes until you get to a point. Work each point by following the instructions for the appropriate size of fluke.

Large Fluke: Coming from the back of the fabric or beadwork, push the needle through the second bead (the last bead added to the most recent picot), add a size 11 seed bead, a 4 mm bicone crystal, a size 11 seed bead, three size 15 seed beads, a crystal drop, and three size 15 seed beads. Skip the last three size 15 seed beads, the crystal drop, and the next three size 15 seed beads. Push the needle back through the size 11, 4 mm bicone crystal, two size 11 seed beads, and in to the fabric (figure f). Turn the needle around and go back

through the closest 11 seed bead. Continue the picot edging to the next point, and then repeat this process.

Small Fluke: Coming from the back of the fabric or beadwork, push the needle through the second bead (the last bead added to the most recent picot), add a size 11 seed bead, a 4 mm bicone crystal, and three size 15 seed beads or charlottes. Turn the needle around and go through the bicone crystal, two size 11 seed beads, and in to the fabric (figure f). Turn the needle around and go back in to the last (closest) size 11 seed bead. Continue the picot edging to the next point, and then repeat this process.

(figure f)
Stack beads at every point on the flukes.

(figure g)
Close-up of large flukes

8 Finish beading the edges of all of the large and small flukes. Add some heat-set crystals, bead stacks such as the Basic Bud and Basic Flower #1 (page 78) and micro (or no-sew) beads to embellish the flukes (figure g). Micro and no-sew beads are applied with glue. Using any tacky glue that dries clear, spread just a small amount on the flukes. Sprinkle the micro beads over the surface and press them gently with your fingers. Lift up the flukes and shake off the excess beads. Scoop the loose beads back into the micro bead container.

9 Thread a hand-sewing needle with strong thread. Place a knot in the end. Use this to close the opening of all of the flukes with a ladder stitch and hand sew all three of the large flukes to the bottom of the tail.

10 Pin the scales to the tail starting at the bottom, above the flukes. Wrap them, one at a time, around the tail in a spiral. Using strong thread, hand sew the scales as you wrap them, making sure they overlap a bit to hide the raw seams. At the top of the tail, hide the raw seam allowances with organza strips. Cut three strips from three different colors of organza, each 3" x 12" (7.6 x 30.5 cm). Use the same organza used to make organza beads (page 196). Cut some vertical slashes along one edge of the length of the strips. Light a candle and carefully seal the edges of the organza. As you run the slashed edge along the candle flame you'll see the organza shrink and create a ruffled effect. Run the straight edge of the organza along the flame to seal this edge too. With needle and thread, hand sew a gathering stitch along the straight edge of each ruffle. Hand sew the strips to the top of the tail, below the waist.

11 Three small flukes are used at the sides and back of the doll's body, at the top of the tail. Hand sew two at each side, below the organza strips. Hand sew one small fluke at the back, above the organza strips. The fourth small fluke will be used later, for the crown.

12 Above the organza at the hips, hand sew freshwater pearls and organza beads (page 196). Scatter and glue a few micro or no-sew beads along the doll's tummy. Use a heat-set crystal for the belly button.

13 Like the flukes, the wings are edged with the picot bead technique (page 200), and accent beads as done in beaded stacks (page 198). Set the wings aside.

SHELLS FOR BUST

1 Collect five colors of Delica beads, Nymo beading thread, size 10 or 12 beading needle, and beeswax. Cut 1½ yards (1.37 m) of beading thread and place this in the needle. There is no knot placed in the single end.

2 Now start peyote stitching as follows: Needle up eight white (color A) Delica beads. Take the beads toward the long end of the thread, the tail. Turn the needle back toward the tail. Add a new color A bead, skip the last bead added (bead #8), and go through #7. Add a new bead, skip #6, and go through #5. Continue this way until you have needled through #1 (figure h). (Note: Each row of the illustration is shown in a different color. Row colors do not represent a change in actual bead color.) Tie the tail and working thread together in an overhand knot. The beads can still be pulled off, but this keeps the beads tightly together. Keep the tail for now. The bead colors are changing to create the stripes of the shells on the doll's bust.

(figure h)
Lay down the base for peyote work.
Rows colored for identification only

Close-up of wings

3 Turn the needle again, heading back toward the beads you just worked. Add a new color A bead and go through the next color A up bead. Changing colors, add a color B and go through the next color A, add a color C and go through a color A. Add a color D and go through the last color A (figure i).

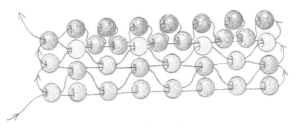

(figure i)
Work an increase over two rows.
Rows colored for identification only

4 Turn the needle again, add a color A, go through color D, add a color A, go through color C, add a color A, go through color B, add a color A, and go through a color A.

5 Increasing is a two-step process. This step is the first increase row. Turn the needle, add a color A and go through a color A, add two color B beads and go through a color A, add two color C beads and go through a color A, and add two color D beads and go through a color A.

Tip:

Watch the threads as you add the two beads. It helps to pull on the thread tightly as you go through the color A beads. When you get to the end of the row, pull on the thread tightly again. This helps keep the beads tightly together and forms the shell shape.

6 For the second increase row, turn the needle, add a color A and go through the first bead of the two color D beads, add a new color D and go through the second bead of color D, add a new color A and go through the first bead of the two color C beads, add a new color C and go through the second bead of color C, add a color A and go through the first bead of the two color B beads, add a color B and go through the second bead color B, and add a color A and go through a color A. (Note: Each row of the illustration is shown in a different color. Row colors do not represent a change in actual bead color.)

7 Turn the needle, add a color A, and go through a color A, add a color B and go through a color B, add a color B and go through a color A, add a color C and go through a color C, add a color C and go through a color A, add a color D and go through a color D, and add a color D and go through a color A.

8 Work a first increase row by adding two beads between the up colors D, C, and B.

9 Work a second increase row by following step 6.

10 Follow step 7. Repeat steps 5, 6, and 7 one more time.

11 Now you work two decrease rows by repeating step 7 twice. You will see the beads pulling in as you pull on the thread at the end of each row.

12 Repeat step 7 with two rows of color A.

13 Work the picot edging as follows: Turn the needle, add three color E beads and go into the next up color A, come out color A and add three color E beads, and take the needle into and out the next up color A. Repeat this all the way to the other side of the top of the shell. Weave the needle and thread down through several beads and do a loop knot (page 198). Cut the thread.

14 Add a starfish (below) and coral (page 195) to the bottom of the shell.

15 To attach the shell to the bust, place a knot in the end of 1 yard (0.91 m) of single thread placed in a beading needle. Attach the thread at the bottom of the bust. Pin the shell to the bust and push the needle in to a bead of the shell and come out that bead. Push the needle back in to the bust of the doll then move through the doll stuffing, over to another side of the bust, and in to the shell. Do this at the bottom and in three places along the top of the shell to secure it to the bust.

Close-up of bust with shells attached

Starfish

1 Cut 1 yard (0.91 m) of beading thread and place this in a size 12 needle. Collect two colors of Delicas (E and F) and a 3 mm bicone crystal that matches Delica color F.

2 Needle up ten Delicas of color E. Leaving a 3" (7.6 cm) tail, tie the threads together to form a circle of beads (figure j). Needle through bead #1, pulling the knot inside the bead. Add five color E beads to the needle. Skip the next bead (#2). Push the needle through bead #3. Add five more beads, skip a bead, and go into the next bead. Continue around the ten original beads in this manner. At the end you will have five picots, each with five beads. (Note: Each round of the illustration is shown in a different color. Round colors do not represent a change in actual bead color.)

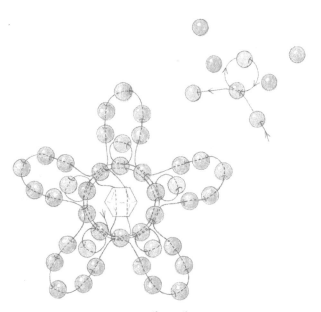

(figure j)
Make five picots around the center beads, then add an accent crystal.

Rounds colored for identification only

3 Push the needle through #1 and into the center bead between a picot (bead #2). Add a color F and go back in to #2. Push the needle through #3 to the next center bead (#4). Continue adding a color B in the center of each picot.

4 Weave the needle through the beads to an inside bead and come out that bead. Pick up the 3 mm crystal and push the needle into a bead opposite where you came out. Needle through that bead, back into the crystal, and then into the bead you came out originally, but into the other side. Going though the other side keeps the crystal from falling off.

5 Attach this starfish to the bust shell by weaving the needle and thread in and out of the beads on the shell and the beads on the starfish.

Coral (Branched Fringe)

1 Cut 1½ yards (1.37 m) of beading thread and place this in a size 10 or 12 beading needle. Weave into the bottom of the shell (see Adding Thread to Beadwork, page 198). Collect the pink size 11 seed beads, the 3 mm bicone crystals, and silver charlottes.

2 Weave the needle to the center of the shell and come out a bead at the edge. Add fifteen seed beads to the needle and thread. This is the main branch. Add a 3 mm bicone crystal and three silver charlottes. Skip the charlottes and go back through the crystal and four seed beads (figure k).

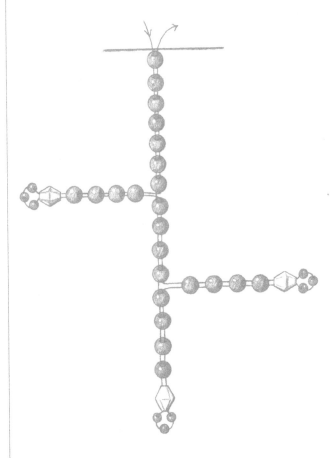

(figure k)
Add short beaded extension to basic fringe to make coral.

3 Coming out the fourth pink bead, add four new seed beads, a bicone crystal, and three charlottes. Skip the charlottes and go back in to the crystal and four pink beads. Push the needle into the main branch and, moving toward the doll, through four more pink beads.

4 Come out this bead and make another small branch with four seed beads, a bicone crystal, and three charlottes. Push the needle into the remaining pink beads on the branch.

5 Push the needle into the beads at the bottom of the shell and move over two or three beads in the shell. Create another piece of coral, but use only thirteen beads for the main branch. When that one is finished, push the needle in to the beads at the bottom of the shell and go to the other side of the center branch. Create another piece of coral with only eleven beads on the main branch.

6 After the dangling coral is completed, push the needle into the bust and come out at the top of the shell. Create coral along the top, using nine or eleven beads for the main branches. This time anchor the beads to the doll's bust.

ORGANZA BEADS

These beads can take on the look of barnacled spiral shells or they can be elegant. The results depend on what you do to make them. They are made exactly like a bead made from Tyvek. Because of the plastic fibers in both, use a dust mask and work in a well-ventilated area or outside.

1 Collect the synthetic organza, wooden skewer (satay stick), metallic thread, and embossing gun. You will also need some acrylic paint and embossing powders.

2 Cut three different colors of synthetic organza into strips that are ½" (1.3 cm) wide to no more than 2" (5 cm) long. Wrap three or four strips of varying colors, one on top of another, around the wooden skewer (figure l). Secure the strips by wrapping the bundle lightly with metallic thread that is tied in an overhand knot.

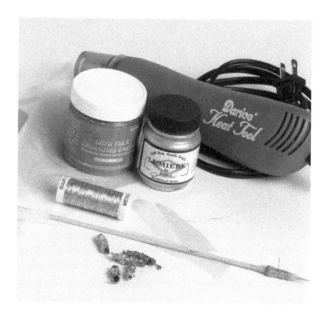

(figure l)
Organza beads in various stages of completion

3 Heat the wrapped organza with the embossing gun until you see the organza starting to melt. Watch carefully, as it heats quickly. You do not want to burn it into a glob.

4 Let the organza cool. Lightly apply a bit of paint to the bead while it is still on the skewer. Dip the damp paint into the container of embossing powder. Apply the heat gun again. The embossing powder will bubble, which lets you know the bead is finished. Quickly remove the bead from the stick. Set this aside. Create as many beads as you want.

BRACELETS

1 Free-form peyote stitch is fun and easy. It uses varying sizes of beads, for an undulating effect (figure m). (Note: Each round of the illustration is shown in a different color. Round colors do not represent a change in actual bead color.) Collect three colors of size 11 seed beads (colors A, B, and C), size 8 seed beads in the same A and B colors as the size 11 seed beads, and one color of size 15 seed beads. Cut the beading thread into a 1½ yard (1.37 m) length and thread this in a size 12 beading needle.

(figure m)
Use a variety of bead sizes for free-form beadwork.
Rounds colored for identification only

2 Place seven size 15 seed beads, five size 11 in color A, five size 11 in color B, five size 8 in color A, five size 8 seed beads in color B, and five size 11 in color C. See if this fits around the mermaid's wrist. If so, you are ready to start the peyote stitching. If not, add a few more size 11 beads in color C. You'll want an even number of beads to work with.

3 Create four rows of peyote stitch beadwork (page 199), changing bead colors and sizes as you work. When finished, place the bracelet on the wrist and weave the ends together.

4 Add some freshwater pearls at the top and coral (page 195) directly to the arm. Some of the coral can hang loose.

PUTTING FRANALIZIA TOGETHER

1 Hand sew the arms to the shoulders with a hand-sewing needle and strong thread. Machine sew a running/gathering stitch down a lengthwise edge of each of two strips of organza. These strips are 2½" x 7" (6.4 x 17.8 cm) in two different colors. They are created in the same way as the organza strips at the waist (step 9 of Wings, Flukes, and Fins, page 192). Pull the threads to gather. Hand sew these at the shoulders, where the arms are sewn. At the same time, add some freshwater pearls using the bead stack technique (page 198) here and there on the doll's shoulders and bust. Add some micro (or no-sew) beads along the doll's shoulders and bust. This makes it look like she has just come out of the water. Heat-set crystals can also be added.

2 Before attaching the wings, hand sew your choice of hair (page 182) to her head. At the forehead, keep the hair behind the seam at the top of her head.

3 Bend back the open end of the fourth fluke until you have the size of crown you want. Using ladder stitches (page 200), hand sew this end to the main part of the fluke to keep its shape. Hand sew this to the doll's head, in front of the hair.

4 With a beading needle and thread, hand sew freshwater pearls, varying sizes and colors of seed beads, and shells to the forehead and sides of head. Create some branched fringe at each side of the head.

APPENDIX

Terms

Needle Over: Weave a threaded needle through one or two beads (as specified) and come out another bead.

Needling/Needle Up/Needle Through: Pull a threaded needle through one or more beads.

Picot: Several beads (usually three) joined by a length of thread that starts and ends in the same position.

Stack: Several beads sitting together, so that one is on top of the next. A short stack is a few beads that sit on the bead or fabric surface. A long stack is fringe. The uppermost bead in a stack is a stop bead.

Step Up: Used mainly in circular peyote stitch. At the end of a row, needle through the first bead in the same row and then add a bead to start the next row.

Stop Bead: Used in two different ways, the function remains the same: to stop other beads from falling off a length of thread. When planning to needle several beads onto a new, loose thread, start by placing only the first bead on the thread, leaving a tail beyond the end of the bead. Use a square knot (page 202) to tie this tail to the opposite, working thread length. Again, pull the needle and thread through the first bead. You have created a stop bead. Additional beads can now be needled as desired, and they will not fall off as you bead. A stop bead can also be a small bead added at the top of a bead stack, so that the ones underneath are snug against one another. For beginner beaders, a stop bead will alleviate the frustration of beads falling off the thread.

Up Bead: Protrudes up or down beyond the current row or the beaded surface. This is commonly found in peyote beadwork, but is not limited to this type of stitching.

BEADING AND EMBROIDERY TECHNIQUES

Adding Thread to Beadwork and Making a Loop Knot (Double Half Hitch)

1 When it is time to end thread, weave the needle and working thread through three beads (figure p). Come out between beads #3 and #4 and make a loop knot with the working needle and thread.

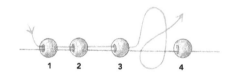

(figure p)
Right: Loop knot
Make a loop knot to start or end thread.

2 To make a loop knot, take the needle under the thread between the two beads; as you pull the thread you will see a loop being created. Push the needle into the middle of the loop and pull tight to create a knot. Do this twice more. Cut the thread.

3 To add thread, after threading the needle, weave through three beads and then make a loop knot.

Backstitch

1 Anchor the thread on the wrong side of the fabric or beadwork. Push the needle through the fabric, coming out on the right side. Needle up seven beads (figure q). Lay this flat against the surface of the fabric. Push the needle into the fabric, coming out on the wrong side.

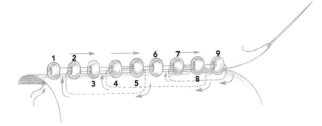

(figure q)
Backstitch
Work beaded backstitching like embroidery backstitching.

2 Move the needle over toward the middle of the row. Push the needle into the fabric and come out between beads #3 and #4.

3 Needle through beads #4 and #5, and then push the needle in to the fabric between #5 and #6. Come back up through the fabric and into #7. Come out #7 and add seven more beads.

4 Continue adding beads, filling in as you please.

Blanket Stitch

This form of blanket stitch is used to cover washers. It is similar to the embroidery stitch, but starts out differently due to the surface it is covering.

1 Cut 2 yards (1.83 m) of an embroidery-like thread. This can be Kreinik ribbon thread or YLI Candlelight thread. Thread a tapestry, or other large-eye, needle with this thread.

2 Tie the thread around the washer, leaving a short tail. Starting from the front, bring the needle into the opening of the washer, under the washer, and then over the thread (figure r). Pull tightly. Continue creating this stitch until the washer is completely covered. Weave the end of the thread through the stitches and cut. Cut the tail too.

(figure r)
Leave the thread crossover at the outer edge for the blanket stitch.

Flat Even-Count Peyote Stitch

1 Begin by needling up an even number of beads; in this example eight are used (figure s). This completes the base. (Notes: In *Creative Cloth Doll Collection*, the first line of beads does not count as a row. Each line of the illustration is shown in a different color. Line colors do not represent a change in actual bead color.)

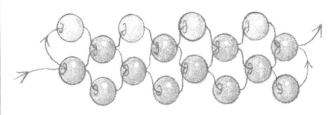

(figure s)
Flat peyote stitch
Skip beads in previous row to create peyote stitch beading.

Rows colored for identification only

2 Turn the needle around, pointing toward the thread tail. Add a new bead (#9), skip the last bead in the base row (#8) and go through bead #7. Add a new bead (#10), skip #6 and go through #5. Continue adding beads in the same manner until you have needled through #1. This completes the first row.

3 Turn the needle around, pointing toward the finished (opposite) end. Add a new bead (#13), skip #1, and go through #12 (an up bead). Add a bead, skip a bead, and go through a bead along the work (as you did in step 2). This completes the second row. Continue adding rows until you have worked the number desired.

Ladder Stitch

1 Stitch down from the front of the piece (#1) (figure t).

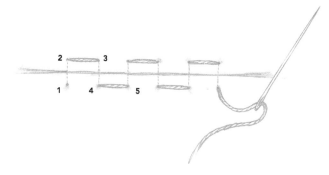

(figure t)
Ladder stitch
Use ladder stitching to join fabric pieces.

Note: Illustration details stitching on the underside of the seam.

2 Hiding the thread, go into and out at the seam (#2).

3 Run the needle under the fabric for a bit and then take the needle out through the fabric (#3).

4 Push the needle into the fabric at #4.

5 Run the needle under the fabric for a bit and take the needle out through the fabric at #5.

6 Continue this process until the seam is finished.

Picot Edging

1 Anchor the thread at the back of the fabric or beadwork. Add three size 11 seed beads and push the needle into the fabric next to the spot you came out. This creates the first picot.

2 Take a small stitch in the back of the fabric and come through the last bead added, bead #3. Add two new size 11 seed beads and push the needle into the fabric next to bead #3 (figure u). Continue adding two beads as you continue along the edge of your piece.

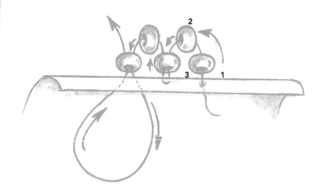

(figure u)
Picot edging
Add two beads for each new picot.

BEADED FRINGE OPTION 1

1. This is not really an embroidery stitch, but if you laid it down flat on the surface of a garment and couched it, it would be. Anchor the thread and come out from the edge of the fabric (A).

2. Add several size 11/12 seed beads, a few size 6/7 seed beads, an accent bead (such as a crystal) and finally a drop bead (B).

3. Skip the drop bead and go back up through the beads and into the fabric (C and A).

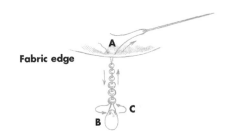

**Option 1
Beaded fringe**

BEADED FRINGE OPTION 2

1. Thread up several size 6/7 beads then 3–5 (or as many you want) size 11/12 seed beads, a drop bead, and an equal number of size 11/12 seed beads.

2. Go through the size 6/7 beads and into the fabric (D).

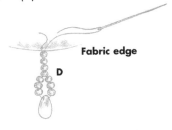

**Option 2
Beaded fringe**

STACKS

1. Stacks can be made with two beads, or as many as you would like to add. They add dimension to the surface you are working on. Anchor the thread and come up from the underside of the fabric (A). Pick up a size 6/7 bead and then a size 11/12 seed bead. Skip the size 11/12 seed bead. Go down through the size 6/7 bead and into the fabric at A.

2. On the underside of the fabric, move along to the desired location of the next stack (B). Insert the needle through the fabric and then repeat step 1.

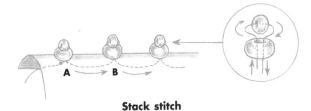

Stack stitch

Simple or Basic Fringe

1   Anchor the thread on the wrong side of the fabric or beadwork. Push the needle through the fabric or out a bead.

2   Needle up an odd number of size 11 beads. At the end, add an accent bead and then a size 15 bead (for a picot) or a stop bead (figure v). Skip the size 15 beads or stop bead and needle through the rest of the beads.

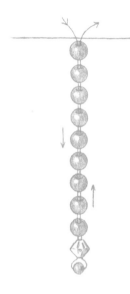

(figure v)
Simple fringe
On fabric or beaded surface, stack beads
to make fringe.

Square Knot

1   Form a loop with the left thread. Bring the right thread through the loop from bottom to top, then underneath the entire left loop.

2   Now bring the right thread through the loop from top to bottom (figure w).

(figure w)
Weave yarn ends to create a square knot.

Blanket Stitch

1. Bring the thread to the front at A. Take the needle to the back at B, and come up at C with the needle over the working thread.

2. Repeat this stitch along the edge of the appliqué.

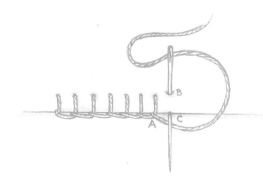

Stem Stitch

1. Bring needle to the front of the fabric at A.

2. With the thread below the needle, take it back into the fabric at B, and out slightly to the right of A.

3. Pull the thread to set the first stitch. Insert the needle at C, keeping the thread below the needle.

4. Work this stitch from left to right, taking regular small stitches along the line of the design.

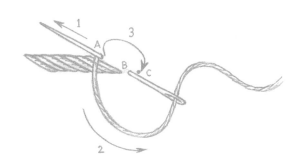

GALLERY

Strelitzia Fuoco

LORRAINE ABERNETHY

The artist writes:

Beading! How else to take this doll right over the top? I like to use materials in my work that aren't necessarily prescribed, for example, using nuts, bolts, and brass screws as if they were fine jewelry. I made my own beads for her hair using plastic drinking straws covered in fabric. I cut strips of fine silk and taffeta about 1" (2.5 cm) wide and the length of the straws on the straight grain of the fabric. I used watered-down PVA glue to saturate each fabric strip, then pressed it firmly with fingers onto the straws. I let the covered straws dry resting across the top of a bowl or jug. When dry, I cut to desired lengths and stitched these to the doll's head using four stitches at the base of the straw bead to secure. I painted the ends of the straws with acrylic paint to match. I wrapped some metallic thread around each bead, crisscrossing all over her head. I then cut 6" (15.2 cm) pieces of fringy yarn, folded in half twice, and using a fine pair of tweezers and PVA glue, I stuffed each bead with a tuft.

Using seed beads to make a netted trim for the ends of her sleeves, I finished the peaks with a large crystal in a contrasting color. I made a three-petal decoration with seed beads using peyote stitch for the front of her bust. I made a little beaded flower for her hair using very small seed beads that made the flower fold over on itself to create a nice contrast to the firm, rigid beads.

The feet were decorated with sequins and small beads in a random pattern. Look closely at her heart-shaped scepters; they are all beaded using a variety of beads, but one of them has brass eyelets stitched around the edge held in place by two beads.

Lady Juliana at Ascot

SHAWN ASIALA

The artist writes:

I had such a good time making this doll! I modified the original pattern by reducing it 25 percent and making the legs straight, enabling the doll to stand and show off her dress. She has a wire armature body, so she's able to stand on her own. I wanted her to be very curvaceous, so I added shapely hips and a bosom. The face was made with pima cotton and is lightly sculpted. I used Prisma- color pencils to shade and color the face. Zig pens were used to outline and accentuate details. The white highlights were applied with gel roller pens. I incorporated "real" eyelashes with the eyeliner, and glued them on the eyelids. A bead in each iris added sparkle to the face. The hair is sewn on the head, and then "styled" with a wool felting needle.

Juliana's hat is made from a ladies' wool hat. I cut out the top part of the hat, and sewed a sturdy wire into the edge, enabling me to shape it. I sewed the hat on the head, and then I added the ribbons, flowers, and feathers.

Her bodice is created from pieces of lace that are sewn on to create a fitted look. Her skirt is an empire design, gathered at the bodice, with a short bustled train in the back.

ADRIENNE AT THE QUEEN'S GARDEN PARTY

Carol Petefish Ayotte

The artist writes:

Adrienne's body is made from 100 percent white Kona cotton, and painted using a diluted solution of sienna, ochre, and white Jacquard Dye-Na-Flow paints. Her face was tinted with oil pastel pencils, Prisma pencils, and Tsukineko fabric markers.

The pantaloons and shoes are made from a frosted cotton fabric painted with aqua and purple dye. They were stamped using Jacquard pads, and drizzled with Jacquard pearl Lumiere paints.

The slip is purple hand-painted taffeta. The net crinoline is a piece of presparkled fabric made into a double layer to add fullness to the outer skirt. I fashioned her outer skirt from a scarf, hand-painted using Jacquard paints and dyes from Things Japanese. The bodice and the hat's body are both made from hand-painted silk; I applied salt to some areas to create a dotted effect. Beads and sequins are added as embellishments.

Adrienne's hat is made using a straw hat crown for shape. I added fusible pellon to shape the brim. The roses on her hat are white organza ribbon dyed to match her dress. Her gloves are made of wedding silk, while her evening bag is made of beads using a right-angle weaving technique to make a smooth surface effect. Her purple necklace and bracelets—an heirloom lent to her by her Aunt Harriet for her special day at Buckingham Palace—are made of seed beads.

Loiseau

COLLEEN BABCOCK

The artist writes:

Silk cocoons gave me the inspiration to create a bird doll sitting in a nest. After making the body, I dyed her using Jacquard Dye Na Flow. I wasn't very pleased with the results, but after working on her face I decided she was okay. I loved her gentle expression and from then on she started to come together.

Dyed silk rods were wrapped around her head, which looked like a bird's crest. Her corset was woven with size 6 seed beads. After I completed it, I was surprised to see that its shape resembled the shadow of a flying bird. The underskirt was created using dyed mulberry bark. I created free-motion, machine-embroidered feathers stitched onto water-soluble stabilizer. These were attached to the mulberry bark.

The bead-embroidered wings and tail are based on a line drawing of a cardinal. I used branched and looped fringing, stacks, couching, and backstitching. Wire was used to create a frame to support the weight. The wings were created in two sections so that the wire frame could be inserted between the two. Finally, micro beads were glued to the feet and eyebrows. Each silk cocoon was edged with these beads.

MAKE A WISH

Darcy Balcomb

The artist writes:

The first challenge was creating movement, as if in flight. The doll was positioned this way, painted with gesso, sanded, and then rubbed with flesh-colored paint. A final coat of spray shellac was used for gloss and dimension. The stand was padded and covered with pieces of vintage sari and silk.

The next challenge was to create clothing that would convey texture and movement. I like to work with scraps. Starting with the upper body, remnants from a recent knitting project were attached. Tan-colored tulle was sewn in place as an overskin and brushed with water-diluted glue. This technique left much of her flesh showing while still providing a top for her dress.

Various scraps of fabric were heat "distressed" and, along with some floral elements and fibers, sewn individually around the waist. Her hair is also made from more than one hundred hand-painted pieces of "distressed" fabric.

The wings are embellished leaves from a silk magnolia tree. She has a glass wand and a whimsical crown made from three hand-knitted triangles. Instead of using seed beads for embellishment, I sprinkled the doll with mini no-sew beads at the base and on the bodice and arms. Rhinestones add further sparkle. She also holds secrets and symbols, some of which reside on the scrolls in her purse.

Jolie Fleur

JUDY BROWN

The artist writes:

On a recent vacation in the south of France, I was amazed by the beautiful colors of the flowers and countryside. This experience became my inspiration for my fairy. I named my doll Jolie Fleur, French for pretty flower.

Her bodice and hat are made of wool felt and her skirt of cotton netting and a floral silk. The wings were fashioned from organza and embroidered with metallic thread, then painted with Lumiere paints. I then attached Swarovski crystals to the edges of her wings. I wanted it to look as though she had a flower bud on the top of her head. I made a hat block with a stem out of aluminum foil and then stretched a wet square of wool felt over the foil form. At the bottom of the form, I gathered the fabric with a rubber band. I then used my steam iron to press the felt until all the gathers had fused together. After the rubber band was removed, I cut the bottom-ruffled edge into pointed petals. I beaded a vine, using size 14 seed beads to encircle the brim of her hat, and then attached eleven small five-pointed flowers. The focal point of her outfit is the beaded floral belt arrangement at her waist. I used peyote, brick, and herringbone stitch to make the flowers and leaves and then attached each component to the peyote belt in a pleasing arrangement. Her sandals are made of felt with leather soles and embellished with silk ribbon trim with a beaded rose at the center and tied with silk ribbons. Finally, she is wearing a Swarovski crystal around her neck, tied with hand-dyed silk ribbon from South Africa, the color of which is appropriately named "Fairies."

Anii

ARTIST: Lynne Butcher

"For this doll I used the advanced pattern and stretched a lycra skin over the cotton body. I then added stuffing between the layers to create contours and fullness where needed. Instead of using the joints, I butted the body pieces together, to give a smooth look to the body. Once the body was finished, I decided not to cover her with bulky clothing. I found an old delicate piece of lace in a secondhand store. I liked the lace's earthy color, and when I cut it into smaller pieces and arranged it on the body, it immediately looked like lichen.

After attaching her 'clothing,' I randomly sewed tiny beads to her body. Ruth Stonely, a well-known Australian quilter and embroiderer, told me that when randomly beading, the aim is to make the beads look as though they've been tipped over the fabric and stitched on just where they lay. I tried to achieve this.

After I made the head, I stretched lycra over the face and needle-sculpted it, adding pieces of stuffing between the layers to form cheekbones, eyeballs, and a stronger nose. I used Prismacolor pencils and a fine Permawriter pen to outline and define features. I embroidered on the eyelashes and used strands of yarns for the hair and threads with beads to tie it all together."

Rosella the Sprite of the Eastern Rosella

JENNY CAMPBELL

The artist writes:

The Australian bush was in bloom when I was thinking about what type of doll to do. Most of the iron bark eucalyptus trees were in flower and a creamy white haze adorned the skyline, the school yard, and the trees close to our house. Among the trees was my favorite bird: the Eastern Rosella. One morning while opening the back gate at school, I watched a mob of Rosella fly down and alight in front of me. They were a flurry of wings and color; there was my doll—a Rosella sprite alighting with her mob of birds. I made the fabric for the body, arms, and legs using a layer of rainbow organza covered in netting with all sorts of toning fabrics cut into small pieces between the layers. The machine embroidery over the sandwich of fabrics was completed with a rainbow-variegated cotton and feed dogs down. Hand-painted Tyvek became her jacket, wings, and shoes.

I love peyote, brick stitch, and threading, but I love the "Campbell" stitch best of all. Don't follow a pattern, simply thread and stitch and add beads wherever you want them; the hardest thing is trying to do the same thing twice. (Maybe that is why one follows a pattern.) I did complete a picot edge on her jacket and several leaf shapes for her hair. The white flowers in her hair represent the blossom on the iron barks, as do the flowers on her bag and at her throat. She has a twisted chain of green beads around her waist and many hanging threads of beads. Once Rosella's head was finished, it was attached and the last few hair feathers were stitched in place.

KATHRYN

Antonette Cely

The artist writes:

What I like most about the fashion of the 1940s is the combination of tailored clothes with feminine frills. It was also an era when women were just beginning to wear pants outside the bedroom. I focused mainly on Katharine Hepburn as my inspiration. She championed women wearing pants in the '30s and '40s and still looked feminine while doing so.

I used a textured woven striped fabric for her suit, and found some lovely pleated cotton lawn for her collar and cuffs. I built shoulder pads right into her shoulders so the suit would have that broad-shouldered look that is so prevalent in this period. The shoes are suede high-heeled loafers, with a matching suede handbag.

I love the fact that this doll pattern has feminine curves, creating a very female silhouette even though she is wearing a tailored suit. The shoes were the most fun, though, and I used the same method I always use for making shoes. I made polymer clay shoe lasts and then constructed the shoes right onto those hard forms. The structure is formed from manila file folders. Suede is glued directly onto the surface. These shoes don't have a stitch of thread in them, except for the traditional hand stitching at the sides of the uppers. That was very freeing for me, since I'm always distracted by making the sewing match.

I decided not to give this doll a hat, because I love the big, exaggerated hairdos of the 1940s and didn't want to hide hers.

Culeoptera

ARTIST: Barbara Chapman

"I began by painting Culeoptera's body with a generous coating of Gesso, but then smoke fairies descended overnight and smeared a layer of charcoal on her body. [*Author's note*: This charcoal effect was from a recent house fire that destroyed much of the artist's beautiful artwork.] Luckily the Gesso layer prevented most of the smoke from seeping through. I then painted her with Jacquard's Dye-NA-Flow paints, which, of course, wouldn't penetrate the fabric in a dye-like fashion because of the Gesso. On parts of her body and face, I used Lumiere metallic paints.

In dressing her, I wanted to show some of the body, so I loosely crocheted a sweater for her and paired it with snazzy handmade felt pants with velvet cuffs. I created jazzy metallic stockings by needle weaving down to the velvet-and-gold-encrusted shoes. I added layers of sleeves, collaging surfaces over each other to create an interesting effect. I collaged some sheer lace and calligraphy papers to her face to create a contemporary fantasy feel and to tie in with the textures in the costume.

Culeoptera was a work in progress. Trial and error with painted leather, needle-woven stockings, and hair styles took her through several identity crises, but everything came together with antique sari border sequins and gilding. With hair wound with lace from India, a few collage elements, and embellishments, she was done. I named my doll Culeoptera in honor of Patti Culea, who brought about her metamorphosis."

Genesis

ARTIST: Marguerite Nelson Criswell

"This doll's face is made from four different pictures that complement each other, which I scanned into my computer. After preparing a piece of silk/cotton fabric with Bubble Jet Set 2000, I cut a piece of freezer paper to A4-size paper, ironed the waxed side of the paper to the fabric, and fed it through the printer. I glued the pieces to the stuffed head and dyed the body with Jacquard Textile, Lumiere, and Neopaque dyes.

The arms represent the heavens. The left arm is dyed blues and purples, with white specks to represent stars and space (night). A bracelet with a star charm is on the wrist. The right arm is dyed reds, oranges, and yellows to represent the sun (day), with a sun charm bracelet on that wrist. The legs represent the earth. The left leg is dyed turquoise blues and greens to represent the sea and encircled with copper wire adorned with seashell beads. The right leg is dyed in muted blues and rusts to represent the dry land and is encircled with copper wire adorned with leaf charms.

The hem of the dress is roller-printed with bronze powder in textile medium. I've added Genesis 1:1, 'In the beginning, God created the heavens and the earth,' to the border. The top and sleeves are embellished with Tyvek film painted with various acrylic paints and dyes and bronze powders in different shades of copper.

The angel's hair is made from Thai mulberry and handmade tissue paper roller-printed with acrylic paints, bronze powders, and fabric medium. It's then glued into a lion's manelike hairdo. Her flowing wings are made from three painted layers of Tyvek film—light-weight, medium-weight, and heavy-weight. The finishing touch was finding a paperweight at a local antiques shop that looked like the universe being formed. I placed it in the angel's hands, and she came to life."

Irulan

ARTIST: Janet Beth Cruz

"To start Irulan, I looked through fashion magazines like *Harper's Bazaar* and *Vogue* to find a stylish outfit for my retro doll. Then I focused on the colors. It's always fun to use bright colors, colors that you love but never find yourself wearing or using in your home. For me, it's bright pinks, reds, oranges, and yellows. When I was ready to dye her body, I used Jacquard's Dye-NA-Flow paints—sun yellow, scarlet, bright orange, and hot fuchsia. For her face I used their salmon, ochre, and white. Although you don't see much of her body, it's just as bright as her outfit.

Her shoes were a dilemma. I knew what I wanted but wasn't sure how to achieve it. I finally drew the design on paper. With help from my mom, Patti Medaris Culea, we added seam allowances, and I was ready to make them from fabric. After sewing and stuffing the shoes, I attached them to her feet and embellished them with beads. Irulan carries a hand-dyed purse and lounges on three beanbags. She's ready to pose for any photo shoot."

Ysanne

VERA EVANS

The artist writes:

My inspiration for Ysanne came from the intense jewel-tone colors of summer flowers in the gardens my mother and mother-in-law tended to with great care every year. The beading of the doll was my favorite part. I started by making the thistle that Ysanne holds in her hand. It is a combination of peyote and fringe that is made into a strip then rolled to form the top of the thistle. A netting stitch covers a painted wooden bead for the base. The tulip-shaped flowers were made using Delicas and size 15s. A vine was created using peyote stitch, and the leaves and flowers were attached. The little berries are 4 mm miracle beads covered in size 15s. The final detail is her dragonfly. This is a pin I made several years ago. The dragonfly went perfectly with the color scheme and is pinned to her hand so I can remove it and still wear it myself.

UMQHAGI

Sue Farmer

The artist writes:

Umqhagi is a Xhosa word for rooster. This was the inspiration for the costume. Generally, I scribble a thumbnail sketch of the costume as a starting point, then I let the fabric dictate what the finished design will be. I tend to drape the fabric on the body or use paper towels to mock up the patterns. This is simpler than taking measurements and flat drafting (For more on draping techniques, see page 135.)

Living in Africa since childhood has strongly influenced my taste in color and costume. Sunrise and sunsets are spectacular here, and the connection with heat, dust, and the early morning cockcrow became the inspiration for the wings and overall coloring.

A rich Batavian print combined with a silk pongee and coarse black tulle was the starting point. The silk needed to be dyed so the colors were painted on with Dye-Na-Flow dyes while wet. Next came antique pleating, which is simple to do and creates a very attractive texture. To keep the soft look, the edges were frayed with a pin.

The bodice was originally intended to be a corset/bib, but the stiff look of the breastplate seemed a more interesting way to go—and led to the topstitched peplum used to disguise the top edge of the skirt.

The length of the neck was perfect for the gold-coiled look, a feature of African women, and a rooster-tail effect made rather interesting wings. Simple bead embellishment connected the print sections. The ankle and wrist beads were used to tie the black stitching of the wings into the rest of the design.

Head dressing in South Africa tends to be a simple bandanna or doek tied at the base of the neck. This was combined with West African drapes and "butterfly ends" for a prettier look.

Beaded Garden

ARTIST: Kathy Gaines

"I used Pimatex fabric for the doll's body and woven silk for her clothes, flowers, and leaves. I also dyed the entire doll using Jacquard's Dye-NA-Flow paints. First I slightly diluted the dyes with water (sulfur green, emerald green, sun yellow, violet, and hot fuchsia), then I applied the dye to fabric that had been moistened with water, to achieve a soft effect.

The lined and seamless skirt is circular with a scalloped edge. The waistline is set off-center. I finished the edges of the skirt and sleeves with a beaded scallop and covered the sleeves with vertical netting. For the necklace, I used circular netting.

I made the collar using free-form peyote beadwork. As I beaded the rows, decreases at the neck edge shaped the collar to fit the neckline. I then layered the collar with flower beads and fluffies. I came out of a bead, added a loop of three to five beads, and back-stitched through the other side.

To make the sandals, I traced around the doll's feet onto a piece of cardboard, and then I glued fabric to the cardboard, tucking under the raw edges. I cut the soles and heels from leather and glued them to the fabric base. Finally, I created a peyote-beaded strip to fit on the top of the doll's foot and embellished it with beaded flowers, flower beads, and leaves."

MELBA

Pam Gonzalez

The artist writes:

The large autumn maple leaves in my backyard in the Pacific Northwest inspired the creation of Melba, the Woodland Fairy. I preserved the leaves using glycerin and then free-motion embroidered on them to show off the leaves' veins. I modified the pattern by giving the doll long toes and only four long fingers. I also modified the pattern by bending her legs so she might sit on her log in the forest.

I began costuming Melba by hand beading the pink and orange spots on her batik fabric body with seed beads. I love working with bright colors. I hand-painted cheesecloth, Venice lace, and polyester crinkle cloth using Jacquard's Dye-Na-Flow and Lumiere paints. I draped the fabric directly on the body to form the clothing. I wrapped cheesecloth around her legs for pantaloons and across her bodice. I also used pink- and copper-colored Angelina fibers fused between the cheesecloth. Her skirt features layers of hand-gathered cheesecloth and crinkle cloth with burnt edges and Venice lace. I added more beads to the skirt to give her a little more sparkle. Velvet leaves, acorns, and miniature pinecones from my yard provide the final embellishments. Melba's namesake is my grandmother who had a passion for gardening.

Wide Open

LI HERTZI

The artist writes:

Because I wanted a standing doll, I straightened one leg, inserted a dowel, and stuffed it. Using my trusty glue gun, I wrapped some bumpy yarn around the doll in places, placed some of my grandmother's old lace strategically here and there (kept in place with the glue gun), crinkled up some paper and put that on, and then put the little glass things on the hands.

I used Natural Sand Texture Gel (from Liquitex) and applied it thickly over the textured parts, and some on the open spaces. Onto that I sprinkled sand, and "smooshed" in fine pumice gel for making pastel paper. I let that dry overnight, and through the next scalding "SoCal" day. Then I used Scribbles dimensional fabric writer to draw the lines and create the dots. That always takes a while to dry, so I left it overnight too. I painted all the parts with gesso and let that dry. (There was a lot of drying!)

Next I painted her mostly blue, but it was too much; it brought me down, sending my wide-open feeling into the cyan paint pot of melancholy. So I painted the face yellow, added the yellow on the leg, and then just let the brush lead me. Here and there I added words and some pictures cut from a laser print. I have to say, I had more fun just painting along than anything else. I added the beads and hair with the glue gun, and then covered the whole thing in Behr Polyurethane.

The best part of this doll was going to the large home-improvement store with her in pieces and getting the young whippersnapper to help me find the right wing nuts to attach the appendages!

Fleur Labeade

KATHRYN HOWAT-FLINTOFF

The artist writes:

Since beading was the focus for this doll, I decided to use the body pattern #2, page 266-268. I wanted to do what I call "free-form" beading.

I took a literal approach to my assignment "flowers for her hair," beading stamens in to ready-made organza and satin flowers. The headdress behind represents the leaves. The odd butterfly landed on the flowers during the process.

I beaded at will (meaning that I picked up beads in no particular order) along and across her shoulders, to a V shape at the back of her neck. I then layered several complementary-colored fabrics on her abdomen and attached the leaf beads and a large peyote flower. The flower was made by first gluing a large glass bauble with the flat side to a piece of felt, and then I made a peyote flower following the instructions in Chapter 6, pages 101-102. Her sandals and gloves are also made with free-form beading. As no self-respecting young woman would be seen out about town without a properly attired under-carriage, she is sporting a G-string made of machine-embroidered freestanding lace with a bead "string" securing it in place. As Fleur Labeade has traveled all the way from New Zealand, she could not resist wearing a paua necklace.

Maeve

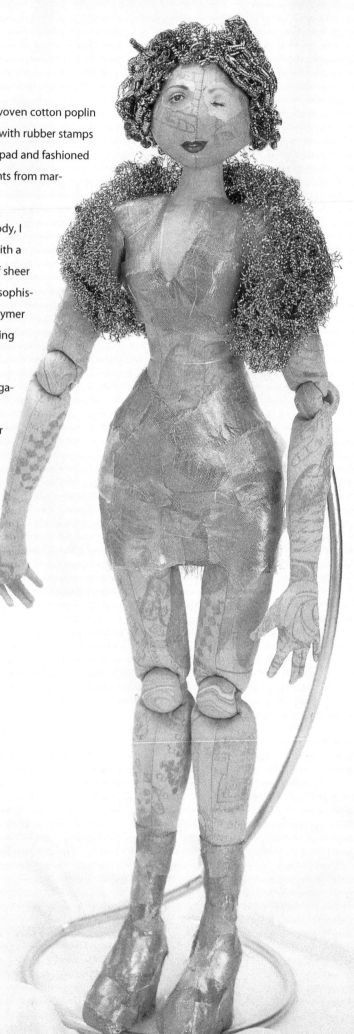

ARTIST: Rosie Francis

"Maeve is constructed from densely woven cotton poplin called Delphina. I stamped the fabric with rubber stamps using a violet-colored 'Memories' ink pad and fashioned the beads for her knee and elbow joints from marbled white and purple polymer clay.

Once I constructed and stuffed her body, I wrapped her in strips of nylon lycra with a holographic print and added layers of sheer and shiny fabric to create a complex, sophisticated-looking cloth. I also added polymer clay 'wedges' to her feet before applying her collaged boots.

I created her face with the help of magazine images. I made her stole from an expanded silver Brillo pad and her hair from the same material, only this time cutting and shaping it to accentuate her shapely lines."

Wishing Fairie

ARTIST: Annie Hesse

"When I teach a class, I always tell my students to find the easiest methods to reach the desired end. So, I followed my own advice and chose the beginner pattern, enlarging it to 110%. I used the advanced hand, though, because I like articulated fingers.

The body shape was so nice that I decided to create my own fabric. I used white 100% cotton fabric and painted it with Jacquard's Lumiere paints—green, gold, and copper. I then stamped images on the dry surface and ironed the fabric to set the colors. I traced the pattern pieces onto the wrong side of my painted fabric, then sewed, cut out, turned, and filled the body with stuffing.

For the beading, I used bead embroidery techniques. I traced my design onto the face and then started laying down my beads and tacking them in place to the fabric. When the face was complete, I attached it to the neck of the doll.

I created the hair with yarns, the skirt and sleeves with tulle, and the necklace with strands of beads. As a final touch, I painted a papier-mâché star and placed it on a stick, which I also painted."

Leading by a Hare

ARTIST: Margaret (Marge) Clok Gorman

"On the day Patti's pattern arrived, I set my imagination loose to make a doll with no limits for painting, stamping, or dying techniques. I had a hare-brained idea: I wanted the doll to be a rabbit with human characteristics. As I began construction, I chose not to incorporate the moveable joints provided in the pattern and instead ladder stitched the arms and legs for a fully posed doll. I eliminated the bust, and I added ears and a fluffy tail.

My idea was to dye all the body parts except the head and hands. I saturated both sides of the doll from the neck to the feet with a spray bottle filled with water. Next came Jacquard's Dye-NA-Flow paints in green, blue, and purple. I dipped a toothbrush into the purple and spattered it all over the doll. I used the spray bottle again and got an exciting watercolor effect. I repeated the process with red, yellow, and orange. With the fabric still wet, I applied a bit of Jacquard Metallic bronze paint. After an overnight of drying, the colors became lighter.

The head is needle sculpted from penne velvet. The ears are painted with metallic white paint and a small amount of blushing. To create the eyelids and mouth, I sculpted penne velvet and formed them with tacky glue. His whiskers are silk threads and wire that are curled around a bamboo skewer. I painted his driving gloves with bronze metallic paint and cut out holes for the knuckles; I used black metallic paint to create stitching lines.

The steering wheel is 15-gauge wire, wrapped with stiffened fabric and then painted. I made the carrot car out of muslin, dying the body orange, red, yellow, and green and the wheels black. I used a carrot stamp to create the spokes. His shoes also have wheels to help him around 'harepin' curves. Once my rabbit had gloves, I had my doll's theme. Now I just do my best to keep him under 65 m.p.h."

Solstice

ANGELA JARECKI

The artist writes:

In making Solstice, I wanted to capture the warmth and whimsy of a summer day. I chose yellows and reds, with just a bit of purple thrown in for my color scheme.

When I use watercolor pencils, I start with a pencil color that is only slightly darker than the fabric color. First, I lay in the shadowed areas, such as the cavity of the eyes, the side of the nose, and under the lips. I gradually darken the shadows, using a pencil that is a shade or two darker than the first color.

Within the shadows, I add a deep, cool color, such as blue or purple. Solstice has purple in her costuming, so I chose to use purple for the shadows to pull the colors from the costume into the face.

Next, I layer a bit of brown pencil into the shadows to blend them with the medium-tone areas of the doll's face. For the lips, I use the cool color that I chose for the shadow to lightly color the top lip, and then add a warmer lip color over that. The bottom lip is usually a warmer, orange-red color. The warmer color makes the lip look as if it comes forward in space. For the white of the eye, I use a medium gray toward the top of the eye, and white near the bottom.

To get the deep black of the iris, I wet the watercolor pencil itself. Wetting the pencils gives you a really rich, deep color.

When the face is almost finished, I lightly mist it with a matte fixative. After the fixative is completely dry, I go back in and add highlights to the eyes, lips, and cheeks. The fixative gives a nice tooth to the material, and the light colors hold very well to this foundation.

Goddess of Fauna

ARTIST: Dorice Larkin

"First I sewed and stuffed the body, dyed it with earth-tone colors, and heat set the colors in the clothes dryer. Then I created her embellishments.

I used some raffia to create a grass skirt. Over this I placed a beaded belt. To create the belt, I beaded over a piece of felt, using random bead embroidery. (This was both simple and quick to do: You lay down a row of beads and then go through every third bead into the felt to hold the design in place.)

The beads at her neck were also easy to make. First I strung enough beads to make the neck piece the length I wanted. Then starting from the end, I added nine more beads in contrasting color. I counted over five beads from my original beads and entered the fifth bead. I continued this to the end of the strand. Then I turned my needle and went back toward the opposite end, going through five beads and adding an accent bead. I placed this bead at the opposite side of the strand from the picot I created above.

I went through five more beads and added an accent bead, continuing this to the end."

SOWMYA

Diane Leftwich

The artist writes:

Making this doll was so much fun. I thought of all the things that reminded me of the "hippie" era and then just went with the flow—kurdas, Indian embroidery, natural fibers, paisley, ponchos, toe sandals, daisy chains, and tie-dyeing.

I gathered all the different types of silk I could find and dyed them using shibori and tie-dyeing techniques. These fabrics were then torn into strips, some were stamped with fabric paint, and pieces were then sewn together to make the pants. The same fabrics were also used for her bag and headscarf. Old Indian embroideries filled with shisha mirrors inspired Sowmya's kurda. I used naïve stitching with different textured threads on layers of colored velvet.

The motifs on her clothes and bag are free-motion embroideries, some using stamps as a base pattern. Motifs on the kurda have had the fabric cut away from behind, allowing you to see through to colors beneath. The poncho was constructed by weaving yarns together with a very finely teased out silk cap overlay. This was sandwiched between water-soluble film and machine stitched to resemble large needle knitting. The daisies were sewn onto georgette and water-soluble film, then cut out and attached to stems made from fabric and thread cords.

Sowmya's sandals are several layers of soft leather glued together. This allowed the straps to be neatly secured between the layers, and decorated with Indian decals. Her hair was made from wefted mohair with a wonderful shibori dyed headscarf tied around her head. Bells and bangles completed the "hippie" feel.

Fionna

ARTIST: Cyndi Mahlstadt

"When picking out my materials for the collage technique, I started with the velvet leaves, which have shades of peach, pink, salmon, and greens, and worked around them. I used those for my primary colors and added different shades of cream. I also added lacy fabrics, buttons, beads, vintage handkerchiefs, ribbon, ribbon roses, and yarns. Using colors to match my color scheme, I dyed the handkerchiefs, the sheer fabric under the skirt, the ribbon roses, and the big flowers on her head. Then I misted the flowers with water, painted on the dye with a paintbrush, and hung them out in the sun to dry. To give the premade ribbon flowers an antiqued look, I gave them a bath in Jacquard's Dye-NA-Flow paint.

I used no-sew beads in very small sizes. Using a small paintbrush, I applied tacky glue in small amounts and sprinkled on the no-sew beads, then I gently pressed them into place with my fingers.

Costuming this doll involved wrapping and tacking. Her sleeves are made of sheer ribbon wrapped around her upper arms and tacked into place with a needle and thread. I created her skirt from strips of sheer fabric, lace fabric, yarns, ribbon, and handkerchiefs tacked at her waist. I wrapped a fine chenille yarn around her lower arms to finish off her sleeves and at her ankles to finish off her shoes."

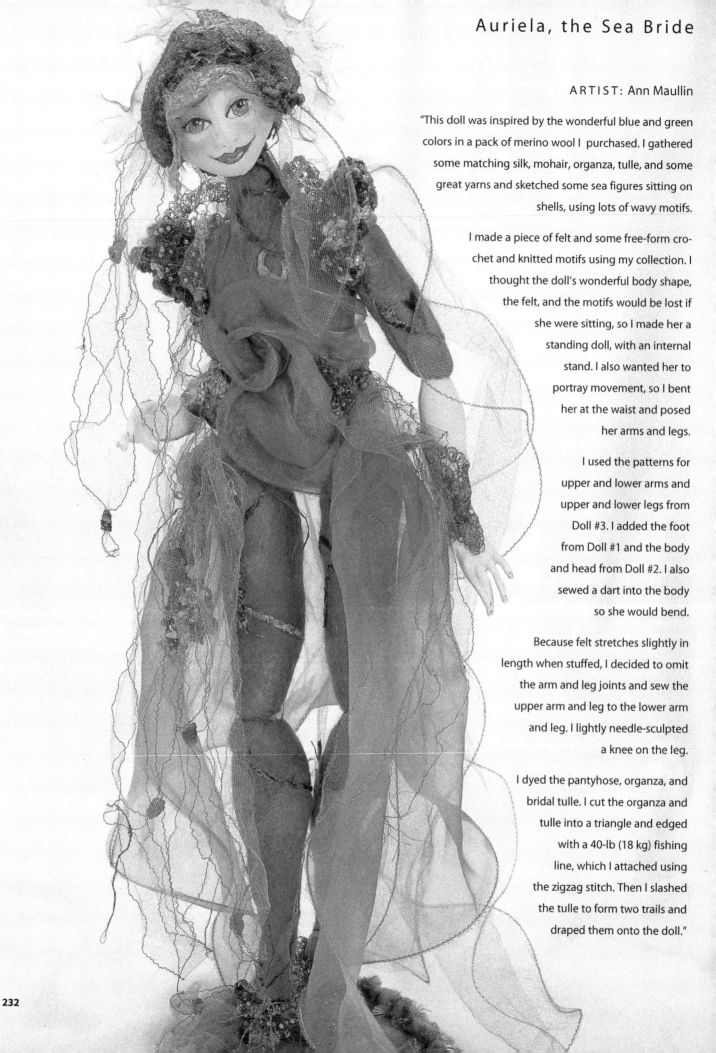

Auriela, the Sea Bride

ARTIST: Ann Maullin

"This doll was inspired by the wonderful blue and green colors in a pack of merino wool I purchased. I gathered some matching silk, mohair, organza, tulle, and some great yarns and sketched some sea figures sitting on shells, using lots of wavy motifs.

I made a piece of felt and some free-form crochet and knitted motifs using my collection. I thought the doll's wonderful body shape, the felt, and the motifs would be lost if she were sitting, so I made her a standing doll, with an internal stand. I also wanted her to portray movement, so I bent her at the waist and posed her arms and legs.

I used the patterns for upper and lower arms and upper and lower legs from Doll #3. I added the foot from Doll #1 and the body and head from Doll #2. I also sewed a dart into the body so she would bend.

Because felt stretches slightly in length when stuffed, I decided to omit the arm and leg joints and sew the upper arm and leg to the lower arm and leg. I lightly needle-sculpted a knee on the leg.

I dyed the pantyhose, organza, and bridal tulle. I cut the organza and tulle into a triangle and edged with a 40-lb (18 kg) fishing line, which I attached using the zigzag stitch. Then I slashed the tulle to form two trails and draped them onto the doll."

Senta's Baggage

ARTIST: Claudia Medaris

"Senta's Baggage is a rubber-stamped doll. Any rubber stamp is suitable with fabric paints, though larger stamps, or ones with fewer details, tend to make a cleaner image on fabric. I suggest you work with tightly woven fabrics and clean the stamps carefully after each use.

I coordinated the primary rubber images for this piece with various larger background stamps. Using fabric paint, stamp dabbers, and masking techniques, I embellished the entire surface of the cloth doll with an array of connecting images. I then inked the main foreground stamp with hues of fabric paint. While wet, these paints blend easily when you dab them on the surface of the rubber image."

Oasis

ARTIST: Michelle Meinhold

"Doll making is my love, but beading is my passion. Oasis, my mermaid, merges these obsessions. With the help of my dear friend Kandra Norsigian, my seed bead colors were chosen. Once the bead colors were in place, I found the fin fabric and fibers for her hair and soon everything went together.

The scales are done in Japanese 14 seed beads. I used a flat peyote stitch to make each row of scales. The scale design is done in a Bargello pattern, with the shading going from a dark purple to a pale yellow green. Once a row was completed, I stitched it to the already stuffed fabric body. I wired her fin using an 18-gauge wire, and then I embellished her fin with Swarovski crystals and amethyst beads along with Japanese 11 seed beads. To finish off her waistline, I did a double-twist stitch with 11s, fresh water pearls, and vintage Swarovski crystals.

I also used 14s and flat peyote to make the seashells that cover her bust. To complete the doll, I made beaded beads with 3-mm Swarovski crystals and 14s for her elbow joints. For her hair I used Prism fibers."

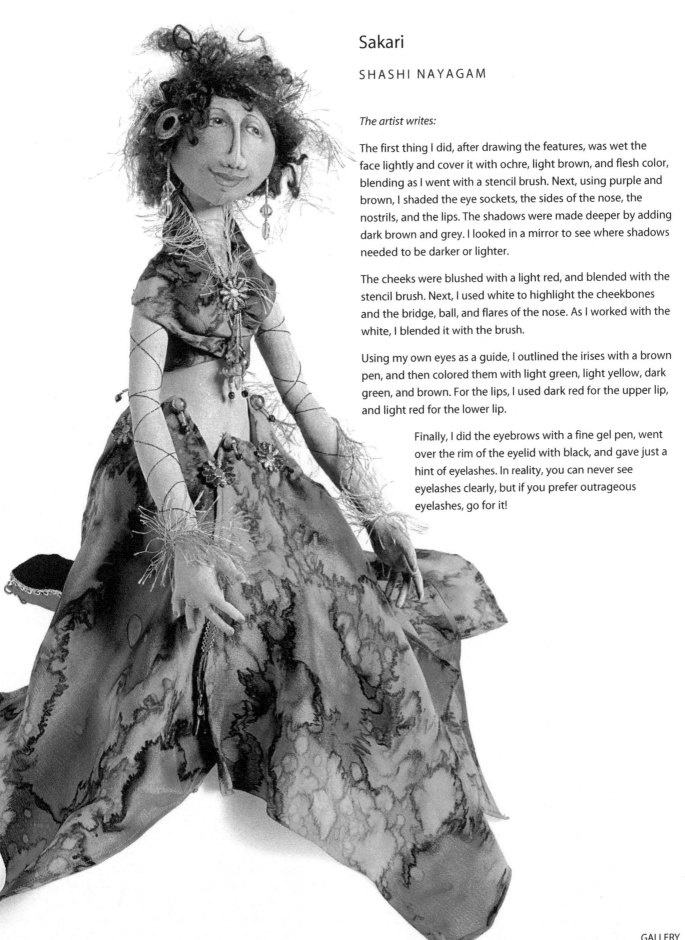

Sakari

SHASHI NAYAGAM

The artist writes:

The first thing I did, after drawing the features, was wet the face lightly and cover it with ochre, light brown, and flesh color, blending as I went with a stencil brush. Next, using purple and brown, I shaded the eye sockets, the sides of the nose, the nostrils, and the lips. The shadows were made deeper by adding dark brown and grey. I looked in a mirror to see where shadows needed to be darker or lighter.

The cheeks were blushed with a light red, and blended with the stencil brush. Next, I used white to highlight the cheekbones and the bridge, ball, and flares of the nose. As I worked with the white, I blended it with the brush.

Using my own eyes as a guide, I outlined the irises with a brown pen, and then colored them with light green, light yellow, dark green, and brown. For the lips, I used dark red for the upper lip, and light red for the lower lip.

Finally, I did the eyebrows with a fine gel pen, went over the rim of the eyelid with black, and gave just a hint of eyelashes. In reality, you can never see eyelashes clearly, but if you prefer outrageous eyelashes, go for it!

CHELSEA

Nancy Palomino

The artist writes:

For extra money while going to college in the late '60s, I made hippie clothing, earrings, and macramé belts. Making this doll brought back memories of that colorful time in my life. After the doll body was sewn and stuffed, I made the clothing patterns by draping, cutting, and basting muslin to fit properly.

Variegated silk velvet and burnout velvet are used for the pants. They are embellished with hand-dyed venice lace and small bells. The cotton T-shirt fabric and all lace embellishments were dyed in one session. A lace heart is hand sewn to the front of the shirt.

For the tunic, I chose the ultimate collage: crazy patch. I love to maintain a stash of buttons, beads, charms, threads, lace, and ribbons for this type of project. Patches of silk, velvet, rayon, and hand-dyed cottons are sewn onto a base fabric that is a bit larger than the pattern pieces. Many hours were spent on appliqué, beading shisha, needle lace, and silk-ribbon embroidery. Machine and hand embroidery was stitched with variegated cotton and rayon threads. Some of the fabric was embellished with bonding powder and metal leaf or stamped with luminescent paint. The tunic pattern pieces were cut from this embellished fabric, stitched together, and lined.

Her hat is made of silk velvet with a ribbon trim and silk ribbon flowers. Free-motion stitched leaves and beads complete the embellishments.

The Birkenstock-style shoes are made with cork and foam soles and buckled, thin leather straps.

Her finished head was sewn on last. Red mohair was attached and braided. Charms were sewn on as earrings. A macramé strap completes the bead and charm embellished purse.

FLOWER

Elise Peeples

The artist writes:

I treated this entire project as a "hippie collage." I reduced the doll pattern to 75 percent. I used lightweight denim from an old tote bag for the blue jeans. To create the appliqué for the blue jeans, I drew a collage picture and colored it with iridescent watercolors. I reduced the image size using an ink-jet printer, then printed it onto fusible fabric. I cut the image apart, fused it to the right leg, and embellished it with machine embroidery and beads. The motifs on the left leg were cut from several printed fabrics, applied to the jeans, embroidered and beaded. I added embroidered trim as fringe around the hems and used tiny brass brads for the button fly. The blouse was made from a discarded gauze top and antique sari border trim. I hand embroidered fifteen shisha mirrors, which were cut from a lightweight metal sheet using a paper punch. The belt is another embroidered trim backed with synthetic suede. The vest is lightweight leather with hand-dyed lace trim. The earrings, bracelet, and peace sign are cut from printed tin. The tote is made from a hand-woven fabric. Inside is a tiny edition of the *Tao Te Ching*, a vial of patchouli, a ball of sea grass, a feather, a pebble from the Washington coast, and a tiny silk bag of crystals.

ODE TO CAROLE LOMBARD

Camille CS Pratt

The artist writes:

The film star Carole Lombard was the personification of glamour for me and the inspiration for this doll. She had a bright spirit, a sincere charm, a sharp sense of humor, and a sparkling presence, to boot.

With this image in mind, I began to research her clothing. I wanted something that embodied all I sensed from Carole and the time she lived in. I found it in a photo of a 1930s-era wedding dress. I wanted to take the simple lines of that dress, add a twist of Hollywood in its heyday, and transform it into something Carole would have been proud to be seen in. Out came paper and pencil, silks and beads, Swarovski crystals, and my imagination. The outcome was a costume I took great pleasure in designing and bringing to fruition.

The doll has elegant sheer silk stockings attached to the garters of a beautiful dupioni silk girdle. Her underbodice is dupioni silk, hand beaded for texture. The overbodice is an antique piece of overdyed silk. Complementing the bodice is a skirt of crepe-backed satin in a rich shade of eggplant with beaded hem and graceful train.

She carries a small silk box purse from the same era, complete with a mirrored lid and beaded handle. A pair of crepe satin gloves add a touch of elegance. She is properly and tastefully bejeweled with crystals right down to her shoes.

WILLOW

Dale Rollerson

The artist writes:

This doll was a tremendous challenge for me as I am not an experienced doll maker but a textile artist. My friend, Jaslyn Pearce, actually made the doll for me to make sure I got started.

I recently purchased an embellisher and used it to make her knickers. I embellished merino wool onto Romeo water-soluble fabric and then reapplied it to scrim (butter muslin) with a few extra trimmings and some hand stitching. They are all hidden—but the added layers will keep her warm!

The bodice was similar to an art to wear piece I was creating at the same time. I machine stitched lots of threads, Angelina, and silk fibers between sheets of Romeo, then soaked it in cold water to remove the film. It was molded to her body and let dry so it would retain that shape.

I knitted some fishnet leg warmers and made a petal overlay with different weights of hand-dyed silk. A machine-stitched cord is wrapped around her waist. I knitted short ends of silk thread for her coat. Her hat is free-motion machine stitched, hand-dyed velvet. Her bag and shoes are both made on the embellisher with some lace stitched on thermogauze that is felted into the surface.

Anapelli

ARTIST: Kandy Scott

"Anapelli has a wonderfully curvy body, so I didn't want to cover it up with too many clothes. She's wearing a modest beaded bodice with a shawl collar that meets in the back with a beaded tassel.

The beads are an assortment of organic-looking beads from thrift store necklaces and Tyvek beads. I made the medallion on her skirt from painted pieces of Tyvek. FirstI cut odd-shaped pieces of the material in various colors, then I heated it from the unpainted side. I stacked various pieces until I came up with a pleasing configuration. Then I glued them together.

For her skirt, I fused my main fabric together so that no wrong side showed. Then I cut long curvy pieces, embellished them with couched yarn, and sewed them all to a band that fits around her hips. I also strung wooden beads, Tyvek beads, and seed beads on pieces of yarn and sewed them to the waistband. Her tree was made of coat hangers and attached to a doll stand base, which was then wrapped with torn strips of fabric and yarn. Two branches were bent in the back to go under her arm-pits so she could relax and feel secure while waiting for the moon to rise and the stars to splash across the sky."

Jillian

SANDRA SIMMONS

The artist writes:

In deciding upon a collage approach for making Jillian, I decided to use fabric collage to create the body. First, I created crazy-quilted fabric from brightly colored batik fabrics, with decorative stitching along the seams. I wanted to add some sparkle, so I used gold metallic thread for free-motion embroidery on top of the crazy-quilted fabric. Beadwork was then added to Jillian's bag, along the flap and shoulder straps, to add interest as well as texture.

The face, hands, and feet were created from hand-dyed fabric in order to provide a skin tone of color. For the face, I took a very standard approach, using the graft method for placement of features. I then penciled them in using a mechanical pencil. Next, I outlined the eyes, eyelid area, the sides of the nose, and the lip area with a brown Pigma pen to give the features more definition and permanency. At this point, I needle sculpted the face using a quilt-weight thread and a 3" (7.6 cm) needle.

After the needle sculpting was complete, I colored the face by using various shades of green for the eyes, and crimsons for the cheeks and lips. A brown Pigma pen was then used to add more definition, place the eyelashes, and draw the eyebrows. Shading was added with sienna and brown tones along the sides of the eyes, nose, mouth, and temple area. Highlights were then placed near the shaded areas, along the nose, and on the bottom potion of the lip, using a cream-colored pencil. A white gel pen was used for highlighting the eyes. After all the coloring was complete, the face was sealed using Createx Textile Medium, and heat set, using a very small Clover iron.

ISABELLA

Ray Slater

The artist writes:

Isabella's inspiration came from the paintings of William Larkin, famous for his full-length portraits of sixteenth-century Elizabethan nobility. I wanted to capture the essence of the costumes worn in the reign of Elizabeth I but with a contemporary twist by using modern embroidery techniques. The body, arms, and legs are metallic silk organza backed with muslin and free-motion machine embroidered into a pattern with metallic thread.

The underskirt is made by stitching textured threads onto silk metallic organza and is trimmed with a deep gold lace edging. Using Elizabethan textile motifs as a reference, the overskirt and bodice front are created by layering two pieces of nylon organza together, free-motion embroidering a motif in metallic thread, and melting away the background with a soldering iron. Strips of knotted nylon organza are used for the hair and more cutwork motifs make a headdress.

Forget-Me-Not Fairy

KAREN SMITH

The artist writes:

Alaska's summers, in which the longest day is more than nineteen hours long, allow my favorite flower, the forget-me-not, to grow in my garden. This is also our state flower. When Patti asked me to make a doll for her book, I knew I had to incorporate this flower into my doll.

My favorite fabric to use for sculpting is Pimatex cotton. I fill my dolls' faces very firmly, and this cotton holds up very well during the sculpting. Before sculpting, I lightly drew in the features with a mechanical pencil, and then outlined them with a brown Micron pen. Following Patti's basic sculpting techniques, I sculpted the eyes, nose, and lips.

Because I wanted the doll to be softly colored, I used a combination of Prismacolor pencils and Micron pens. Sienna brown was used for the shading, along with Peach. The lips were colored with Magenta and Scarlet Lake. The eyes were a combination of Olive Green and Periwinkle. For the blush on her cheeks, I used my own "people" blush.

When I had completed the doll head that captured what I had envisioned, I looked out my window just beyond my sewing table, and watched the setting sun. It was 11:30 pm!

Huldra, Troll Maiden

ARTIST: Ute Vasina

"Considering that I'm used to making all my dolls from doe suede and with troll-like features, this doll posed an interesting challenge. The first thing I did was make her nose larger. (I have this thing about noses.) The next step was the torso. I really liked the womanly figure! She didn't resemble any of my troll figures. I decided she would be 'Huldra,' appearing like a fair maiden—a beautiful seductress from the outside, but very much a troll from within. After all, some female trolls will do that to find or catch a husband.

With this is mind, she took on a great form, right down to her toes. I almost hated putting clothes on her. With her strong personality, I had a sense right from the start what she wanted, so her clothes are very simple, her sweater hand-knit, and her hair made from mohair.

Finally, I love to recycle old or used things. For some dolls, I'll use a piece of clothing. For others, I'll add something old, such as an old skeleton key, a piece of jewelry, or another great find. In Huldra's hand I've placed a very special key.

This doll has a real peaceful elegance about her. Maybe it's the beauty shining from within."

ARTIST: Betts Vidal

"What would this doll that I was to create be? The answer came when I saw a tiny newspaper ad for a Thai restaurant with a drawing of a graceful, leaping dancer. This would be my inspiration—Thailand! I needed to add my own personal touch, so I began by reducing the given pattern to a size I felt comfortable working with—not too tall, not too small. The pattern featured a broad-cheeked face, a shapely torso, ball-jointed limbs, and squared-off toes. I decided to capitalize on these features.

I began creating the doll with the torso because of the unique piecing. While playing with the pieces, I decided to leave the center panel in a skin-colored fabric. The addition of the lavender bra was a last minute inspiration. This would emphasize her curves and introduce another color. For the face and limbs, I chose a fine ivory silk faille, instead of a traditional flesh color, to emphasize the yellow and lavender silks. I also added my trademark eyelids and eyelashes.

For the beading, I rummaged through my many boxes until I found the perfect vintage lavender bugle beads, yellow and rose crystals, and seed beads.

Part of my creative effort is to name a completed project. Thoughts of the music from *The King and I* and Thailand's original name became 'Song of Siam'—and so my doll was named."

Phoebe

ARTIST: Barbara Willis

"It was interesting to watch this doll develop step-by-step. I chose to embellish her with knits and crochet as part of my challenge category. Because I don't knit or crochet, I needed to be inventive. As I sat down with Patti's pattern, I realized that I needed to make a few adjustments to the pattern so it would work for my vision of this doll. I reduced it by 20% at a copy center, then I cut away the seam allowances on the torso to slim her up a bit.

As I began to think about her costume and construction, I decided to use a knit fabric to cover the paper clay mask I created for the face. Knit is a perfect fabric to use for this purpose because it molds itself around facial structures. I chose one with a fine-gauge knit, and I used the mesh side of the fabric to represent the skin. It takes color well and works with fine-tip pens. Her legs were made from a small printed cotton fabric. After adding color to the face, I glued the mask in place and button jointed on her arms and legs.

Her costume began to fall into place when I chose silks as the base fabric for the skirt, sleeves, and chest and open-weave gauze for her pantaloons. Using a knitted, man's dress sock, I created a chemise. I cut the sock and added lace to the cut edge. I slipped it up onto her, covering the lower torso and hips over the silk skirt. The knitted sock formed itself to her beautifully, showing off her shape. I added a tassel to embellish the knit chemise and small vintage crochet buttons to embellish the front of the silk bust. Using the leftovers of the sock I created a small knitted cap to cover the back of her head and wrapped silk ties around her face to complete her headdress."

Maeve of the Midnight Court

LUANNE WYKES

The artist writes:

Maeve is a fairy princess inspired by the fairies of Celtic mythology. As usual with my dolls, she let me know who she was going to be and turned out a little more benevolent in nature than the fairies who sparked her creation.

After making up body pieces from Pimatex ready-to-dye cotton, dyeing them, and painting her face, I began the process of embellishing with fabrics and beads.

Right-angle weave was used for her choker, upper arm trims, and the trim on her bodice. Decorative fringing was added to the choker and upper arm trims. The bodice trim was woven (in a string), then couched in place. Peyote stitch with picot edging was used for her wrist cuffs, belt, and headband. A drop bead was added to the center of the headband, and simple threaded bead strands each side with a flower bead toward the bottom of each strand.

One of the meanings of the word maeve is "purple flower," so she had to have a beaded flower or two. I used peyote stitch, brick stitch, and simple threaded strands of beads for stamens and stems, then attached to the lowest point of the belt.

Her tiara was made by threading beads onto beading wire, which was woven through central beads (during the threading process) and into a firm base of two strands of twisted florist wire to interlock and stabilize the whole structure.

The shoe decoration began with a cluster of simple fringing on the vamp, then the topline was edged with Patti's cuff trim. A picot was added to the tip of the toe. I wound strings of beads around the ankle and held in place with a couple of stitches. The last touch was to thread a few beads on to the wing wires before they were coiled.

EO THE ARBER

Melinda Small Paterson

The artist writes:

Eo needed a nose, ears, and feet that were larger than what the pattern provided. For her green woodsy costume, I laid a combination of fabrics around her and chose the darkest for her tunic, a textured one for the hat and shoes, and a shimmery one for the blouse. Pieces were pinned in place and then trimmed or gathered to fit. The blouse scraps were just enough to wrap her neck, front, and arms. Each pant leg is a tube equal to her hip measurement and gathered below her knee. Her tunic is a rectangle with a neck hole in the center and a cut down the front. A felt lining, cuffs, and trims were sewn while it was flat, then the sides were sewn closed and the waist gathered.

For the felt soles of her shoes, I traced around her foot, then sewed a triangle at the heel and a long triangle for the toe. The hat is a longer slim triangle with another tapering piece for the brim and side dangles. Stuffing went into the toes and hat, with gathering stitches to make them curl.

The wings started with Mylar pinned to cardboard over my drawing. Clear acrylic medium was brushed on to secure layers of netting and lace bits. Black lines were machine sewn and florist wire was satin stitched on the top edge using a cording foot. Then they were cut out along the outline.

When I'd sewn all I could by machine, the clothes were sewn onto the doll. The tunic was sewn last. An opening was cut in the neck back to fit around the wings, then sewn shut.

CONTRIBUTING ARTISTS

Lorraine Abernethy

Coromandel, New Zealand
liadolls@ihug.co.nz
www.lorrainesartdolls.com

Lorraine has designed and constructed garments for the theater and worked for designers in the fashion industry, and in retail fabrics. For the past ten years, she has drawn on her lifelong passion for fabrics and textiles and has been teaching adults screen-printing and surface design for fabrics at a variety of art schools and workshops. Lorraine has been a doll maker since 1982. She began making reproduction antique porcelain dolls back then, but after several years felt the need to return to her fabric/textile roots. Inspired by elinor peace bailey's book Mother Plays With Dolls, Lorraine began to design and make her own work. Lorraine now sells through galleries to collectors, conducts workshops, and designs a range of dolls for patterns. She is a full-time doll maker and is living her dream.

Shawn Asiala

Delray Beach, FL
USA
shawnasiala@bellsouth.net

Since childhood, Shawn Asiala has adored dolls. Her father, a USAF officer, traveled around the world, collecting beautiful handmade dolls for Shawn from many countries. Before she was eight, Shawn began sewing clothes on a Singer Featherweight. She soon loved it, and quickly moved on to other sewing projects.

Shawn lives with her loving husband Tom and beautiful daughter Jenny. She works and teaches at Quilters Marketplace in Delray Beach, Florida. To share her love of doll making, Shawn is a member of an inspirational South Florida doll club called the Sandollr's.

Carol Petefish Ayotte

East Sandwich, MA 02537
USA
carolayotte@adelphia.net

Born in the Midwest, Carol resided in many parts of the Unites States and Europe. She retired in 1995 after thirty-five years of teaching and supervising art and art history in public schools in the United States and military-dependent schools in Europe. She holds a bachelor of fine arts from the University of Illinois and a master of education from Towson State University in Maryland.

Since her retirement, Carol has been pursuing her life-long interest in soft-sculpture figures which combines her love of fiber arts with a longstanding interest in the plastic arts, color, and design. She has made dolls of one kind or another for most of her life.

Carol currently resides near the water on Cape Cod, with her husband, who is a retired army officer.

Colleen Babcock

London, UK
colleenbabcock@uwclub.net

Colleen has always enjoyed making things. She majored in theater design and production at York University in Toronto, Canada. This led the way to creating costumes for polymer clay dolls and now cloth dolls. Colleen finds cloth doll making magnetic because it never limits you to any one technique, material, or style. Colleen's husband, John, and parents, Barry and Kitty, are by now pros at shopping for fabric, critiquing dolls, and stoking the creative fires.

Darcy Balcomb

Darcy was consistently drawn to textiles, paints, beads, and trinkets, but she never thought of putting them all together to create a doll until she became a stay-at-home mom. She sold her work in galleries, taught workshops, and won awards for her entries in various doll exhibits. Always unusual, her one-of-a-kind creations combined many types of artistic media and involved much experimentation. She lived in San Diego with her husband and two children.

J. Arley Berryhill

Albuquerque, NM
USA
arleyberryhill@aol.com
www.arleyberryhill.com

Arley Berryhill has been making dolls, both cloth and clay, for ten years. With a background in art, design, theater, fashion, and costuming, he feels all his skills are being utilized in doll making. For the past twenty-five years, Arley has made a living creating costumes, props, masks, and jewelry for television, stage, commercials, and film. He's worked on costumes for Broadway shows, including The Phantom of the Opera, puppets for the Jim Henson Muppet Shop, and headdresses for the Ringling Bros. Circus. He spent five years making hats, armor, and accessories for the Seattle Opera Company, and recently worked on costumes for Disneyland and Universal Studios. Arley now lives near Las Vegas, and is in charge of wardrobe for a hotel show.

Judy Brown
Twinsburg, OH
USA
brownth@aol.com

Judy Brown has always loved sewing, painting, and creating. Doll making is the perfect outlet for her as it combines her passion for sewing, painting, sculpting, and beading. She majored in art at Kent State University where she met and married her husband, Tom. Tom's army career enabled Judy and their three daughters to move around the country. While living in St. Louis in 1990, she founded her company, Make Believe. In 1994, the family moved to Virginia where Judy enrolled in an elinor peace bailey class and immediately became enthralled with cloth doll making. Her business and talents shifted to this facet of doll making, which quickly became her creative focus. She currently resides in Twinsburg, Ohio, and teaches doll making at several local quilt shops. She is a member of two cloth doll clubs and recently won a first-place ribbon for her doll in the Lake Farmpark quilt show.

Lynne Butcher
Queensland
Australia
lynnebutcher@dingoblue.net.au
Pattern designer, workshops

Lynne Butcher has been designing and teaching cloth doll making for many years. She began her career as a schoolteacher, specializing in art, and now spends much of her year on the road selling her patterns, teaching workshops, and designing.

Lynne is a member of the National Original Doll Artists of Australia. She has won many awards, among them the Diamond Gold Seal by NODAA. In 2000, she was inaugurated into the Doll Hall of Fame at Doll-O-Rama.

Jenny Campbell
Victoria, Australia
acjc6@bigpond.com

Jenny is a primary school teacher who has always loved sewing and creating. She designs and makes clothes for herself and her family. She is intrigued by all types of crafts, but patchwork was the craft she embraced seriously for many years. The progression to making artistic dolls seemed quite natural. Jenny was at a quilting day and met a woman who had a wonderful book showing pictures of dolls created by American doll artists. She was hooked on the craft and found she was able to use all the leftover bits from her quilts. She found several doll groups on the Internet and has been making and experimenting with cloth and polymer clay dolls ever since. She beads and experiments with all types of fabric to create new and unusual pieces. Jenny's latest venture has been making lampwork beads and altered books. She loves to attend workshops and learn different techniques—always looking at how she can simplify the process for children. Jenny teaches art as well as Asian and environmental studies with a focus on Indonesia. Jenny lives with her husband, Alan, in their house in the Australian bush with their two dogs, lots of kangaroos, wallabies, and birds. Their two children are grown. Their son, Ben, is married and they are to be grandparents very soon. Their daughter, Anna, is doing what most young folks do these days—working and having fun around the world.

Antonette Cely

Atlanta, GA
USA
noni@cely.com
www.nonidolls.com

Antonette Cely is a well-known cloth doll artist whose dolls are bought by serious collectors around the world. Richard Simmons has the largest single collection of her work. Antonette has written and self-published books on doll making, including Cloth Dollmaking. She frequently writes for doll magazines, such as Soft Dolls and Animals! and Doll Crafter. She designed costumes and did make-up for the stage and screen for many years before turning to doll making. Her dolls are considered to be among the best in the medium of cloth. From the hand-dyed fabric used for the skin, to the internal structure that attaches each doll to her base, Antonette's meticulous attention to detail is what makes her sought after by doll makers and collectors alike. Her dolls can be seen in such books as Here Come the Bride Dolls, The World's Most Beautiful Dolls, The Doll: By Contemporary Artists, and Anatomy of a Doll: The Fabric Sculptor's Handbook, among others.

Barbara Chapman

Solana Beach, CA
USA
Workshops

Barbara Chapman has been a fiber arts teacher in the San Diego area for more than 30 years. She and her husband, Wayne, a potter and glass bead artist, open their home twice a year to sell their work as well as the creations of other artists exhibiting wearable art. Barbara avoids sewing machines whenever possible, preferring hand sewing. In fact, many of her early dolls were collaged together with glued fabrics and much embellishment.

She now enjoys paper clay as a medium for creating faces, because it accepts paint so well. Surface decoration is her first love—fantasy expressed in color and texture. Her journey continues in search of that little spark that invites her into a magical world. It's there where her imagination becomes reality.

Marguerite (Margie) Nelson Criswell

Oxford
UK
criswell@btinternet.com

Marguerite (Margie) Nelson Criswell began making dolls in 1988 and painting in 1994 as creative outlets for stay-at-home motherhood. As she discovered that art was a means to express her identity and calling, she developed a desire to use it to communicate her Christian faith. She works with fabric sculptures, watercolors, pastels, and colored pencils. Her fabric sculptures incorporate fabric sculpting, painting, wire work, beading, stamping, collage, printing, and embroidery. Born and raised in Ellenton, Florida, she now lives in Oxford with her husband and two children. Her artwork can be found in private collections in England, Canada, and the United States. The Isis Gallery in Oxford represents her artwork. She holds a Bachelor of Science in Business Education and a Master of Arts in Religion.

Janet Beth Cruz

Belle Isle, FL

USA

jblacruz9@aol.com

From an early age, Janet Beth Cruz had a passion for creating something from nothing. In high school, she won first place at a local county fair for her first oil painting. Like her mother and others from her family, portraits were of great interest to her. One of her high school classes was in sewing, and she really loved that—especially the fashion design element. Today she continues to learn and experiment in both fine and fiber arts. Janet made a doll for each bridesmaid who was in her wedding.

Vera Evans

North Olmsted, OH

USA

veraevans@adelphia.net

Vera lives in northwestern Ohio with her husband, Bill, and their two children. Her passion for dolls began about ten years ago. She had taken a class with elinor peace bailey and met other people who shared the same interests. Beading began as just another embellishment technique for dolls but soon became an obsession. She is never without her beads and frequently takes beading classes to learn new techniques. The jewelry she creates is sold locally and when the time is available she also teaches. The best of both worlds collide when she can combine beading with doll making.

Sue Farmer

Capetown

South Africa

sufarmer@iafrica.com

Sue arrived in central Africa, from England, at the age of six. She grew up on a small holding, the only girl, with three brothers. Her mother taught her to use a treadle sewing machine and, by the age of eleven, she was able to make simple items. Sue has always found pleasure in working with fabric, so it was natural that she should drift into dressmaking, which occupied her for many years. Sue went to London to complete a diploma patternmaking course. She and her family then moved to South Africa, where she worked for the Nico Malan Opera House in Cape Town as a costumer for five years. After that, she ran her own costume shop for eighteen years. She recently retired, and has been making dolls for three years.

Rosie Francis
Surrey
UK
rosiered@usa.net

Rosie Francis has been interested in textiles since her early years. Her passion grew as she spent more time exploring the skills that her mother and grandmother imparted to her as a young girl. After leaving Australia and traveling to the Middle East, she further explored art and culture, allowing these things to influence her work and art. Today Rosie is part of the Tri This Design Group with Janet Twinn, Dianne Robinson, and Hilary Gooding.

Kathy Gaines
Huntington Beach, CA
USA
gainesx2@thegrid.net

Kathy Gaines's first remembrance of sewing was on a doll for charity as a young girl in Sunday school. Things really haven't changed much for her: She still sews on her little baby sewing machines, only now it's with her collection of baby Featherweights.

She has always loved the needle arts and believes that she can apply everything she has learned in the past—china painting, ceramics, porcelain dolls, needlepoint, machine knitting, crochet, stained glass, silk ribbon embroidery, quilting, beading, silver work and jewelry making—to doll making. She especially loves to make dolls that are movable and depict the innocence of childhood. She's a member of various cloth doll clubs and has never lost her enthusiasm for making dolls for children.

Pam Gonzalez
Renton, WA
USA
pammster12@yahoo.com

Pam has always had a passion for sewing and creating. Encouraged by her sister, Kathy, she took a class with Elinor Peace Bailey and has been making dolls ever since. Her dolls have been featured in Quilting Arts Magazine and Somerset Studio. She received third place for Amateur Doll in the 2001 and honorable mention for Professional Doll 2004 in the Sulky Challenges. She has also won several awards for her dolls at the Western Washington Fair. When not in her studio, Pam loves doing art projects with her son, Evan.

Margaret (Marge) Gorman
Sacramento, CA
USA
mgo1414087@aol.com

Margaret (Marge) Gorman was born in and now resides in Sacramento, California. She's a wife and mother of four who owns and operates Mrs. Sew & Sew, a home-based business dedicated to designing original cloth dolls. Marge is President of Tayo's Doll Works morning Doll Club.

She teaches doll making and has won numerous awards for her whimsical dolls. She has been published in several *Cloth Doll Magazine* articles. One of her dolls was featured on the July 2000 cover of *Soft Dolls & Animals* magazine and another was accepted in the 1999 national Hoffman Exhibit.

Li Hertzi
Cleveland, OH
USA
lihertzi@lihertzidesign.com
www.lihertzidesign.com

Li Hertzi is an artist, designer, computer adventurer, teacher, and maker of decidedly funky dolls. She grew up on a farm in Greentown, Ohio, land of wide landscapes, white farm houses, lakes, and weather that leads you to look inward for light.

She studied at Parsons School of Design and the New School, both in New York City. She is interested in the figure as an icon, with a focus on the basic sculptural elements found in African, Pre-Columbian, Native American, and primitive art. By creating patterns, she invites everyone to play in the richness of the creative experiment, and to be amused in the process.

Annie Hesse
Daphne, AL
USA
dolls@zebra.net

Annie Hesse has been making and selling mixed media and fabric figures since the mid-eighties. Before that she was a basket maker, which eventually led her to doll making. Annie says it was the knarly vines and branches she used. Each day she'd look at them and wonder. Finally she grabbed a bunch of them, tied them together, lashed another one across for an arm, added a huge lichen-like fungus that resembled a head, and called it her first doll. After that, she just let it flow, making figure after figure and adding other mediums, like fabric, to these sculptures.

Annie has given up her secure, tenured job as a high school teacher to make dolls for a living. She now teaches her techniques worldwide, exhibits in galleries, does a few art shows a year, has pieces at the White House, and does commissioned work for movies and television shows.

Kathryn Howat-Flintoff
Te Awamutu, New Zealand
flinthowat@xtra.co.nz

Kathryn has had a love of sewing, arts, and crafts since childhood, making her first garment at the age of ten. Her creativity has gathered momentum since then, resulting in a serious addiction (of absolutely the best kind) to cloth doll making, patchwork/quilting, and machine embroidery. She is largely self-taught, but has in later years been able to attend conferences, tutorials, and classes, and has gathered valuable techniques, tips, and good friends. Books and magazines have also enabled her to broaden her outlook. Kathryn is currently designing her own cloth dolls. She lives in rural Waikato on the North Island of New Zealand, on a dairy farm with her husband. They are building a new house and have incorporated a specifically designed studio to support her habit and some teaching.

Angela Jarecki
Sugar Land, TX
USA
ajareck1@comcast.net

Angela Jarecki was a greeting-card artist with Hallmark Cards for ten years. She now freelances for them and other card and publishing companies. Angela has always loved dolls, fibers, fabrics, yarn, beads, and embellishments of all kinds. She had lots of creative "stuff" in her stash but no real direction until about five years ago, when she found the fantastic world of doll making. She has taught art classes for children, creativ-ity workshops for adults, and several Internet classes on making dolls. Angela lives outside of Kansas City, Missouri, with her husband and four children.

Judi Korona
St. Cloud, FL
USA
korona@kua.net

Judi lives in the Orlando, Florida, area and learned much of her fashion design skills while working for the Walt Disney Company. She has worked in a quilt shop called Queen Ann's Lace in Kissimmee, Florida, for many years. There, she became a Bernina expert and teaches many classes, especially on embellishing techniques using the various sewing machines in the store. She has designed for the Bernina Fashion Show. She loves doll costuming, since they wear everything well—costumes that no one would be able to wear in real life.

Dorice Larkin
Yorba Linda, CA
USA
DoriceL@aol.com

Dorice Larkin, in a humble understatement of her gifts, says she has been "playing with art" all of her life. In college Dorice studied textile design and theater arts. Her devotion to starting a family put her art on hold for many years, and now she and her husband, Bill, have five adorable girls. It was while playing with her daughters that she was drawn back to her art, this time through doll making.

What draws Dorice the most to doll making are the people involved in this art form—including their love of sharing their ideas as well as their "stash." Dorice finds most of her inspiration from her dreams, her books, and her daughters. She has a commercial line of patterns that are both whimsical and realistic.

Diane Leftwich
NSW,
Australia
diane@leftwich.info

Diane has always loved textiles. Her journey in the textile arts started in knitting, designing, and selling garments in galleries. She also enjoys embroidery, felting, quilting, and shibori. Doll making has allowed to incorporate of all these textile techniques and meet other special artists. Diane is married, with two children, and is thankful to her family for putting up with her continual creative clutter and always encouraging her. She lives in natural bushland in NSW Australia, where she teaches doll making and shares her joy of textiles.

Cyndi Mahlstadt
Iowa
USA

Art has always been Cyndi Mahlstadt's passion—sketching, sewing, and making things. In 1995, Cyndi started making cloth dolls, teaching herself the basics. After that she started exploring different techniques, in an effort to develop her own style. In January 2001, she discovered wire armature figures, and a whole new world opened. Overnight, she was hooked!

Cyndi enjoys making fantasy figures. Much of her inspiration comes from her garden and from nature. She often includes a touch of whimsy and humor in her work. The technique she enjoys most is "cloth over wire" for bodies and needle sculpting for faces. Going back 20 years, Cyndi says that "making dolls as an art form never crossed my mind." Today, it's her joy and passion!

Ann Maullin
NSW,
Australia
annmaullin@cardiovasc.com

Ann Maullin lives in the Hunter Valley vineyard region in the state of New South Wales in Australia. She's married to a wonderful man, Greg, and has two children and two grandchildren. A figurative fiber artist who loves creating with this medium, she has been designing her own dolls since she started making them 6 years ago.

Claudia Medaris
Albany, CA
USA
medaris@hotmail.com

Claudia Medaris graduated from the University of California at Berkeley, where she studied ceramics with Peter Voulkos. She produced pottery in the San Francisco Bay area for many years and now continues to produce graphic art, mainly rubber stamp creations. Her work has been published in *Somerset Studio, Rubberstampmadness,* and the *San Francisco Chronicle.*

Claudia is an active member of the Capolan Exchange, a renowned Mail Art group, and her personal essays on the nature of the artistic mind are a regular feature of *The Studio* and the *BrainWaves OEZine.* Residing in Albany, California, Claudia is married and the mother of two daughters.

Michelle Meinhold
Fresno, CA
USA
meinhold@csufresno.edu

Michelle Meinhold discovered her love of color while studying fine arts at the University of California Santa Cruz. The color choices in textiles and beads have helped fuel her creative fires. At first she used beads to embellish the dolls. One day the obsession took over, and beads became her medium of choice. To satisfy her need to make dolls, her Floral Tassel Doll series came into bloom. She has been a cloth doll artist since 1985; she began teaching cloth dolls and beading in 1998.

Stefania Morgante
Cagliari, Italy
customerservice@gufobardo.com
www.gufobardo.com

Stefania is an Italian doll designer and pattern creator. Originally a painter, sculptor, and photographer, Stefania has an Arts, Music, and Show Degree. Her passion for dolls began after working as a theater editor, drawing teacher, and advertising designer. With her fabric sculptures and teddy bears, her honors include first prize at the National Teddy Bear Contest (March 2002), second prize for the Canadian Doll Artists Association (CDAA), and first prize at the National Dolls and Teddy Bears Contest (May 2005).

Shashi Nayagam
Surrey
UK
shashi.nayagam@ntlworld.com

Shashi Nayagam was born and raised in a small hill station in India. It was there that she met a friend of her mother's who made cloth dolls. As a child, Shashi spent many hours looking at these beautiful dolls. She dreamed of someday making her own dolls. After growing up, getting married, and moving to England, Shashi decided to make her dream of doll making come true. With the help of the Internet and online classes, she developed her own style of doll making. Drawing and painting were among Shashi's favorite childhood pastimes. She is now able to use those skills in creating beautiful dolls.

Michele Cokl Naylor
Cottonwood, AZ
USA
michele@dollsbymichele.com
http://cokl.wordpress.com

Michele was given a special doll by her grandmother, who had made it along with its entire wardrobe. This was her introduction to sewing. She began making dresses for her dolls and eventually those of other children. Her artistic gift has come without formal art training but by taking classes from various doll designers. She has developed her own style making contemporary art dolls with a feel for the Arizona desert where she resides. Her dolls represent people she has known, seen, or met in her imagination.

Nancy Palomino
Corbett, OR
USA
palomino@cascadeaccess.com

Nancy lives in a beautiful Douglas fir forest near Portland, Oregon, with her handsome and talented husband, David. She started sewing doll clothes at the age of four and got her first machine, a treadle, at age six. She still owns it, along with seven others, and sews almost every day. About six years ago, after her two boys were grown, she started making doll clothes again, this time along with cloth dolls to wear the garments. She is a founding member of the Depot Dolls doll group, whose members inspire and encourage her.

Melinda Small Paterson
Portland, OR
USA
melinda@smallwork.com
www.smallwork.com

During art school, Melinda was a face painter for the Simpich Character Dolls Ltd. in Colorado, and then for ten years she built doll houses and scale wicker furniture replicas. Costuming followed, followed then by her porcelain fairy dolls and their twig furniture. That led to dragon companions made of fabric, cloth dolls, and patterns. Her doll making is inspired by folklore and mythology. It satisfies her because it combines a variety of materials and multiple skills. Knowing when to stop adding details is the hardest part for Melinda. She continues to take art courses and has been teaching doll-related classes for twenty years. For her classes, she brings layouts with samples that show every step of the process. Also, she brings her "duds" to show how each piece evolved and how many times she tried again to get what she wanted.

Elise Peeples
Vancouver, WA
USA
epeeplesdolls@comcast.net

Elise is a fiber artist who works with the human form. She employs appliqué, beading, felt making, collage, stitchery, painting, and weaving in her doll making. Her dolls have many textures, and she loves the sensual nature of fabrics and fibers, as well as the opportunities for surface design that these materials offer. While she enjoys the challenge of creating a realistic figure, her dolls tend to be quite abstract.

Elise's background is in art, dance, and theater. She is married, with two grown daughters. A recently emptied nest allows her more time to devote to her art.

Camille CS Pratt
Richmond, TX
USA
hericane@ix.netcom.com

Camille has always loved color, creativity, design, and texture. She is a self-taught artist working with many mediums. All of her skills and interests such as watercolors, writing, and reading have an impact on her primary love—doll making. Camille's work has been featured in numerous magazines and several exhibits. She teaches doll making, and enjoys sharing her knowledge to help others achieve their artistic goals.

Camille lives outside of Houston, Texas, with her patient husband and four fine daughters, each one a prolific and profound artist in her chosen medium.

Dale Rollerson
Perth
Western Australia
mail@thethreadstudio.com
www.thethreadstudio.com

Dale is a teacher, textile artist, and writer living in Perth, Western Australia. Dale has been working with threads and other fibers all of her life and loves to share her ideas with others. Her dedication to textile arts led her and her husband, Ian, to start a business that specializes in hand- and machine-sewing threads, textile art supplies, and online classes. The Thread Studio is a thriving business. You will find this couple at most of the sewing and craft shows throughout Australia, and at the Knitting and Stitching Show in London, England. They plan to travel to the United States soon.

Kandy Scott

Phoenix, OR
USA
kandyscott@earthlink.net

Born and raised in Oregon, Kandy Scott began her creative life as a hair dresser, then moved into the fiber arts. She and a partner started a pattern design business in the 1980s and traveled throughout the United States, Australia, and New Zealand. Today, Kandy prefers teaching to designing her own patterns, as motivating others to create has become a passion of hers. Her classes are inspiring because she believes there are no mistakes, just creative readjustments.

Kandy Scott's dolls are eclectic and incorporate many different techniques—a style that she attributes to her short attention span disorder. Taking workshops in free-motion surface design, fabric dyeing, and beading has also helped her create fun dolls. She says she wants the viewer to look closer and discover the surprises in each piece. Using old jewelry, sewing on soda cans, manipulating painted Tyvek, and attending to details makes her dolls fun to look at again and again.

Kandy now teaches workshops on her techniques, makes dolls for auctions to benefit local interests, and does some consignment work for family and friends. At the time of this writing, Kandy is preparing for her first one-woman show at a gallery near her home in Texas.

Sandra Simmons

Columbus, OH
USA
raggedysan@aol.com

Sandra Simmons has always had a love for art. She remembers drawing and painting from a very young age, and as a teenager was especially drawn to the world of fashion design. After exploring a gamut of art-related interests, she started realizing her love for textures, colors, and then textiles. She soon knew that her primary interests were those in the fiber arts.

Sandra discovered doll making through a magazine article about elinor peace bailey that showcased many of elinor's dolls. It was this article that spurred her desire to one day to create and surround herself with such delightful characters. She soon found a class that elinor taught, and it was absolute bliss. Sandra's love for doll making was just beginning.

Ray Slater
Plumstead,
UK
ray-.slater@virgin.net

Sewing has always been a part of Ray's life, from making doll clothes from the scraps of fabric left over from her mother's dressmaking, to making costumes for television and theater. She trained in embroidered textiles and theatrical costuming before working in repertory theater companies and television. She now uses her skills to create period reproduction costumes and fantasy embroidered costumes for half-scale porcelain mannequins. For the last few years, Ray has been involved with making fabric dolls and also in promoting this craft throughout the United Kingdom. She teaches in Europe and the United States.

Karen Smith
Anchorage, AK
USA
momarchy@yahoo.com

Sewing has been a long-time love of artist Karen Smith. She makes most of her own clothes, and clothing for her two sons and daughters. Karen fell into doll making when her mom, who collected antique dolls, asked her to make some doll clothes. The first cloth doll she made came from a magazine, and the pattern had to be enlarged by drawing it on a grid. This started her on her journey into cloth doll making.

In 1976, three days after their wedding, Karen and her husband moved to Anchorage, Alaska, from Southern California. She writes, "The long, dark days of winter have helped me create dolls, and experiment with different techniques."

Ute Vasina
Lincoln, NE
USA
ute@neb.rr.com
www.enchantingdelights.com

Born and raised in Germany until age 12, Ute Vasina never had much interest in sewing—until her daughter was born and she got the urge to sew her a dress. But it wasn't long before she went from sewing dresses for little girls to sewing dolls.

She attended a doll show with her mother, where she saw cloth dolls up close. Soon after, she joined a local doll club known as the Mad Dollmakers; this group helped her grow as a doll maker and designer. Because of her fascination with trolls, she started researching these characters and creating them herself. Each of Ute's trolls is uniquely different and full of life. Ute's creations have been featured in *Soft Dolls & Animals* magazine and the Figure in Cloth doll exhibit.

Betts Vidal

26163 Underwood Ave.
Hayward, CA 94544
510-782-9390
bettsvidal1@earthlink.net
Pattern designer, workshops

When Betts Vidal was at the tender age of 18 months, her parents placed a small chalkboard 18" (45.5 cm) from the floor to encourage her to draw. To this day, she can sketch a thought easier than she can articulate one. Studying art, painting, drawing, interior design, pottery, basketry, lapidary, and quilting—as well as having a love of natural elements, richly textured fabrics and surfaces, luscious colors, Americana, buttons, and found objects—all led her to the world of doll making. Dolls are a lifelong way of incorporating all she has experienced into a most rewarding form of creativity. The dolls have taken her to many new places, to other countries, and to treasured friendships. And best of all, her husband, children, grandchildren, siblings, and parents all share in her delight of dolls.

Barbara Willis

Mt. View, CA
USA
bewdolls2@aol.com
www.barbarawillisdesigns.com

Dolls have been a part of Barbara Willis's life for as long as she can remember. She settled on cloth dolls after a few seasons with porcelain and never looked back. She comes from a creative family that sewed, decorated, painted, and loved fabric. She has fond memories of haunting the fabric stores with

her grandmother and mother. She has been creating these treasures for many years and enjoys the pleasures of teaching in the United States as well as internationally.

Luanne Wykes

Victoria, Australia
luanne@luannewykes.com

Luanne is a self-taught multimedia artist, best known for her decorative art. She has dabbled in most fields of the art and handicraft world since childhood. Her cloth doll journey began in 1998, when her daughter was diagnosed with Type 1 diabetes at eight years of age. Cloth dolls, new to Luanne at the time, became a coping device and wonderful therapy, and still are to this day. She uses her painting skills in doll making, particularly in the creation of unique faces. In fact, cloth dolls combine all of Luanne's creative passions in one package. She is a popular and sought-after designer and teacher for her innovative techniques and original work. Her designs have been published in many magazines and books.

FURTHER READING

Cloth Doll Artistry
Barbara Willis, Quarry Books
ISBN 1-59253-513-2

Cloth Doll Workshop
elinor peace bailey, Patti Medaris Culea,
Barbara Willis, Quarry Books
ISBN 1-59253-621-4

Creative Cloth Explorations
Patti Medaris Culea, Quarry Books
ISBN 1-59253-463-0

Art Doll Adventures
Li Hertzi, Quarry Books
ISBN 1-59253-267-4

PATTERNS

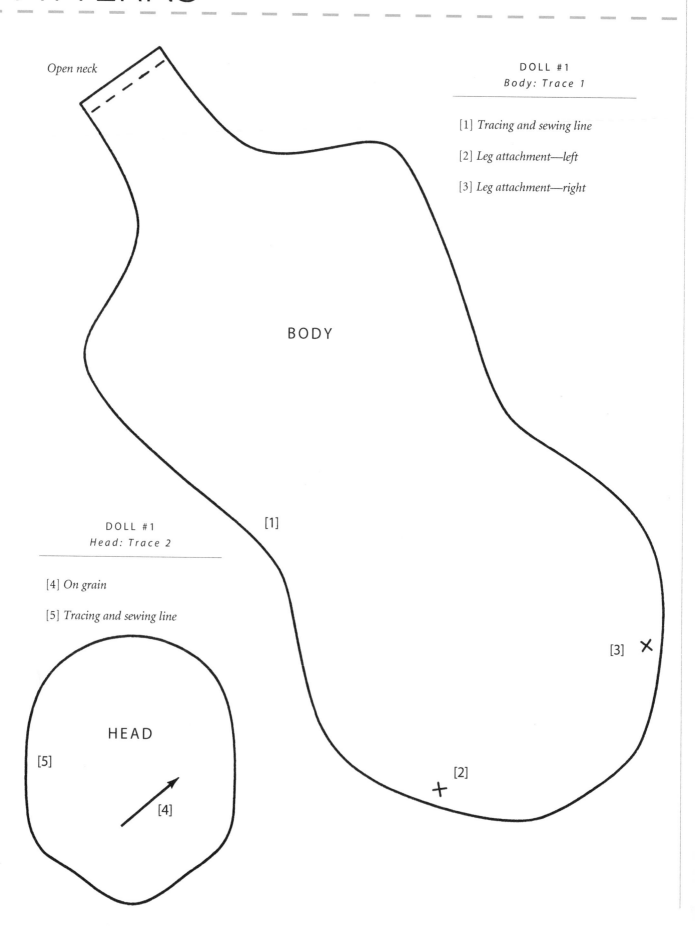

Open neck

[1] *Tracing and sewing line*

[2] *Leg attachment—left*

[3] *Leg attachment—right*

BODY

[1]

DOLL #1
Head: Trace 2

[4] *On grain*

[5] *Tracing and sewing line*

[3] ✕

HEAD

[5]

[2]

✕

[4]

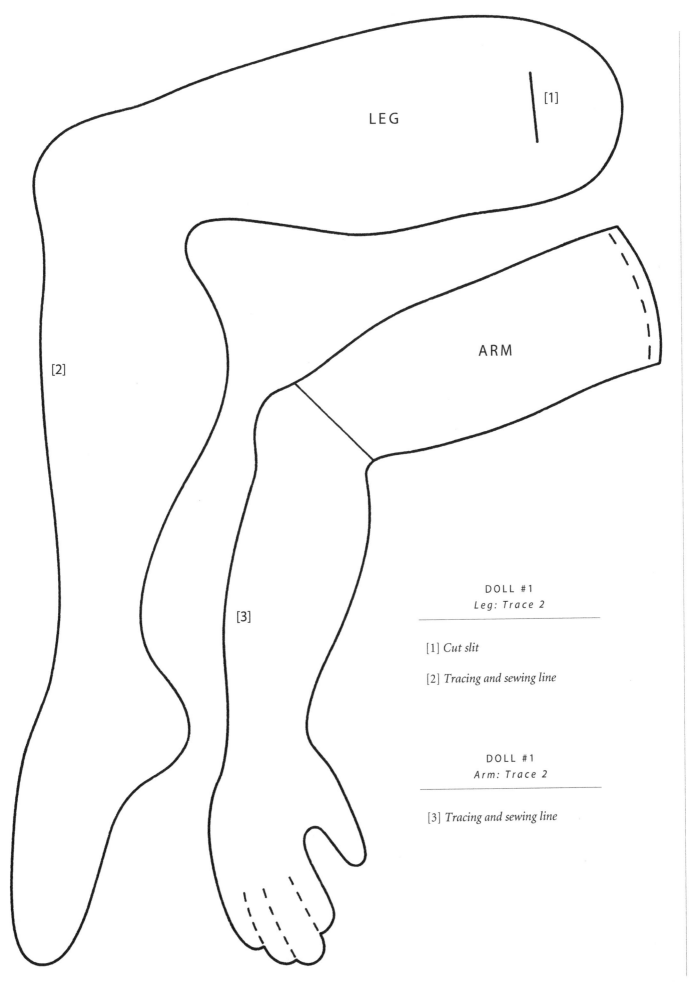

LEG

[1]

[2]

[3]

ARM

DOLL #1
Leg: Trace 2

[1] *Cut slit*

[2] *Tracing and sewing line*

DOLL #1
Arm: Trace 2

[3] *Tracing and sewing line*

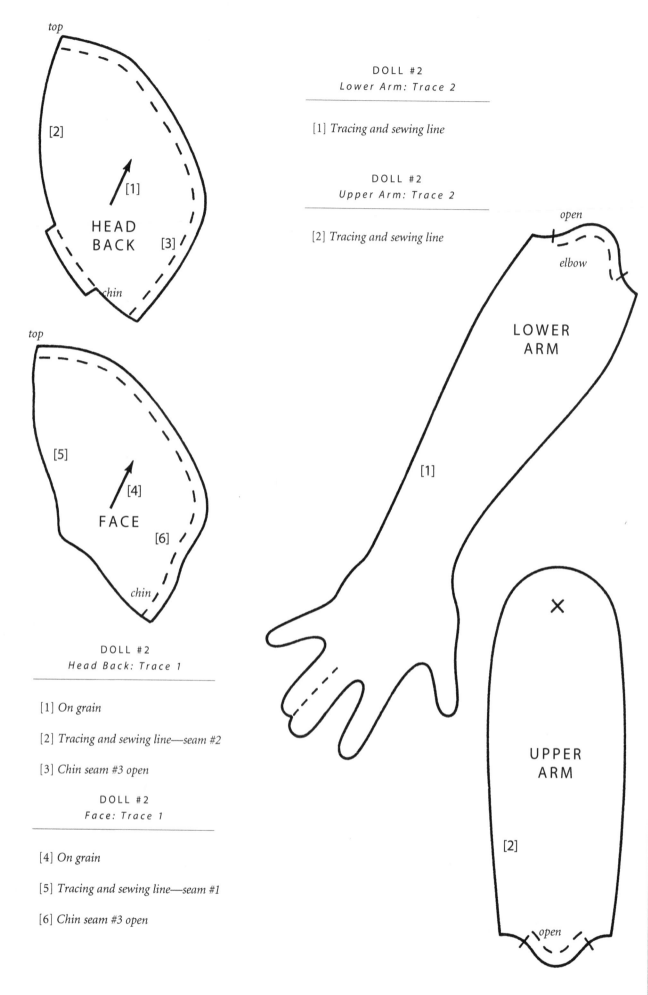

top

[2]

[1]

HEAD
BACK

[3]

chin

top

[5]

[4]

FACE

[6]

chin

DOLL #2
Head Back: Trace 1

[1] *On grain*

[2] *Tracing and sewing line—seam #2*

[3] *Chin seam #3 open*

DOLL #2
Face: Trace 1

[4] *On grain*

[5] *Tracing and sewing line—seam #1*

[6] *Chin seam #3 open*

DOLL #2
Lower Arm: Trace 2

[1] *Tracing and sewing line*

DOLL #2
Upper Arm: Trace 2

[2] *Tracing and sewing line*

open

elbow

LOWER
ARM

[1]

✕

UPPER
ARM

[2]

open

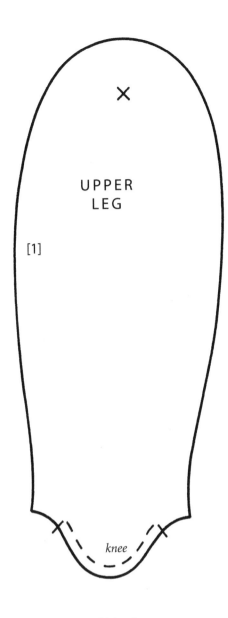

UPPER
LEG

[1]

×

knee

DOLL #2
Upper Leg: Trace 2

[1] *Tracing and sewing line*

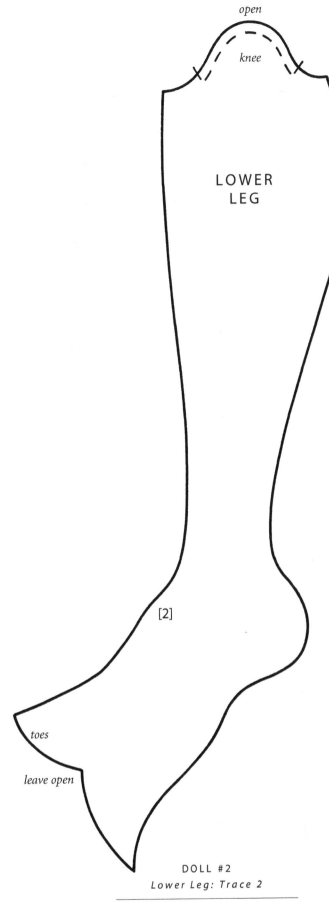

open

LOWER
LEG

knee

[2]

toes

leave open

DOLL #2
Lower Leg: Trace 2

[2] *Tracing and sewing line*

[1] *Tracing and sewing line*

[3] *Place on fold*

[2] *Seam #5*

[4] *Seam #4*

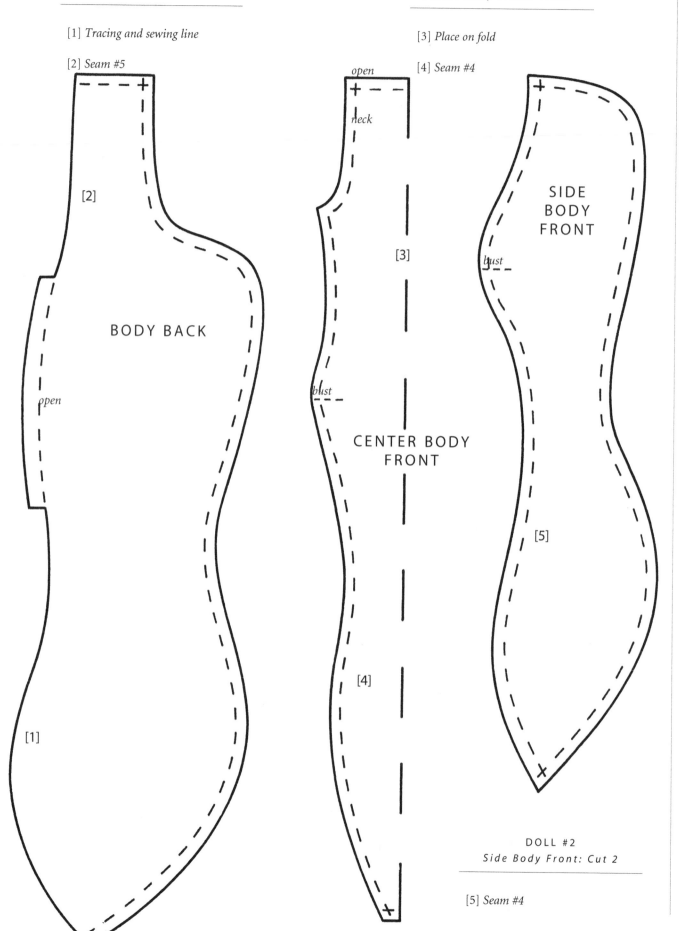

open

neck

[2]

[3]

BODY BACK

bust

SIDE
BODY
FRONT

open

bust

CENTER BODY
FRONT

[5]

[4]

[1]

×

DOLL #2
Side Body Front: Cut 2

[5] *Seam #4*

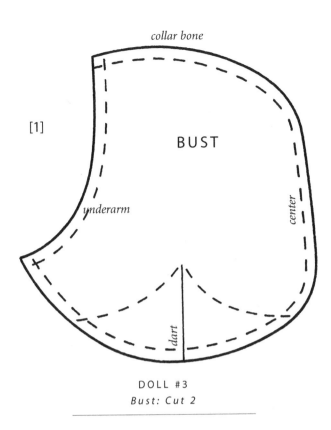

collar bone

BUST

underarm

center

[1]

dart

DOLL #3
Bust: Cut 2

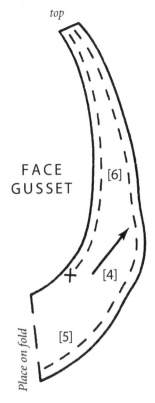

top

FACE GUSSET

[6]

[4]

[5]

Place on fold

DOLL #3
Face Gusset: Trace 1

[4] *On grain*

[5] *Seam #3*

[6] *Seam #4*

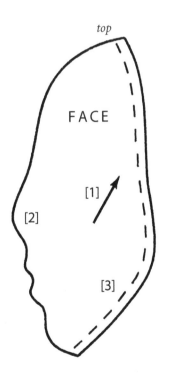

top

FACE

[1]

[2]

[3]

DOLL #3
Face: Trace 1

[1] *On grain*

[2] *Seam #3*

[3] *Tracing and sewing line—seam #1*

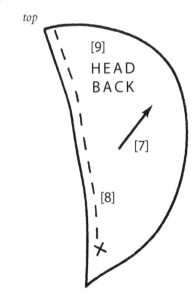

top

[9]

HEAD BACK

[7]

[8]

DOLL #3
Head Back: Trace 1

[7] *On grain*

[8] *Seam #4*

[9] *Tracing and sewing line—seam #2*

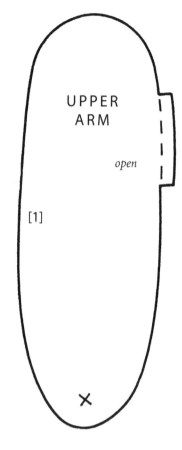

UPPER ARM

open

[1]

✕

DOLL #3
Upper Arm: Trace 2

[1] *Tracing and sewing line*

ARM & LEG
JOINTS

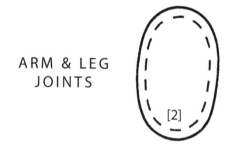

[2]

DOLL #3
Arm and Leg Joints: Trace 2

[2] *Cut 8*

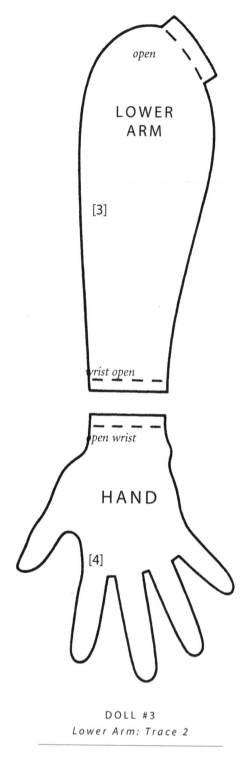

open

LOWER ARM

[3]

wrist open

open wrist

HAND

[4]

DOLL #3
Lower Arm: Trace 2

[3] *Tracing and sewing line*

DOLL #3
Hand: Trace 2

[4] *Tracing and sewing line*

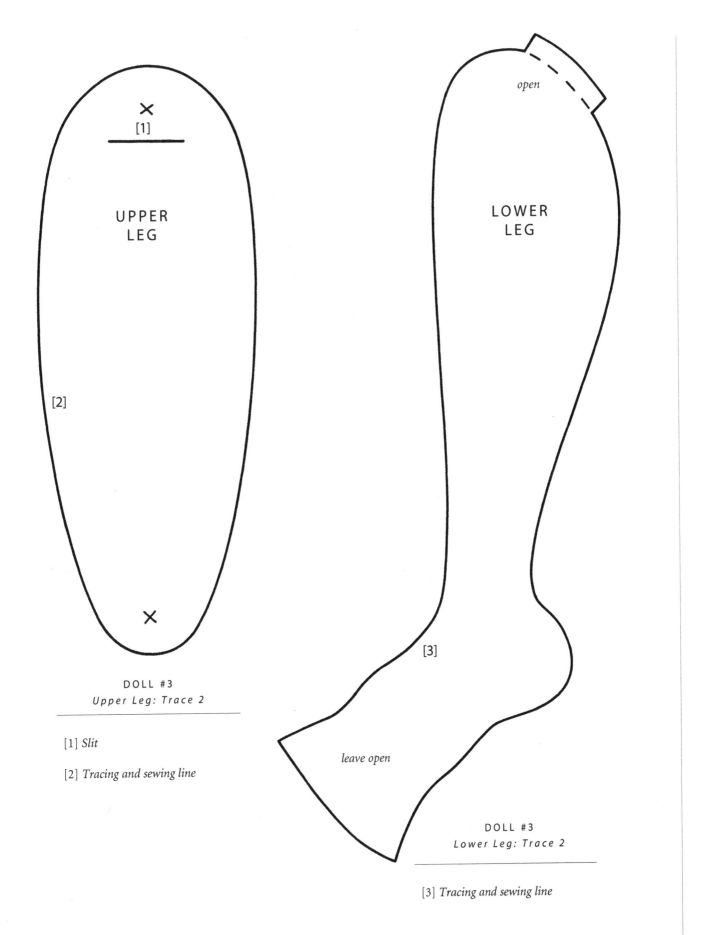

UPPER
LEG

✕
[1]

[2]

✕

DOLL #3
Upper Leg: Trace 2

[1] Slit

[2] Tracing and sewing line

open

LOWER
LEG

[3]

leave open

DOLL #3
Lower Leg: Trace 2

[3] Tracing and sewing line

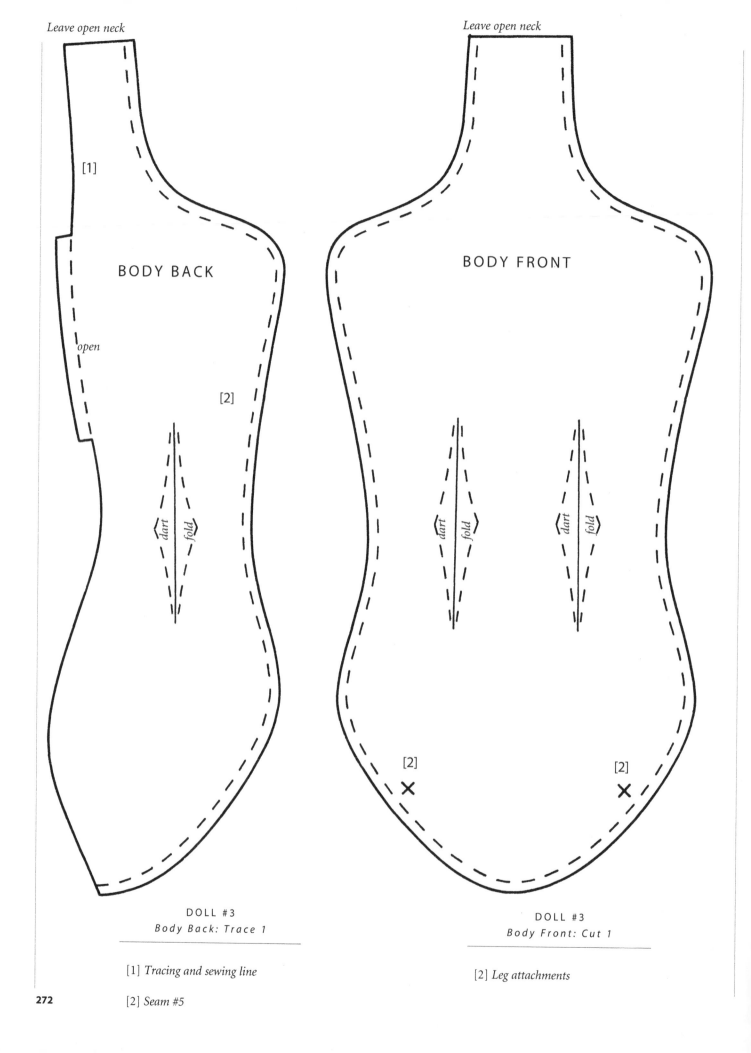

Leave open neck

[1]

open

[2]

BODY BACK

dart *fold*

DOLL #3
Body Back: Trace 1

[1] *Tracing and sewing line*

272 [2] *Seam #5*

Leave open neck

BODY FRONT

dart *fold*

dart *fold*

[2]
✕

[2]
✕

DOLL #3
Body Front: Cut 1

[2] *Leg attachments*

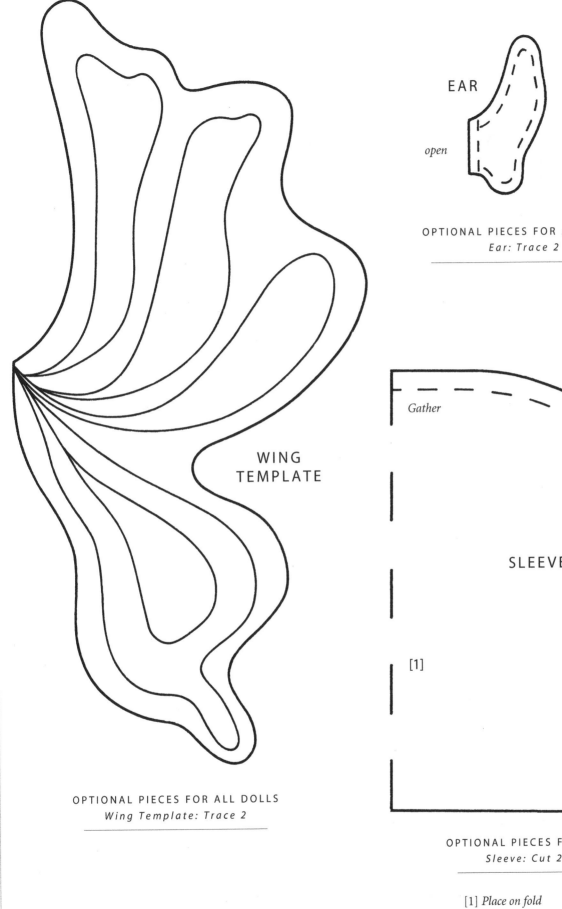

WING TEMPLATE

OPTIONAL PIECES FOR ALL DOLLS
Wing Template: Trace 2

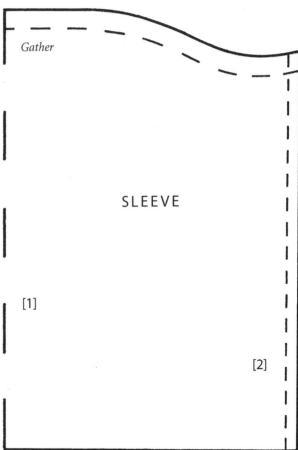

EAR

open

OPTIONAL PIECES FOR ALL DOLLS
Ear: Trace 2

Gather

SLEEVE

[1]

[2]

OPTIONAL PIECES FOR ALL DOLLS
Sleeve: Cut 2 on fold

[1] *Place on fold*

[2] *Seam #1*

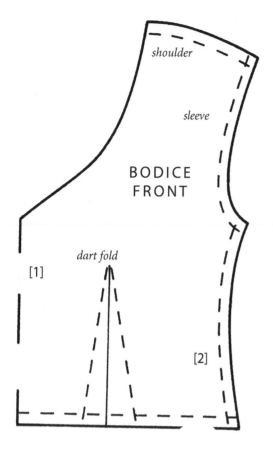

shoulder

sleeve

BODICE
FRONT

dart fold

[1]

[2]

OPTIONAL PIECES FOR ALL DOLLS
Bodice Front: Cut 1 on fold

[1] *Place on fold*

[2] *Side seam*

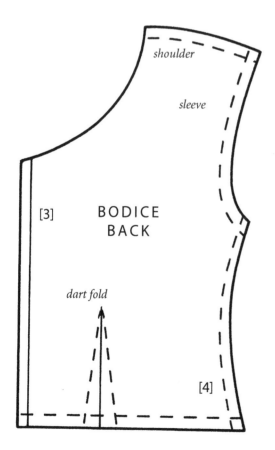

shoulder

sleeve

[3]

BODICE
BACK

dart fold

[4]

OPTIONAL PIECES FOR ALL DOLLS
Bodice Back: Cut 2

[3] *Back opening*

[4] *Side seam*

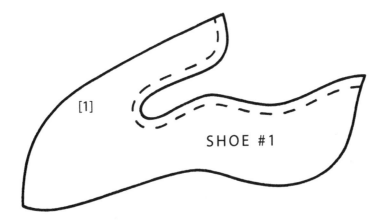

[1]

SHOE #1

OPTIONAL PIECES FOR ALL DOLLS
Shoe #1: Trace 2

_____

[1] *Tracing and sewing line*

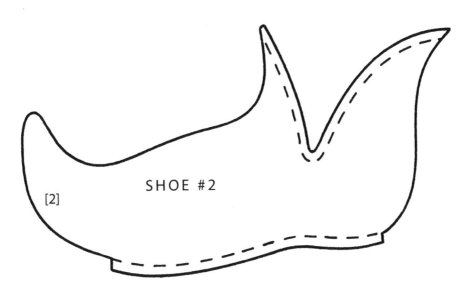

SHOE #2

[2]

OPTIONAL PIECES FOR ALL DOLLS
Shoe #2: Trace 2

_____

[2] *Tracing and sewing line*

SHOE #2
SOLE

OPTIONAL PIECES FOR ALL DOLLS
Shoe Sole: Cut 2

_____

Tania (Intermediate doll)

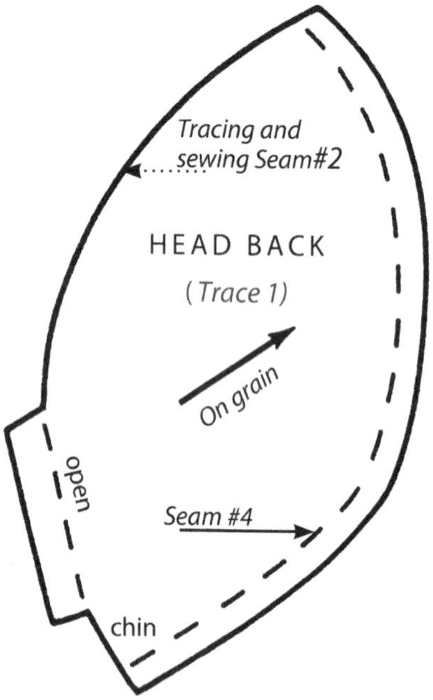

Neck

Tracing and sewing Seam#2

HEAD BACK

(Trace 1)

On grain

open

Seam #4

chin

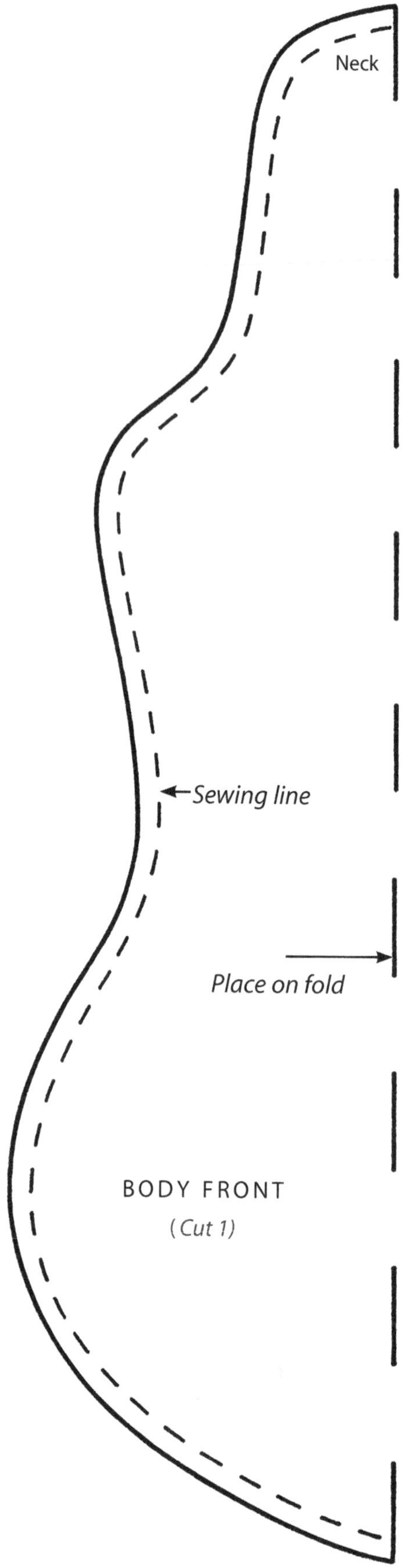

←Sewing line

Place on fold

BODY FRONT

(Cut 1)

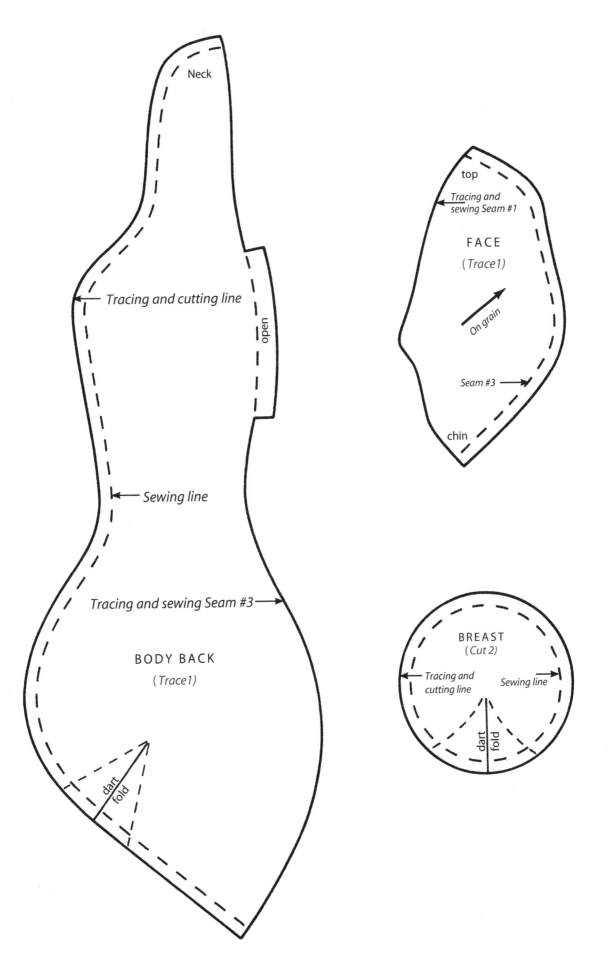

Neck

Tracing and cutting line

open

Sewing line

Tracing and sewing Seam #3

BODY BACK

(*Trace1*)

dart
fold

top

*Tracing and
sewing Seam #1*

FACE

(*Trace1*)

On grain

Seam #3

chin

BREAST

(*Cut 2*)

*Tracing and
cutting line*

Sewing line

dart
fold

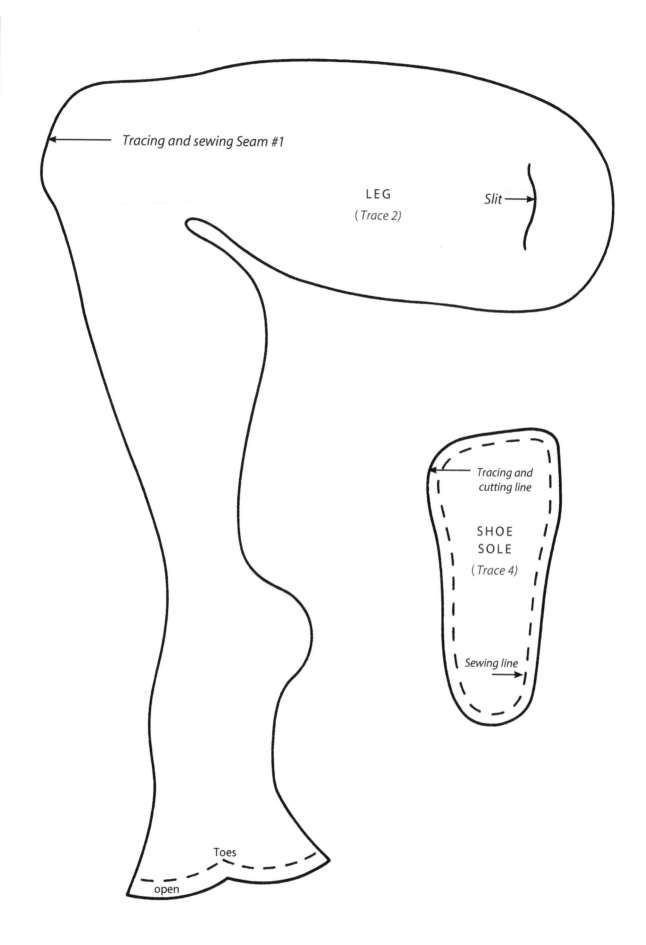

Tracing and sewing Seam #1

LEG
(Trace 2)

Slit

Tracing and
cutting line

SHOE
SOLE
(Trace 4)

Sewing line

Toes

open

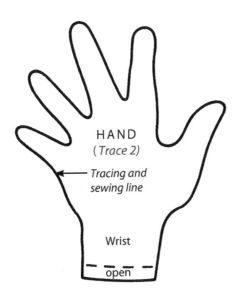

HAND
(*Trace 2*)

*Tracing and
sewing line*

Wrist

open

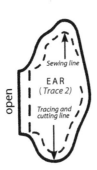

Sewing line

EAR
(*Trace 2*)

open

*Tracing and
cutting line*

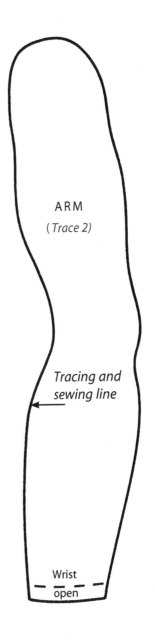

ARM
(*Trace 2*)

*Tracing and
sewing line*

Wrist

open

Magdalene (Advanced doll)

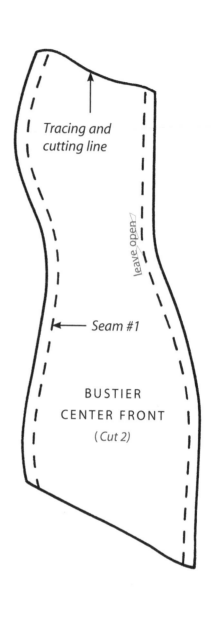

Tracing and
cutting line

leave open

← Seam #1

BUSTIER
CENTER FRONT
(Cut 2)

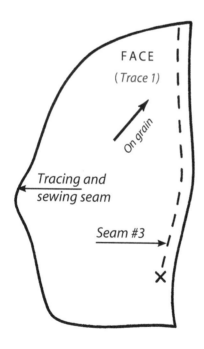

FACE
(Trace 1)

On grain

Tracing and
sewing seam

Seam #3

✕

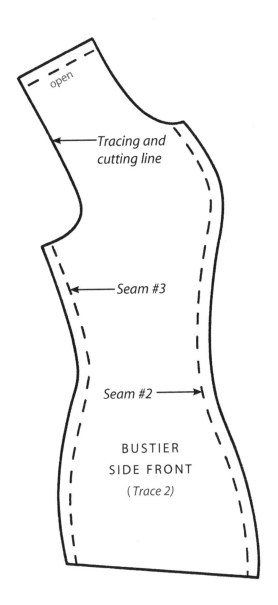

open

Tracing and cutting line

Seam #3

Seam #2

BUSTIER
SIDE FRONT
(*Trace 2*)

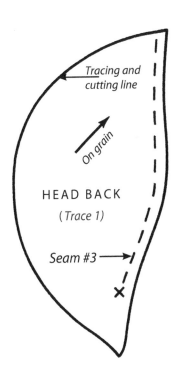

Tracing and cutting line

On grain

HEAD BACK
(*Trace 1*)

Seam #3

×

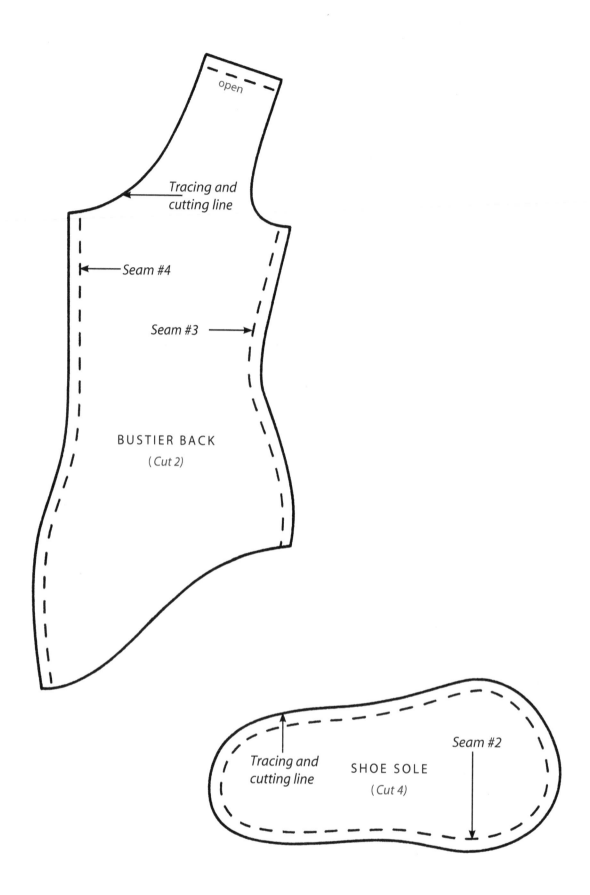

open

Tracing and
cutting line

Seam #4

Seam #3

BUSTIER BACK
(Cut 2)

Tracing and
cutting line

Seam #2

SHOE SOLE
(Cut 4)

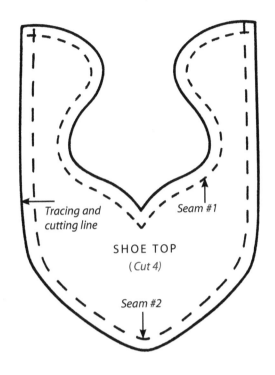

Tracing and
cutting line

Seam #1

SHOE TOP
(Cut 4)

Seam #2

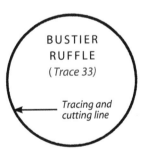

BUSTIER
RUFFLE
(Trace 33)

Tracing and
cutting line

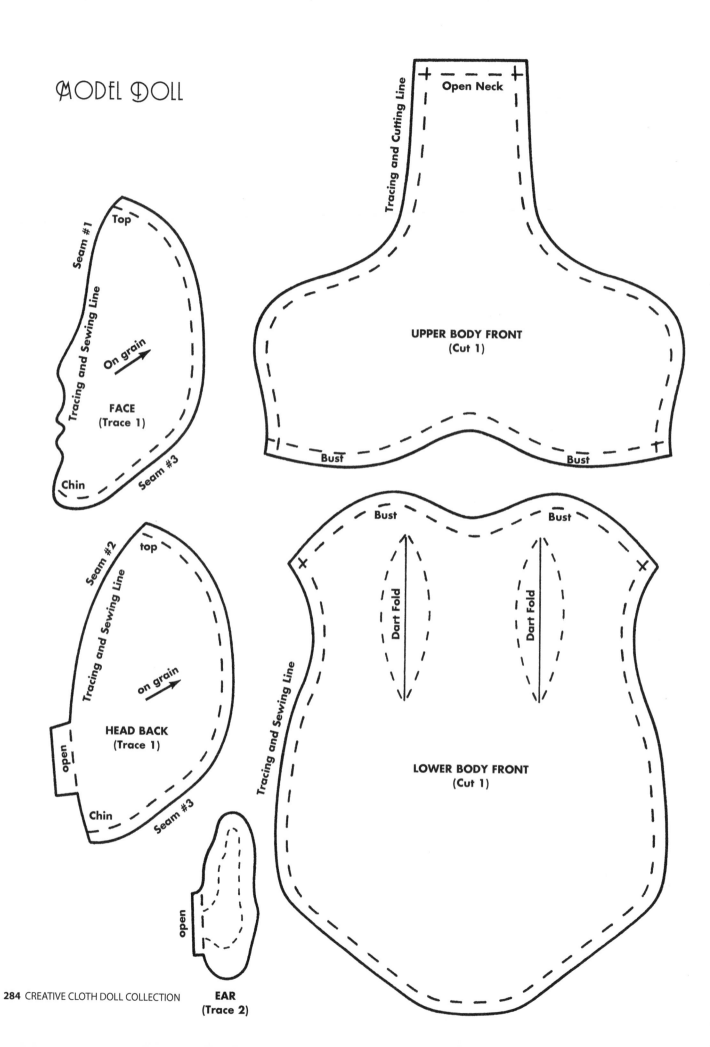

MODEL DOLL

Open Neck

Tracing and Cutting Line

UPPER BODY FRONT
(Cut 1)

Bust   **Bust**

Seam #1

Top

Tracing and Sewing Line

On grain

FACE
(Trace 1)

Chin   Seam #3

Bust   **Bust**

Dart Fold   Dart Fold

Seam #2

top

Tracing and Sewing Line

on grain

HEAD BACK
(Trace 1)

open

Chin   Seam #3

Tracing and Sewing Line

LOWER BODY FRONT
(Cut 1)

open

EAR
(Trace 2)

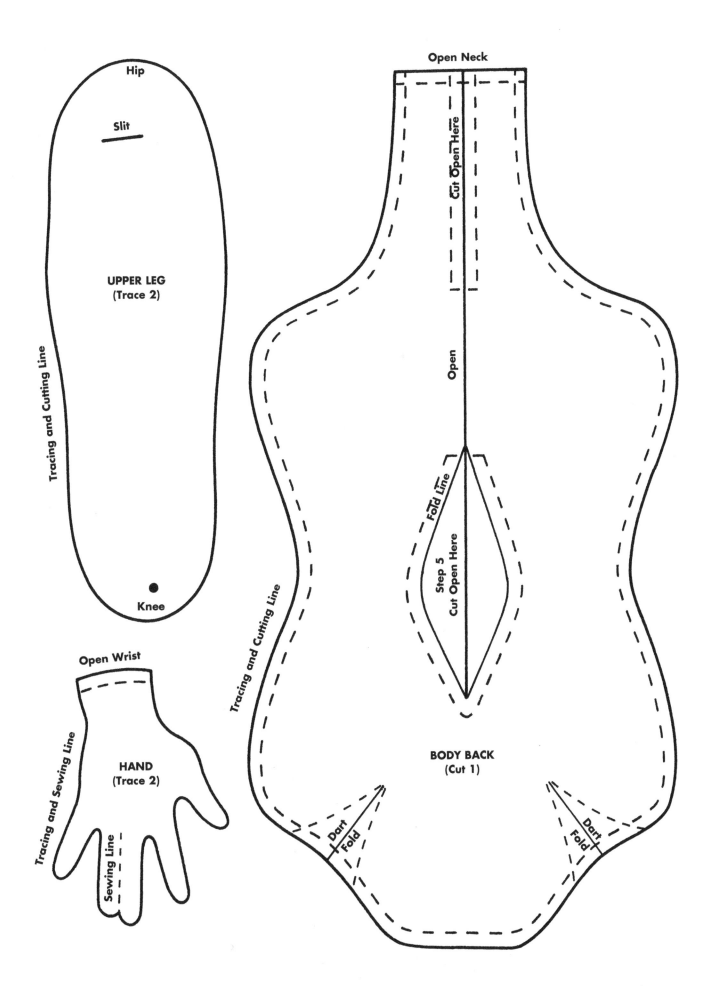

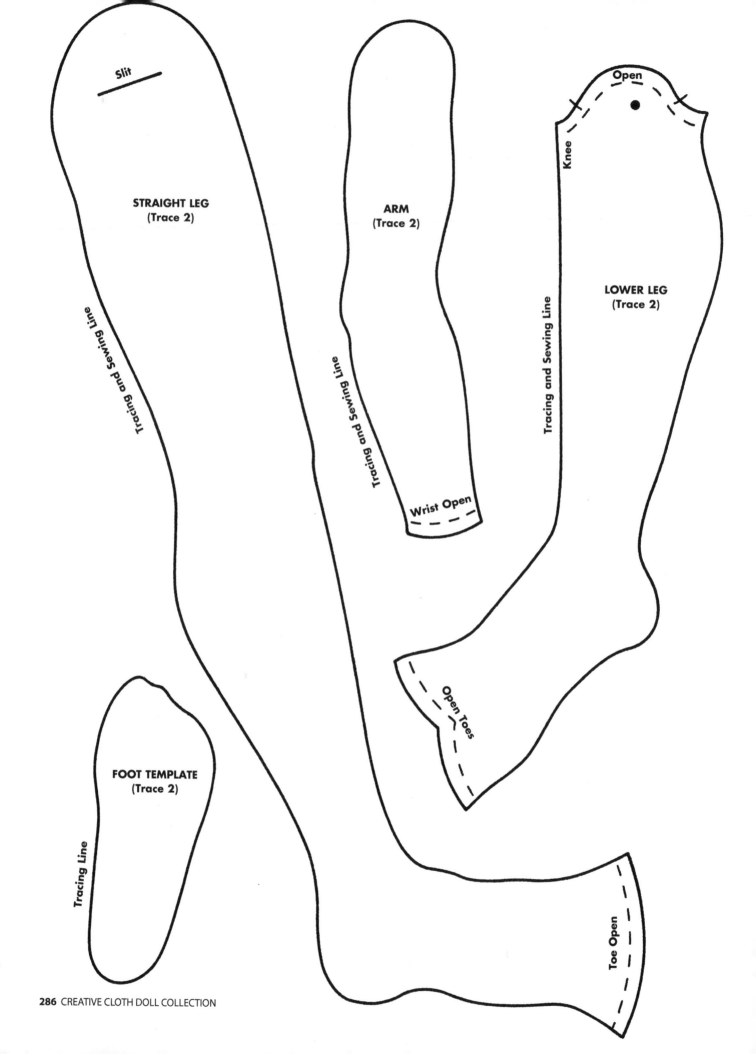

Slit

STRAIGHT LEG
(Trace 2)

Tracing and Sewing Line

ARM
(Trace 2)

Tracing and Sewing Line

Wrist Open

Open

Knee

LOWER LEG
(Trace 2)

Tracing and Sewing Line

Open Toes

FOOT TEMPLATE
(Trace 2)

Tracing Line

Toe Open

HELEN'S SUIT

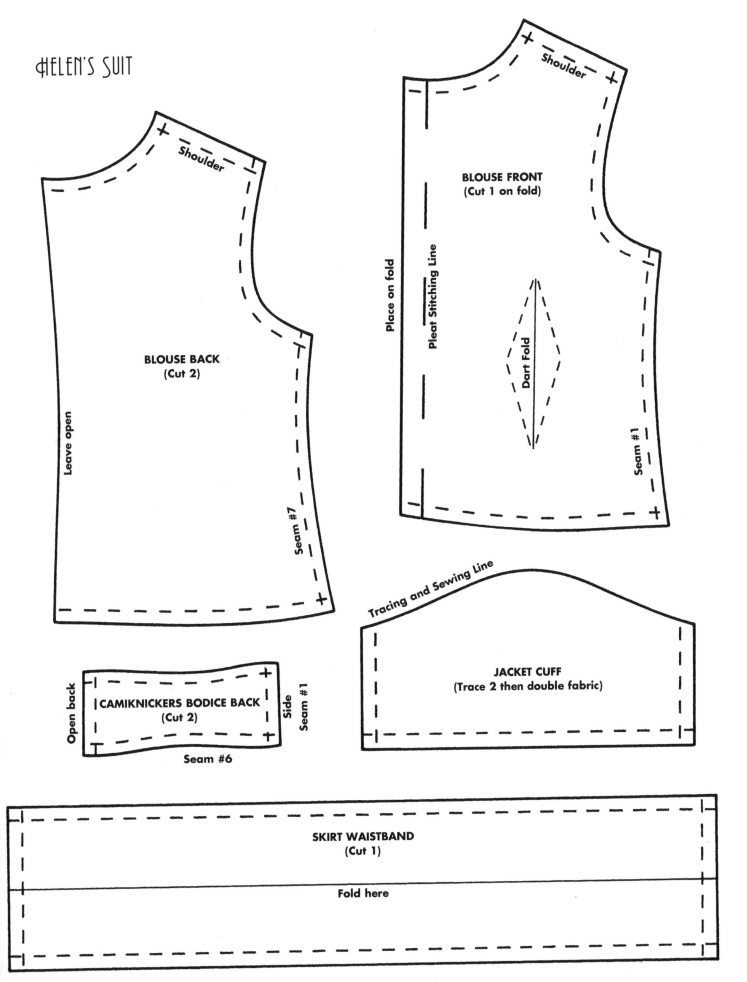

BLOUSE BACK
(Cut 2)

Shoulder

Leave open

Seam #7

BLOUSE FRONT
(Cut 1 on fold)

Shoulder

Place on fold

Pleat Stitching Line

Dart Fold

Seam #1

CAMIKNICKERS BODICE BACK
(Cut 2)

Open back

Side
Seam #1

Seam #6

Tracing and Sewing Line

JACKET CUFF
(Trace 2 then double fabric)

SKIRT WAISTBAND
(Cut 1)

Fold here

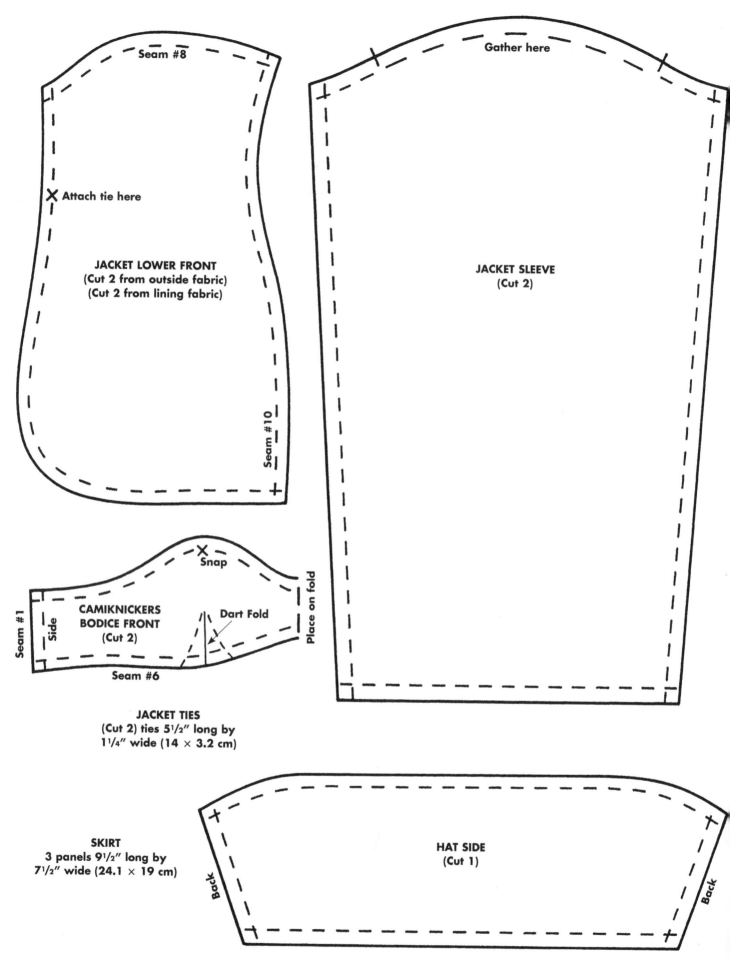

Seam #8

X Attach tie here

JACKET LOWER FRONT
(Cut 2 from outside fabric)
(Cut 2 from lining fabric)

Seam #10

JACKET SLEEVE
(Cut 2)

Gather here

X
Snap

CAMIKNICKERS
BODICE FRONT
(Cut 2)

Seam #1

Side

Dart Fold

Place on fold

Seam #6

JACKET TIES
(Cut 2) ties 5½" long by
1¼" wide (14 × 3.2 cm)

SKIRT
3 panels 9½" long by
7½" wide (24.1 × 19 cm)

HAT SIDE
(Cut 1)

Back

Back

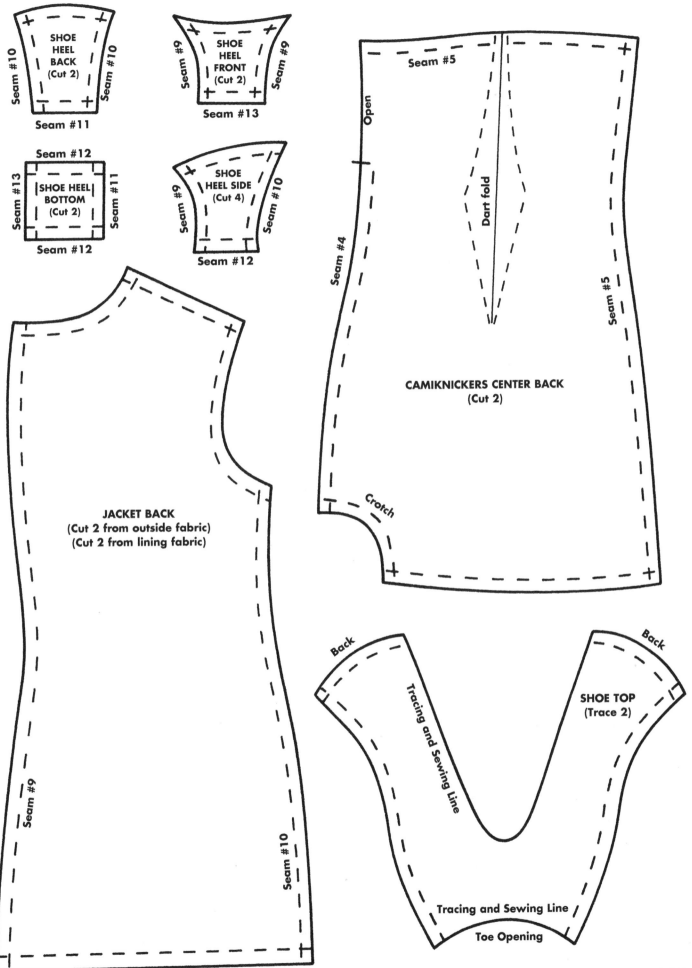

SHOE
HEEL
BACK
(Cut 2)

Seam #10

Seam #10

Seam #11

SHOE
HEEL
FRONT
(Cut 2)

Seam #9

Seam #9

Seam #13

Seam #12

SHOE HEEL
BOTTOM
(Cut 2)

Seam #13

Seam #11

Seam #12

SHOE
HEEL
SIDE
(Cut 4)

Seam #9

Seam #10

Seam #12

Seam #5

Open

Seam #4

Dart fold

Seam #5

CAMIKNICKERS CENTER BACK
(Cut 2)

Crotch

JACKET BACK
(Cut 2 from outside fabric)
(Cut 2 from lining fabric)

Seam #9

Seam #10

Back

Tracing and Sewing Line

Back

SHOE TOP
(Trace 2)

Tracing and Sewing Line

Toe Opening

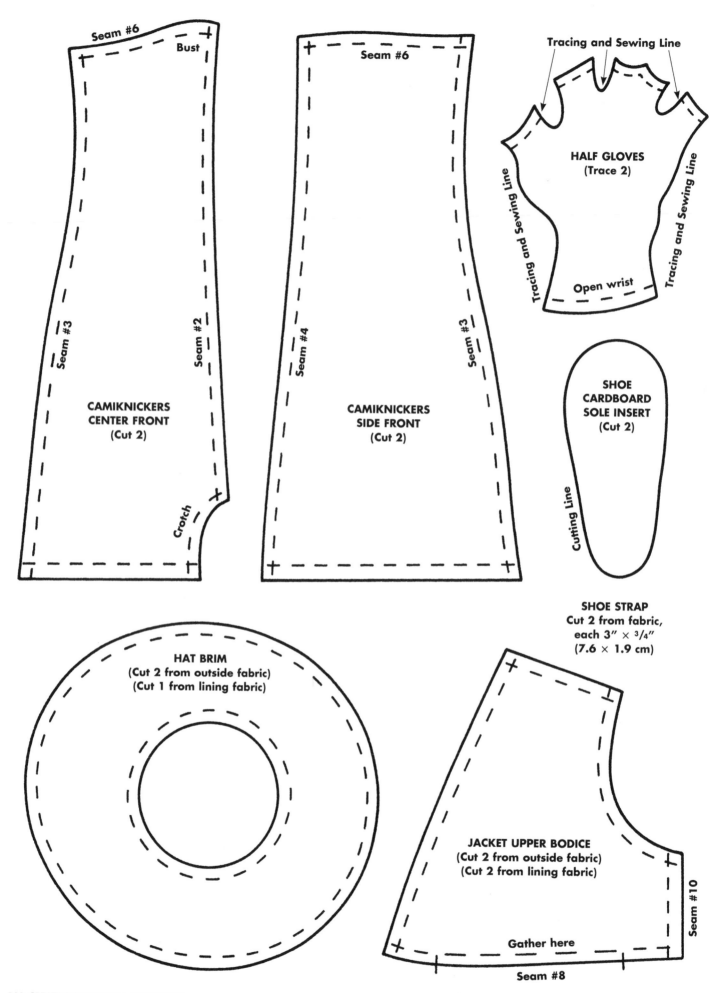

Seam #6

Bust

CAMIKNICKERS
CENTER FRONT
(Cut 2)

Seam #3

Seam #2

Crotch

Seam #6

CAMIKNICKERS
SIDE FRONT
(Cut 2)

Seam #4

Seam #3

Tracing and Sewing Line

HALF GLOVES
(Trace 2)

Tracing and Sewing Line

Tracing and Sewing Line

Open wrist

SHOE
CARDBOARD
SOLE INSERT
(Cut 2)

Cutting Line

SHOE STRAP
Cut 2 from fabric,
each 3″ × ¾″
(7.6 × 1.9 cm)

HAT BRIM
(Cut 2 from outside fabric)
(Cut 1 from lining fabric)

Bust

JACKET UPPER BODICE
(Cut 2 from outside fabric)
(Cut 2 from lining fabric)

Seam #10

Gather here

Seam #8

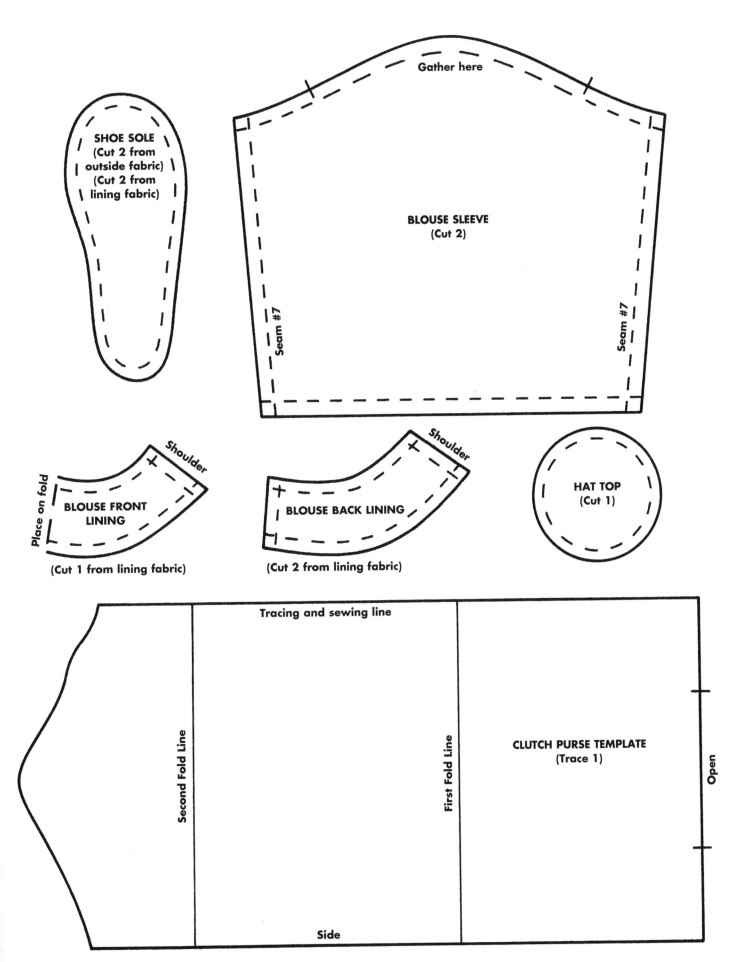

SHOE SOLE
(Cut 2 from outside fabric)
(Cut 2 from lining fabric)

BLOUSE SLEEVE
(Cut 2)

Gather here

Seam #7

Seam #7

Shoulder

BLOUSE FRONT LINING

Place on fold

(Cut 1 from lining fabric)

Shoulder

BLOUSE BACK LINING

(Cut 2 from lining fabric)

HAT TOP
(Cut 1)

Tracing and sewing line

Second Fold Line

First Fold Line

CLUTCH PURSE TEMPLATE
(Trace 1)

Open

Side

ELIZABETHE'S ACCESSORIES

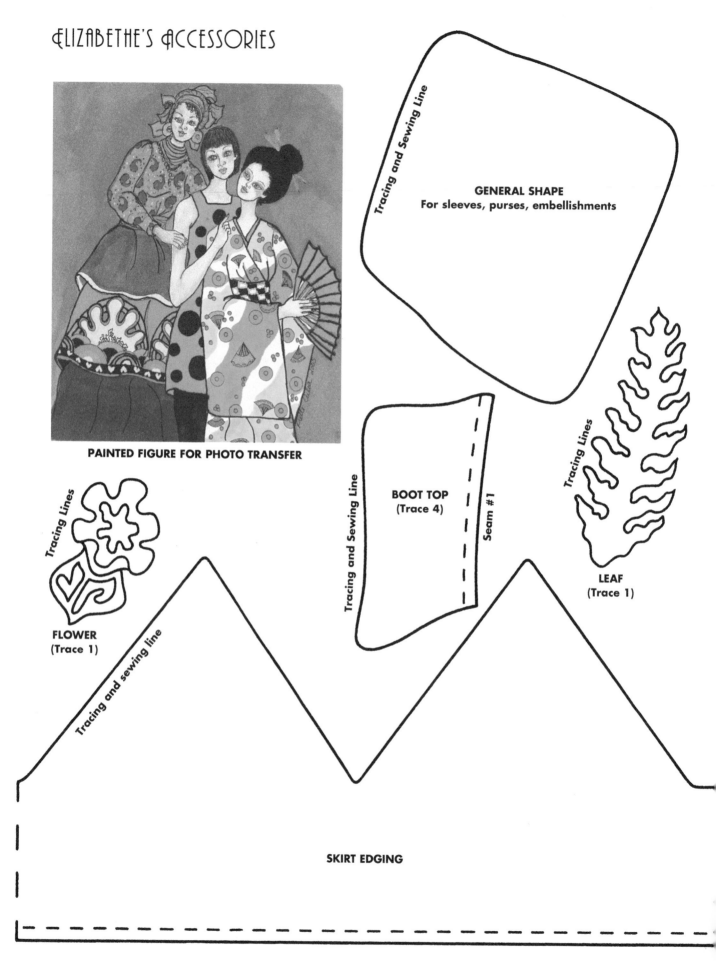

PAINTED FIGURE FOR PHOTO TRANSFER

GENERAL SHAPE
For sleeves, purses, embellishments

Tracing and Sewing Line

Tracing Lines

LEAF
(Trace 1)

Tracing Lines

FLOWER
(Trace 1)

Tracing and Sewing Line

BOOT TOP
(Trace 4)

Seam #1

Tracing and sewing line

SKIRT EDGING

GOLENDRIAL'S FAIRY OUTFIT

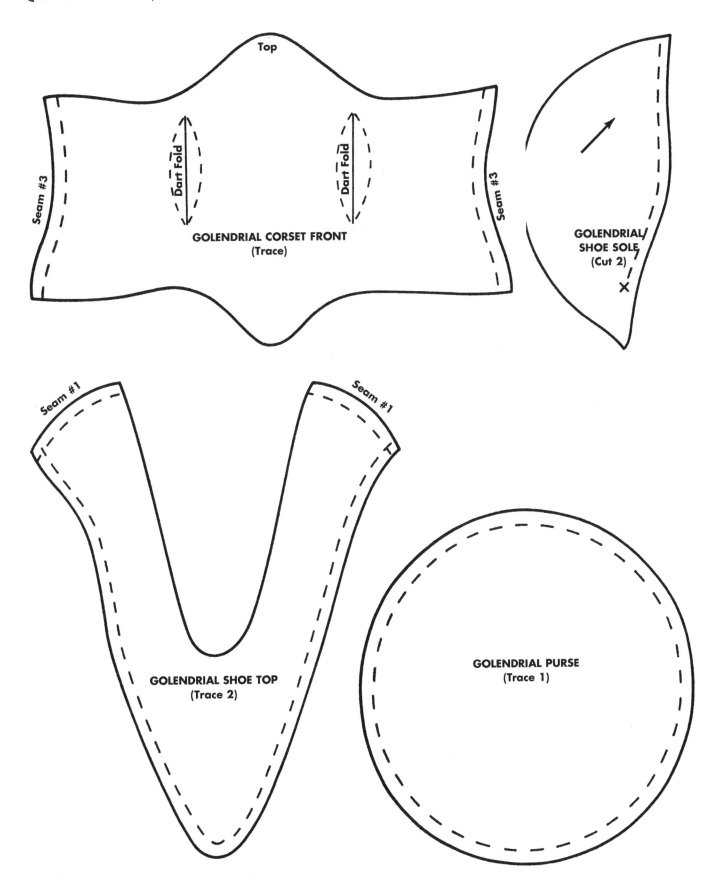

Top

Dart Fold

Dart Fold

Seam #3

Seam #3

GOLENDRIAL CORSET FRONT
(Trace)

GOLENDRIAL
SHOE SOLE
(Cut 2)

Seam #1

Seam #1

GOLENDRIAL SHOE TOP
(Trace 2)

GOLENDRIAL PURSE
(Trace 1)

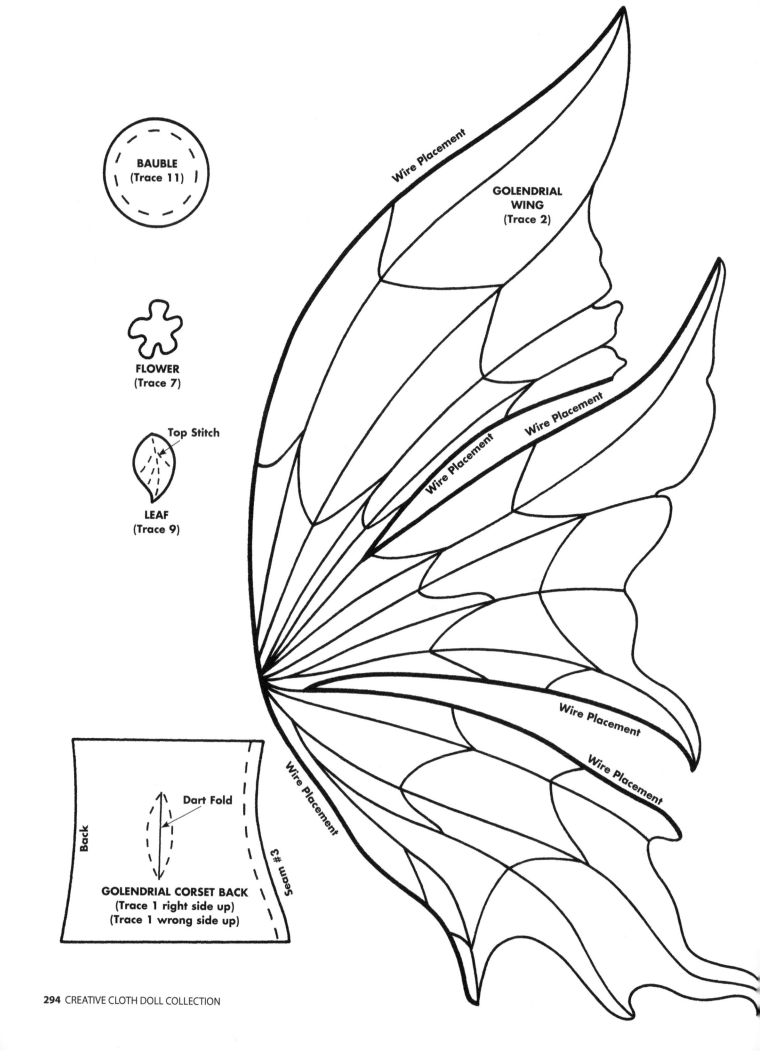

BAUBLE
(Trace 11)

FLOWER
(Trace 7)

Top Stitch

LEAF
(Trace 9)

GOLENDRIAL
WING
(Trace 2)

Wire Placement

Wire Placement

Wire Placement

Wire Placement

Wire Placement

Wire Placement

Wire Placement

Back

Dart Fold

Seam #3

GOLENDRIAL CORSET BACK
(Trace 1 right side up)
(Trace 1 wrong side up)

BASIC DOLL BODY

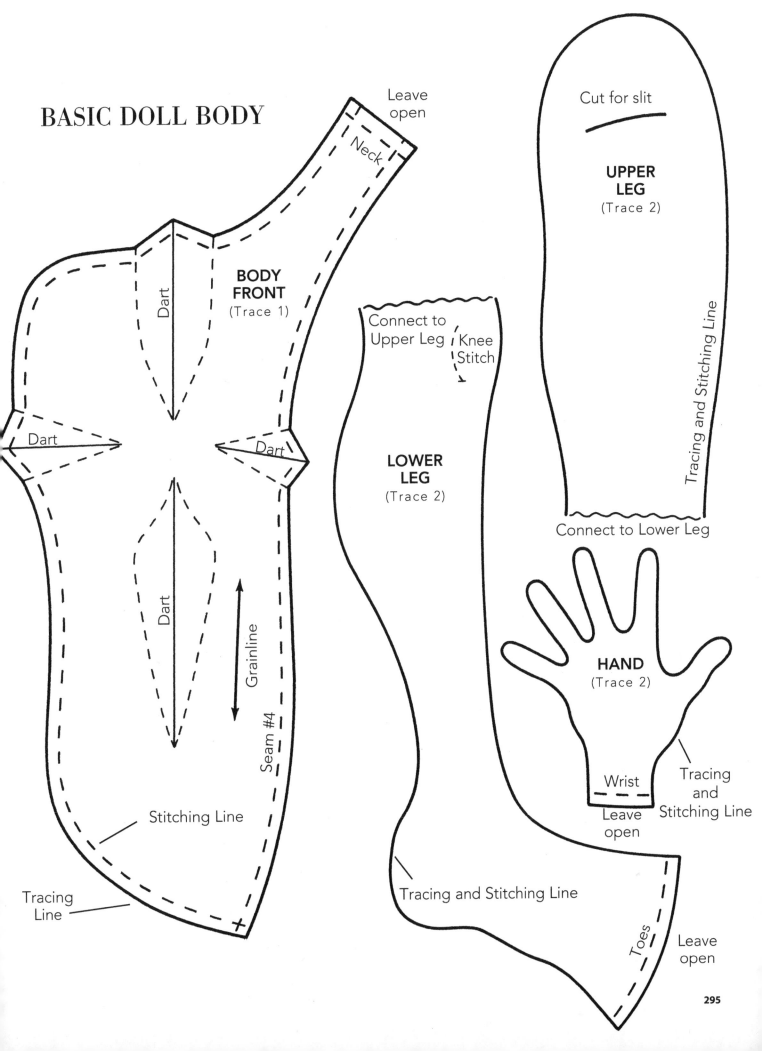

Leave open

Neck

BODY FRONT
(Trace 1)

Dart

Dart

Dart

Dart

Grainline

Seam #4

Stitching Line

Tracing Line

Cut for slit

UPPER LEG
(Trace 2)

Tracing and Stitching Line

Connect to Lower Leg

Connect to Upper Leg

Knee Stitch

LOWER LEG
(Trace 2)

Tracing and Stitching Line

HAND
(Trace 2)

Wrist

Leave open

Tracing and Stitching Line

Toes

Leave open

295

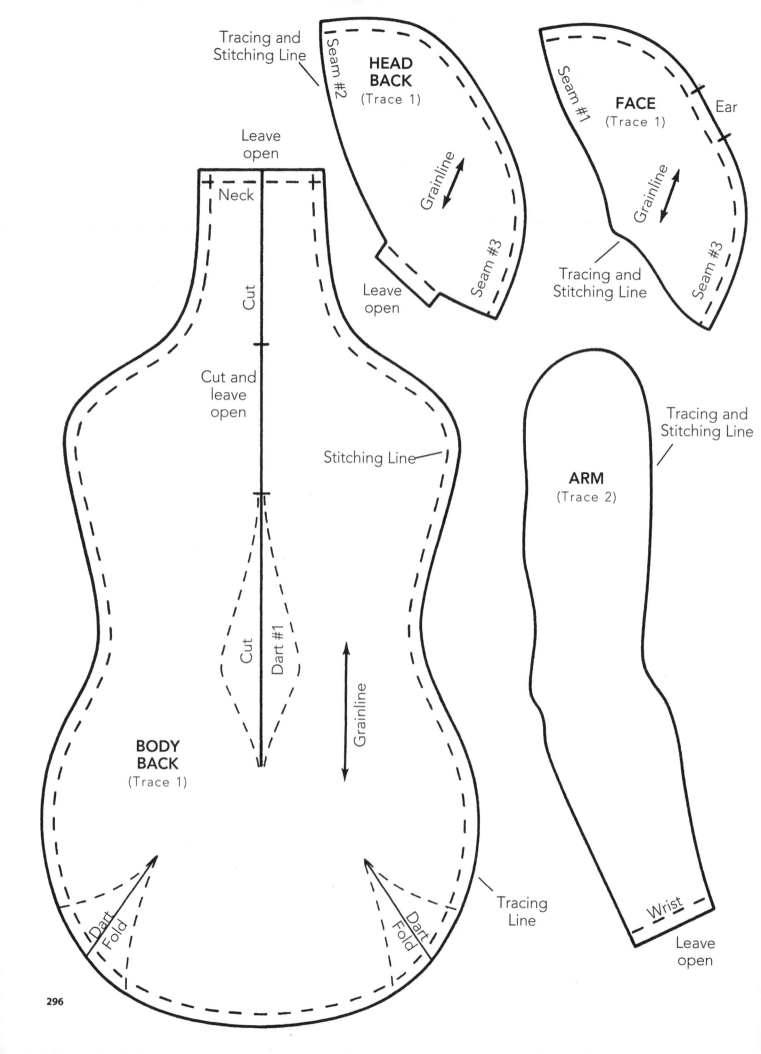

Tracing and Stitching Line

Seam #2

HEAD BACK
(Trace 1)

Grainline

Seam #3

Leave open

FACE
(Trace 1)

Seam #1

Ear

Grainline

Seam #3

Tracing and Stitching Line

Leave open

Neck

Cut

Cut and leave open

Stitching Line

Tracing and Stitching Line

ARM
(Trace 2)

BODY BACK
(Trace 1)

Cut

Dart #1

Grainline

Dart

Fold

Dart

Fold

Tracing Line

Wrist

Leave open

296

VIVIANA

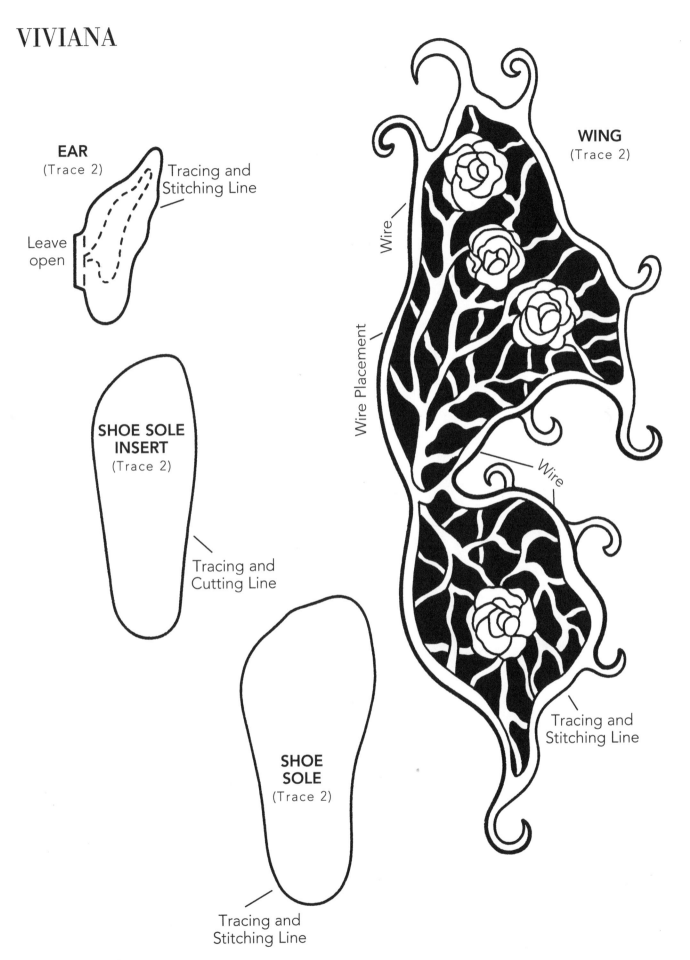

EAR
(Trace 2)

Tracing and
Stitching Line

Leave
open

WING
(Trace 2)

Wire

Wire Placement

Wire

**SHOE SOLE
INSERT**
(Trace 2)

Tracing and
Cutting Line

Tracing and
Stitching Line

**SHOE
SOLE**
(Trace 2)

Tracing and
Stitching Line

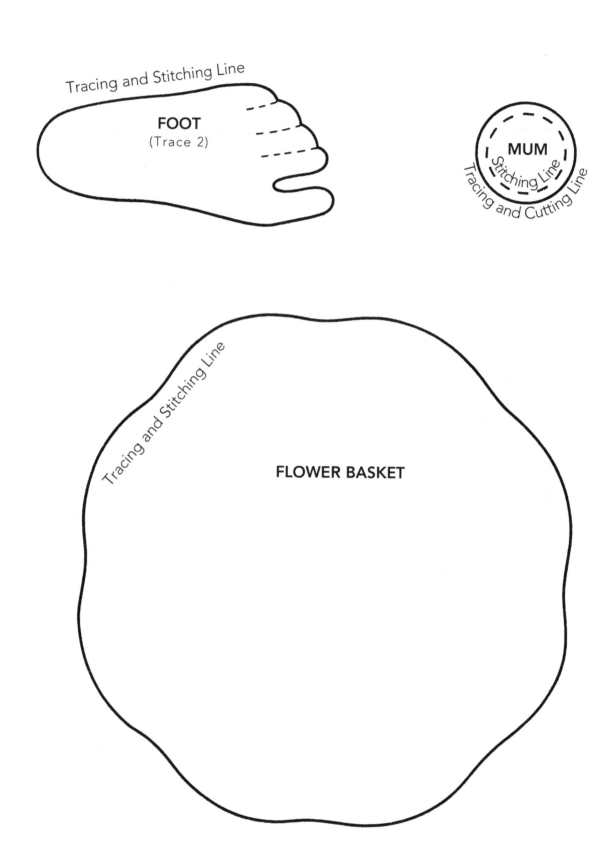

Tracing and Stitching Line

FOOT
(Trace 2)

MUM
Stitching Line
Tracing and Cutting Line

Tracing and Stitching Line

FLOWER BASKET

FRANALIZIA OF THE NORTH SEA

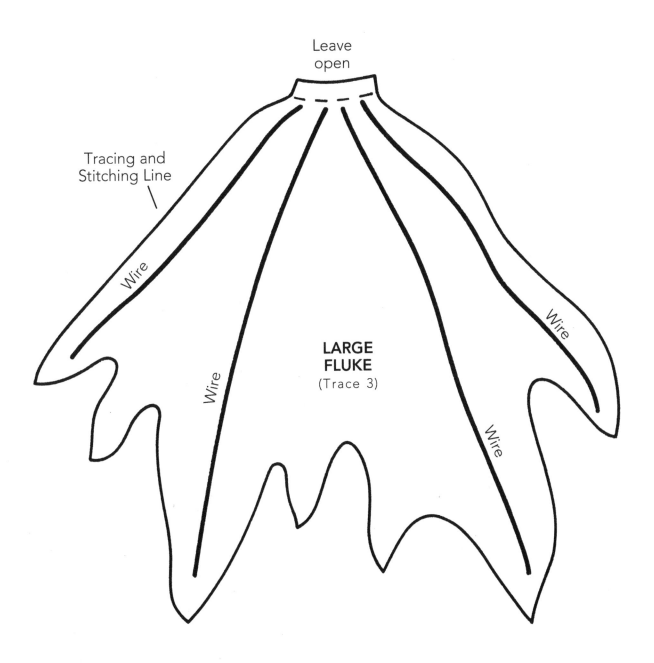

Leave
open

Tracing and
Stitching Line

Wire

Wire

Wire

Wire

**LARGE
FLUKE**
(Trace 3)

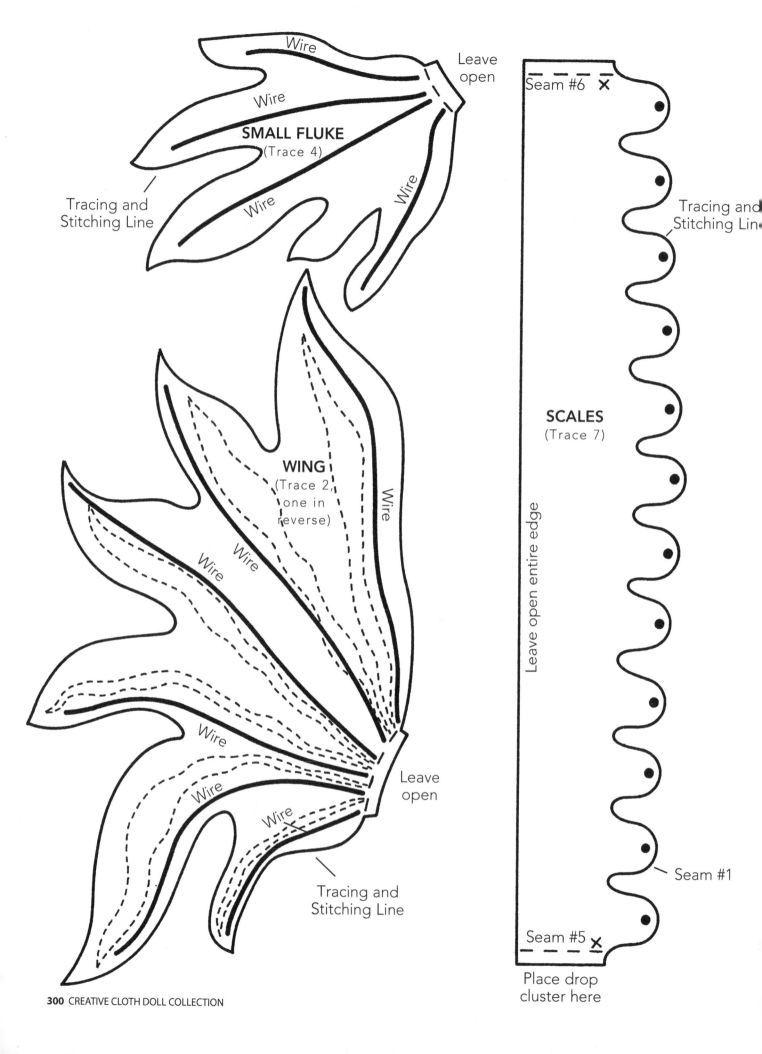

Wire

Wire

SMALL FLUKE
(Trace 4)

Leave
open

Tracing and
Stitching Line

Wire

Wire

Wire

Wire

WING
(Trace 2,
one in
reverse)

Wire

Wire

Wire

Wire

Wire

Wire

Leave
open

Tracing and
Stitching Line

Seam #6 ✗

Tracing and
Stitching Line

SCALES
(Trace 7)

Leave open entire edge

Seam #1

Seam #5 ✗

Place drop
cluster here

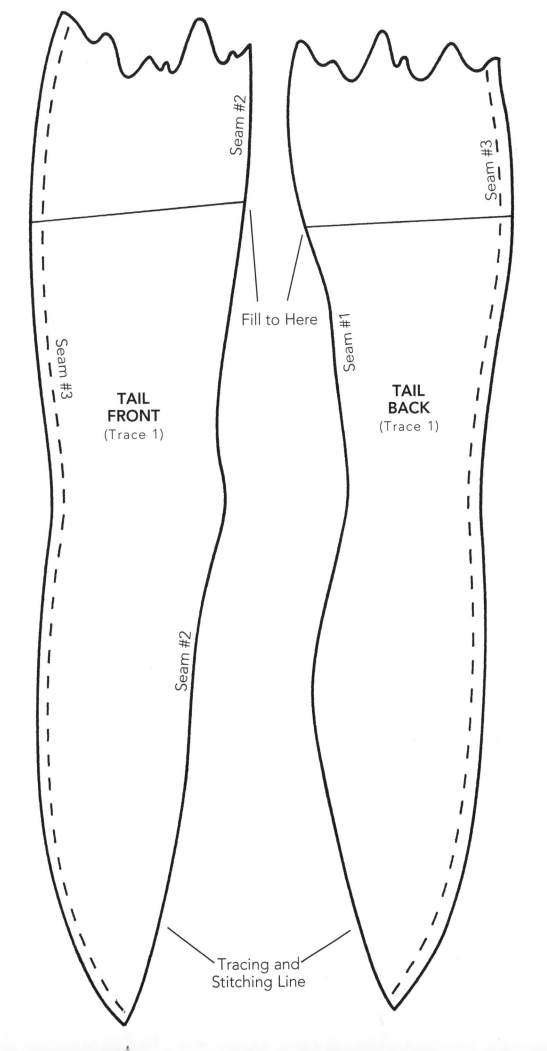

Seam #2

Seam #3

TAIL FRONT
(Trace 1)

Seam #2

Fill to Here

Seam #1

Seam #3

TAIL BACK
(Trace 1)

Tracing and
Stitching Line

RESOURCES

United States

Caravan Beads, Inc.
Portland, ME
www.caravanbeads.com
Complete line of beads, retail and wholesale

Cloth Doll Connection
www.clothdollconnection.com
Online doll-making classes, links, calendar of events

Dollmaker's Journey
www.dollmakersjourney.com
Books, patterns, and supplies for the contemporary doll artist

Joggles, Inc.
www.joggles.com
Beads, books, fabrics, mohair and other fibers, patterns

Just Let Me Bead
Noank, CT 06340
www.justletmebead.com
Bead kits, beads, classes, newsletter

Kandi Corp
Clearwater, FL
www.kandicorp.com
Heat-set crystals and Kandi Kane applicator

Meinke Toy
Troy, MI
www.meinketoy.com
Angelina fibers, books, stabilizers, threads

PMC Designs
San Diego, CA
www.pmcdesigns.com
patti@pmcdesigns.com
Classes, heat-set crystals and applicator, newsletters, patterns, rubber stamps, tools

Quilting Arts, LLC/*Cloth Paper Scissors*
Stow, MA
www.quiltingarts.com
Beads, books, Jacquard products, magazines, rubber stamps

Rio Grande
www.riogrande.com
Large catalogue of jewelry-related supplies in all categories

Rupert, Gibbon & Spider, Inc.
Healdsburg, CA
www.jacquardproducts.com
Jacquard products: Dye Na Flow, Lumiere, textile paints

Tsukineko, Inc.
Redmond, WA
www.tsukineko.com
Fantastix, stamp pads

Canada

Opus Framing & Art Supplies
www.opusframing.com
Books, Jacquard products, workshops

Australia

Anne's Glory Box
Hamilton, NSW
www.annesglorybox.com.au
Beads, books, dyes and paints, fabrics, mohair, stabilizers

Idyll Pleasures
West Pymble, NSW
www.idyllpleasures.com
Beads, books, dyes and paints, doll patterns, Jacquard products

The Thread Studio
Perth, Western Australia
www.thethreadstudio.com
Threads, stabilizers, paints, books, beads, online classes

New Zealand

Fabric Arts
Keriview
Northland
www.fabricarts.co.nz
Fabrics, embellishments, books and magazines, doll patterns

Zigzag Polymer Clay Supplies Ltd.
Christchurch
www.2dye4.co.nz
Jacquard products, Prismacolor pencils, rubber stamps

United Kingdom

Art Van Go
Herts
UK
www.artvango.co.uk
Books, Jacquard products, Stewart Gill paints

Crafty Notions
Newark
UK
www.craftynotions.com
Angelina fibers, beads and bead supplies, books, paints, stabilizers

Fibrecrafts and George Weil
Surrey
UK
www.fibrecrafts.com
Angelina fibers, books, paints, workshops

Rainbow Silks
Bucks
UK
www.rainbowsilks.co.uk
Beads, books, classes, embossing powders and tools, Jacquard products, rubber stamps

Yorkshire Art Store
North Yorkshire
UK
www.yorkshireartstore.co.uk
Books, embossing powders and tools, Jacquard products, paints

Europe

Bernina Creative Center
Prague,
Czech Republic
www.bernina-dani.cz
Books, fabrics, Jacquard products, workshops

ABOUT THE AUTHOR

Patti Medaris Culea studied art in Los Angeles and Japan and began as a painter and portrait artist. Her interest in the human figure evolved into working with cloth. Today, she combines her love of silk and dyes by creating extraordinary fairies, mermaids, and other one-of-a-kind dolls. She has a full-line of cloth doll patterns and her work has appeared in books, magazines, and galleries. In demand as a teacher, she travels throughout the world. She is the author of *Creative Cloth Doll Making*, (Rockport Publishers, 2003), *Creative Cloth Doll Faces*, (Quarry Books, 2005), *Creative Cloth Doll Couture*, (Quarry Books, 2006), *Creative Cloth Doll Beading*, (Quarry, 2007), *Creative Cloth Explorations: Adventures in Fairy-Inspired Fiber Art* (Quarry Books, 2009).

ACKNOWLEDGMENTS

In your hands is a work of love; a condensed collection of four books on doll making that I have been privileged to write during the past eight years. There are still more projects in the works and in my mind; however, this book allows me to share with you what has been such a satisfying part of my life to date.

A woman who has been a guiding light through the creative process is Mary Ann Hall of Rockport/Quarry Publishers. From her initial contact came four books on doll making and one on fiber art. Thank you, Mary Ann for being appropriately enough, a "ROCK" of sup"PORT."

There are family fingerprints (and perhaps smudge marks) on this book. While I take care of the art elements, my husband, John has helped me with writing many pages, especially the introductions to each chapter. Our daughters, Janet Beth and Heidi, were involved. Heidi worked on the editing of contributors text while teaching middle school in Brussels and JB, made a doll for the first book. That was a real challenge—working on the doll with one hand and coping with our then, two-year-old granddaughter with the other.

The special dimension and vision for the books are the result of contributing artist friends. Their creative works are rightly showcased for the world to see. All of us find our greatest satisfaction in bringing happiness to people who are kindred spirits in this specialized form of art.

To the person who has this book in your hand: I hope you will find its contents a resource for your library and an inspiration for future projects. Please know that I am humbled and encouraged that people like what I create. God bless you.

CPSIA information can be obtained
at www.ICGtesting.com
Printed in the USA
LVHW071519050720
659782LV00012B/832